Unlock the Door-Beyond Sexual Abuse will be of special interest to anyone looking for a greater understanding of sexual abuse and the recovery process. Deb Maybury opens the door to a source of collective energy when she unites her work with some very courageous people. The stories shared in her book will bring you on a journey towards love and compassion.

Sexual abuse survivors are wounded in unhealthy relationships, and it takes healthy relationships to transform and heal from the past. The author welcomes all victims, caregivers, and their communities into a circle of compassion. I encourage you to use the wisdom learned from this book and shed your light in dark places.

Tom Wilken Author of *Rebuilding Your House of Self Respect: Men recovering in group from childhood sexual abuse*

This is a book that raises consciousness on the whole issue of sexual abuse. I loved the Sylvia Fraser interview - memories are always waiting to come back. An ignored memory can create a variety of symptoms that could interfere with your life A symptom that is ignored can run or ruin your life. They whisper, talk, shout then shake you till your teeth rattle.

Abuse is sometimes an uncomfortable topic. However, Deb skillfully presents with a wisdom, compassion and sensitivity that makes for a smooth, comfortable and informative read. It is a must read for victims, parents, workers in the field, and those who wish to make a difference.

Sandra Fecht M.A., Psychotherapist and Co-author of *Trigger Your Happy*

After reading a few chapters of *Unlock The Door*, Deb Maybury does it again. Her ability to listen and hear people's voice can't be put into words. She provides a safe environment with her gentle openness and willingness to be present while people share their trauma. I have had the pleasure to be a part of this incredible book in my healing and complete two phases of group with her as my facilitator at The Gatehouse. This book will be valuable to so many in their journey of healing and bring awareness to all about sexual abuse.

Stephanie Breckon, Early Childhood Educator

Please put this book on your list to buy. It's truly eye-opening to the sexual abuse epidemic. I don't have any personal (known) experiences or ties to sexual abuse, and I think if you are the same way - you need to read it more than people who do have experiences with it. It's important for all of us to understand the prevalence, the impact and the prevention measures.

Jacki Flynn, Editor

Deb Maybury has drawn on personal experience and exhaustive research to assemble a must read book for all. Her genuine care to educate and help others heal from the trauma of sexual abuse is evident in each word, sentence and paragraph.

Ross O'Donnell President & CEO. Fitness Kickboxing Canada Inc.

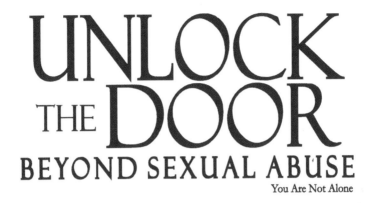

UNLOCK THE DOOR

BEYOND SEXUAL ABUSE

You Are Not Alone

Reveal, Connect and Heal

Deb Maybury

Unlock the Door – Beyond Sexual Abuse

The author of this book does not dispense any therapeutic advice or prescribe the use of any technique as a form of treatment for physical, emotional or medical problems without the advice of a physician. The intent of the author is only to offer information of a general nature to assist you in your quest for emotional and spiritual well-being. In the event you use any of the information in this book for yourself, which is your constitutional right, the author and publisher assume no responsibility for your actions.

DISCLAIMER – Private practice individuals are listed for informational purposes only. Although the author has done her best to ensure that only qualified professionals are listed in the resource directory, she does not have the ability to individually screen every listing. Prior to contacting or seeing any individual, it is recommended that you check his or her qualifications with the appropriate professional organization.

Maybury, Deb
Unlock the Door – Beyond Sexual Abuse

ISBN-13: 978-1484993804
ISBN-10:1484993802

Printed in United States of America.
Published by Deb Maybury/CreateSpace self-publishing.
Cover Design: Ranilo Cabo: rcabo.co.nr

For more information:
deb@debmaybury.com
unlockthedoorbeyondsexualabuse.weebly.com
debmaybury.com

Dedications

This book is dedicated to three precious souls who, each in their own special way, have blessed my life.

First, my birth mom. Through her love and acceptance I have not only my life, but I have a family nothing short of the greatest gift I have ever received.

Second, Becky. To fulfill my promises, "If you have to go, I will have to accomplish enough for both of us," and "You won't be forgotten because I won't stop talking about you." I have written your name in the sands of Asia, Spain, California and Texas and from Vancouver to Halifax, and I will continue to share your story to inspire others to never give up. I miss you more than words can say. Thirty-three years of friendship is as wonderful to remember as it is difficult to be without.

Third, Offie. You were here for eighteen years. You were truly the epitome of unconditional love. You spent hours lying beside me and sitting on my lap as I worked endlessly on this book. You always made me smile, even when you behaved poorly. I never felt alone when you were next to me. Puppy heaven sure got lucky the day you arrived. Thanks for being my baby.

Don't give up. Remember, it's always the last key on the key ring that opens the door.
Paulo Coelho

Contents

Acknowledgements   ix
Foreword by Gabor Maté M.D   11
Preface   17

Unlock The Door   Deb Maybury   19

Family Secrets

A Father's Lament   George   23
Parents in Turmoil   Jane and Mark   25
My Father's House:
a Memoir of Incest and of Healing Sylvia Fraser   39
My Brother   Jenni   59
The Emotions of Not Feeling   Tabitha   65
My Husband Raped Me   Laurie   75
Why Me?   Dorothy   85
I Thought I Could Trust Him   Jamie   99
Behind The Bushes   Dorina   113
I Am Here Now   Allison   125
Searching for a Safe Place   Kelly   129
Sleeping with a Stranger   Patricia A. Wiklund   145
Lyrically Speaking –
How the Years Burn   Ruth Brainis   167
Loving My Sinner, Hating His Sin   Charmaine   171
Naming It to Tame It   Kalin   187
A Victim's Statement   Hope   191
Where's the Justice? –
A Victim's Statement   Author's note   197
Unforgive You Now   Kristen   201

Trusted Others

Love You Like a Brother   Paulie   203
A Child's Perspective   Tim C.   219

Author and Thriver	Dana	233
Daddy's Hands	Colleen Laylon	237
I Want to Tell My Story	Lynne	239
A Sign on My Head	Stewart	253
Coach or Predator?	Bonnie	265
I'm Not Gonna Hide	Fayth	275
Scout's Honour	Bob	277

To Punish, To Protect

Sergeant Shelley Tarnowski	Sgt. Shelley Tarnowski	293
Shame on You	Lorraine	311
It's Pretty Dismal	Ted	313

A Time to Heal

Sword and Wand	Alyssa Wright	329
The Gatehouse	Arthur Lockhart	331
Harmony Integration Therapy	Satyen Raja	349
Shifting Paradigms about the Martial Arts	Brad Hutchinson	355
Emotional Freedom Technique	David Rourke	357
The *Demartini Method*®	Dr. John DeMartini	369

Advocacy

Respect Group Inc.	Sheldon Kennedy	391
Making a Difference – Erin Merryn	Deb Maybury	401
The FACSA Foundation	Connie Lee	403
Final Thoughts		405
I Am Who I Am	Stephanie	411
Deb Maybury and *Unlock the Door*		413
Potential symptoms of sexual abuse		415
Resources		417
Little girl, young boy		419

ACKNOWLEDGEMENTS

I feel more like the messenger of *Unlock the Door* than the author.

My heart and gratitude go out to the storytellers, advocates and healers in this book: George, Jane, Mark, Fayth, Hope, Jenni, Charmaine, Kelly, Stephanie, Dana, Allison, Dorothy, Colleen Laylon, Arthur Lockhart, Lynne, Satyen Raja, Tabitha, Jamie, Ruth, Tim C., Paulie, Dorina, Kalin, Dr. Patricia A. Wiklund, Bob, Stewart, Laurie, Bonnie, Alyssa Wright, Lorri, Ted, Sgt. Shelley Tarnowski, Erin Merryn, Brad Hutchinson, Kristen, Connie Lee, David Rourke, Sheldon Kennedy, Sylvia Fraser and Dr. John Demartini.

To those who read, edited and re-edited: Gerry Jenkison, Sandy Stubbert, Deb Adams, Jacki Flynn, Yvonne Danjuma, Maria, Paula, Kristin, Nikki and Kelly, thank you very much.

Thank you to Gabor Maté for writing the forward. You are wonderful and do amazing work. Thank you for your insight and dedication, and for making a huge contribution to so many.

To Arthur Lockhart for all your support and help along the way, as well as your vision, passion and commitment to The Gatehouse and all those who have benefited from your tireless work – thank you.

To my peers at The Gatehouse, I love and believe in you all and feel privileged to be on this healing journey with you by my side. Your encouragement, support and ability to make me accountable has been immensely appreciated.

Thank you to my amazing family, who never discourage me from taking on anything out of their comfort zone and who always smile with the look of *here she goes again* when I share my latest project. Thank you all for your support and encouragement. Love you all.

Thank you to my family at Dradalm Promotions, Deb, Patsy, Angie, Marina, Sandy, Amanda, Sarah and Shannon for tolerating my endless enthusiasm and constant discussions about this project – as well picking up my slack during book and work multitasking.

Thank you for all the encouragement from far too many to thank – including personal friends and everyone following the progress of *Unlock the Door* via social media.

A special thank you to Charmaine who went out of her way to contact Sheldon Kennedy and Gabor Maté when I was running out of steam.

Thank you Racquel for hours and hours of transcribing!

Thank you to everyone who recommended a contributor and to anyone else I may have missed thanking!

Thanks to Fayth for telling her auntie, "You're doing good work." I am more proud of you than you can imagine. Through your honesty and openness you will make a difference to other children your age!

Deb Maybury
March 18, 2013
Toronto

FOREWORD

The way to begin resolving trauma is to talk about it, to bring it to the light of day. As one of the contributors to *Unlock The Door* states, "When one person's words flow and another person listens, magic can happen." In this book people speak and we, the readers, listen. And listen we must.

For twelve years I worked as a physician in Vancouver's Downtown Eastside, notorious as North America's most concentrated area of drug use. Within a few square blocks thousands of human beings chase the chimera of oblivion through the injection, ingestion or inhalation of mind-altering substances, seeking an evanescent escape from the pain of their existence. It's a quest that often leads to their death, whether through overdose, suicide, HIV or a multiplicity of other diseases. In those twelve years I did not meet a single female patient, out of hundreds, who had not been sexually abused in childhood. Many of these same women prowl the streets offering cheap sexual favours in exchange for drug money, an endeavour that is more than a financial transaction: having been objectified sexually as children, they may have little valuation of themselves other than as sexual beings. Sexuality is the only aspect of them that ever received attention. Among the men, at least a significant minority had been sexually abused as well.

No one should think, therefore, that the consequences of sexual abuse are only psychic – although those would be devastating enough, as I discuss below. Addiction is one frequent outcome, both because sexual abuse generates searing emotional pain that substances like opiates, cocaine and alcohol temporarily soothe, but also because abuse alters the developing brain in such ways that make it more receptive to intoxicants.

We know something about how specific kinds of childhood trauma affect brain development. For example, the vermis, a part of the cerebellum at the back of the brain, is an area thought to play a key role in addictions due to its influence on the motivational system in the midbrain. Imaging of this structure in adults who were sexually abused as children reveals abnormalities of blood flow, and these abnormalities are associated with symptoms that increase the risk for substance addiction. In one study of the electro-encephalograms (EEGs) of adults who had suffered sexual abuse, the vast majority had abnormal brain waves and over a third showed seizure activity.

According to a review published by the US National Institute on Drug Abuse in 2002,

> … the rate of victimization among women substance abusers ranges from 50% to nearly 100%... Populations of substance abusers are found to meet the (diagnostic) criteria for post-traumatic stress disorder... those experiencing both physical and sexual abuse were at least *twice* as likely to be using drugs than those who experienced either abuse alone.

Similarly with alcohol: those who experienced sexual abuse were three times more likely to begin drinking in adolescence.

As with addiction, so with diseases of the body. Men sexually abused have a threefold risk of heart attacks, while people abused in childhood have a nearly fifty per cent risk of cancer as adults. And this last fact points to the importance of the present volume of painful recollections and revelations: the men are thought to incur the elevated risk not only because of their trauma, but because they tend to repress or suppress their traumatic memories, fearing to share them with others. Such suppression stresses the cardiovascular system, and other body functions.

An Australian study also found that men who had been sexually abused in childhood were up to ten times more likely to have suicidal tendencies. One of the researchers said,

> Men are particularly vulnerable because they don't like to talk to others about their problems... It's difficult for anyone to come to terms with traumatic experiences such as childhood sexual abuse, but for men the stigma is worse because they don't tend to confide in their friends as much. Many suffer feelings of failure and isolation and think that it is a sign of

weakness to discuss their past abuse with others.

While such shame may affect men more, women are very much vulnerable to it as well.

I have often considered why sexual trauma should be so particularly debilitating, both psychologically and physically. What makes it more corrosive than other forms of psychological or physical abuse? I believe the answer lies in the need of the human being for autonomy, for an existence in which one's body and soul can both glory in their full individual expression. Sexual abuse, more than other forms of hurt, robs the person of autonomy, reducing her or him to the status of an object whose body exists only to serve the desires of another, whose emotional needs are seen not to exist, whose soul is disregarded. Such objectification threatens to deprive us of our very humanity and, as many stories in this book attest, forces us to split our psyche: the surface façade we present to the world, and the inner, hidden milieu of shame, confusion, pain, anger and bottomless sorrow. We become not ourselves. And then we compensate in ways that can never make up for the loss of ourselves. Addiction is only one of them.

The most corrosive impact of sexual abuse is shame, toxic self-rejection. Children are narcissistic, in the purest sense of the word. Their world revolves around them; everything happens to them and because of them. If the caregiving adults are able to respect the child for who she is, as she is, the child will come to accept and honour herself. If they hurt and objectify her, it is because she is unworthy to be a full human being. That shame becomes the central dynamic of the psyche. Not recognized and integrated, it needs to be compensated for – if not by drugs, then by a desperate drive to be accepted by others at all costs, or even by the relentless striving for worldly achievement that, attained or not, leaves the person as hollow as the most abject failure.

As attested by many of the stories in this book, even if unseen by their narrators, the tragedy of the abused child is that she experienced herself as a failure even before the abuse began. The reason is simple: by the time the child was traumatized sexually, she had already been isolated from the emotional nurturance and protection of the adult world. In my healing work with abuse survivors I ask a simple question: "All that time that your body was physically invaded and your emotions violated, who did you talk to, from whom did you seek help?" The near universal answer: "No one." In short, well prior to the onset of the abuse the child knew she was alone. There was no one to keep her safe and no one to rescue her. That is what made the abuse possible, since the predator senses with laser precision which child is left vulnerable, alone, without succour.

"There is trauma from the abuse and the first thing that disappears is a person's voice because they don't know what to do with the trauma," asserts one of the interviewees in *Unlock The Door*. Yes, but not quite so. That voice had already been silenced – that is why they don't know what to do with the trauma: in fact, that *is* the trauma.

There is an encouraging example in this book of how a sexual incident need not become traumatic, a story in which a three-and-a-half-year-old girl is subjected to inappropriate sexual touching and display from a twelve-year-old cousin. The child immediately tells the grandmother who promptly informs the parents; the entire family gathers around, and the problem never recurs. This child, we may rest assured, has not been traumatized.

Even the astute and eloquent Sylvia Fraser overlooks this essential point. Sexually exploited by her father, she never tells anyone until in adulthood the repressed memories flash into consciousness. But they were repressed only because there was no one to whom the child Sylvia could have revealed what she was having to endure, not even her mother. Instead, she berates herself:

> Unfortunately, when I was growing up, I was always raging at my mother who functioned as a kind of doormat for my father because she was an easy target and I was so full of the fury that helped me to survive. She was a good woman, very dutiful, absolutely moral and upstanding. So, what relatives saw when they looked at me was a little brat who was always having temper tantrums. I certainly expected no sympathy from anybody.

There was no little brat, and the raging was not unfortunate. It was the proper emotional expression of a hurt child enraged at the blindness and indifference of the adults who ought to have seen and prevented her suffering.

We need truth to emerge from shadow into light. This brave volume of stories, interviews, poetry and, above all, truth-speaking, will unlock the door to the light for many. And it will bestow the blessing of helping people still entrapped in shame to find their own courage and strength, as many of the contributors here have been able to.

Gabor Maté M.D.
Author, *In the Realm of Hungry Ghosts: Close Encounters with Addiction*

Working through trauma requires the right balance of assimilation and accommodation.
Stephen Joseph

Preface

The truth is, the epidemic of sexual abuse is no longer a secret – yet, it remains a taboo. We have been socialized to remain silent and to deny or be skeptical about its pervasiveness and emotional impact. The stories in this book are not isolated cases nor individuals seeking to defame and persecute innocent people. They are but a handful of an endless volume surfacing now, as a swing in societal support encourages those violated to speak out.

I imagine the worst thing, more than not being able to speak out, is speaking and not being heard. The most impactful statement I have heard since embarking on this book was, 'When I told my mother her boyfriend raped me she said, "He must have thought you were me".' Sexual violations maim, torture, haunt and cripple us long after the physical experience ends.

A child trusts openly and implicitly, until trust is broken. Once it's severed, it never returns to its original healthy state. The psychological damage is perpetuated and deepens with silence and social and familial disregard. As I write this, yet another teenager has taken her life as a result of the fallout after a rape. How do we as a civilized society ensure that the authorities (police, courts and schools) deal with abusive situations in a timely, sensitive and systematic manner? Failing to take action or sweeping these cases under the rug is no longer an option we can tolerate or justify.

We are all responsible, first to become aware, second to listen, third to hear and fourth to act. We are far beyond denial. It is time to contribute to solutions to reduce the prevalence of sexual abuse, and to promote healing processes for all individuals affected.

Unlock the Door
Deb Maybury

We weren't supposed to be here. He stepped out of the car and headed toward his apartment door. I could hear my heart pound. He turned when he realized I was not following and sent me an encouraging wave to join him. I remained in my seat and shook my head, *no*. He smiled as I read his lips that said "Come on." I repeated my gesture, as determined as a ten-year-old could be. I was not going in there; it was not a safe place. He began to walk back to the driver's door and I sensed he was coming to *get* me. As quickly as possible I slid across the front seat and slammed the lock down as he grabbed the handle. With the door locked, I felt a wave of relief wash over me. I forced myself to smile in an attempt to bring humour to a frightening situation — I hoped he would find humour also. I was immediately concerned, as I wondered what he would do next.

"Debbie, unlock the door," he said firmly. That afternoon was in 1973 and I can still feel the sickness in my stomach when he smiled at me and repeated, "Debbie, unlock the door." No way, no more, I thought. I smiled like I was playing a game, his game. He turned and I hoped he would continue walking toward his apartment. However, when he got to the front of the car, he quickly jumped to the right and headed toward the passenger side. Without hesitating, I slid back to my original position and pushed the lock down before he reached the side of the car. I was locked in with the keys safely in the ignition. I felt panic at not knowing what he would do next. Once again, I smiled – the look on his face indicated he was not pleased.

He did his best to encourage me to open the door and accompany him. I remember him saying something like, "Come in, just for a bit." Like a bit would be okay with me. I knew what it meant and I was not giving any more bits of me to him! Not now, not ever.

He had tricked me into agreeing to go with him that day. Probably with a promise to buy me some toy — that was his style. A dollar for this or that, a reward I paid dearly for. He built trust and provided attention that was lacking for me at home. I regretfully asked myself why I had gotten into the car.

He created memories I wished I could forget.

I waited for his next move. I was afraid but I didn't let on. I remember thinking I could open the door and run across the street, run all the way home, but it was a long way and I wasn't sure I knew the directions. I was too shy to consider asking for help.

I didn't care what he was thinking — I was not going to let him touch me again. He pleaded, "Debbie, unlock the door." I smiled and shook my head, *no*. He seemed to give up and turned and walked toward his apartment. My thoughts raced and I wondered what he was going to do when he returned. I waited for what seemed like a long time.

Finally, he reappeared and approached the car. I looked straight ahead as I was afraid to make eye contact. It made me feel sick to even look at him. When he reached the driver's door he apologized and said he wasn't going to do anything to me. "Unlock the door. I'm going to take you home." *Really?* I thought. Could I trust him? He had not openly lied to me before. One last time he repeated, "Unlock the door."

I opened the door and prayed he was telling the truth. It did not cross my mind that he would *really* hurt me since he wasn't physically violent. He took me home. I remained silent, secretly hating him.

I never saw him again after that day. I did not ask my mother why her friend stopped coming around. I didn't care since I was happy to be without him. I admit that I had wished him dead more than once.

A short time later that wish became reality. My mother told my brother and I that he'd had a massive heart attack and died, even though his brother, who was a nurse, had heard him scream and tried to revive him. My brother looked as upset as I felt relieved. In my mind, I was jumping up and down in celebration, though outwardly, I remained still and silent.

I slept much better knowing that sounds at my bedroom window would not be him attempting to break into my room. I felt relieved that rides in the boat would not turn into unknown destinations and dirty experiences.

That was the end of it. No more sick games with older people wanting a piece of me. My innocence and trust were gone and moving forward I would have to be the one to take care of me.

Family
Secrets

A Father's Lament
George

My daughter was raped. I'm not here to tell her story – I would never presume to be a spokesperson for her. I know I could never properly express her feelings as a survivor and I know that the struggle I went through does not compare to her difficult journey. This is my story: a story about the absolute worst days of my life and how my daughter's sexual assault impacted me as a father who loves his daughter deeply.

I became aware of something being wrong a couple days after it happened. We were always close but she was shutting me out and locking herself in a room for hours at a time, more so than is expected of a seventeen year old. When I first heard the rumours I had no idea how to react. I wanted to stay calm.

At first I handled it poorly. When I confronted her about what I had heard, emotions boiled over and I became furious. How could my little girl *not* come to me about this? What an idiot I was. Here was my baby pouring out her pain and my first reaction was so selfish. We cried together and as we calmed down, we hugged and just sat together without speaking. That was the only time I ever raised my voice to my daughter and I am still disappointed in myself. I was lost. I cried for the next three days while locked in my office at work. What should I do? I began calling around to find out about support programs, not just for her but for our family. We were able to get my daughter into a program within the first month or so, but there was nothing for our family. I searched the Internet looking for support programs for the family but I found nothing. We would have to self-heal. The wound is still there.

Unfortunately I knew a little about abuse as I saw my mother being abused while I was growing up. I turned my back on my mother but there was no way I was turning my back on my daughter. I needed to *fix* this — after all that is what parents do, they fix things for their children. What a fool I was!

I believed in my heart and soul that she was going to need to take back the control in order to heal. As with many survivors, she didn't want to relive the experience for anyone. I felt I had to convince her to file a complaint. I was prepared to risk our relationship. I lovingly but firmly guided her into speaking to the police. She pushed back but eventually agreed. I kept asking myself, "Was I doing the right thing?"

As I sat at the police station with her and a friend she brought along for emotional support, I continued to think about how to react. I had to be strong for her but what about *him*. I wanted him dead. After she had told her story while in another room, the police officer pulled me into that room and suggested that I not do anything stupid. I remember saying, "My daughter needs me more than I need him dead." That is the sole reason her attacker is still alive today.

I spent the next few weeks sleeping on the floor beside her bed. She was afraid to close her eyes. I would just lie there. We wouldn't talk. I needed her to know I'd be there when she needed to talk. In time, she started and sometimes we would chat late into the night and get no sleep. Then, after a few weeks, one night she said, "I can sleep tonight, dad. You can go to bed." Those words made me feel like maybe I had done something right to help her.

For years afterwards, I didn't share her story with our family. I felt it was her story to share, when she was ready. She asked me once if I was ashamed of her and if that's why I hadn't told anyone. Surprised, I explained that I felt it was up to her to tell those who she wanted to know. She understood afterwards but WOW, I missed that one.

I failed to protect my baby. We still talk about it from time to time. I am always looking for reassurance that she is able to live with what happened. I know she will never forget and will never be the same person that she was. I certainly know that I will never forget. After about a year, her attacker was convicted and registered as a sex offender but I got no real satisfaction out of that.

It has been six years since it happened. I still tear up when I talk about it. I often wonder how I could have handled the whole thing better. She has learned to live with the emotional scars and I think about what happened almost every day. I still think of killing him. I worry about running into him somewhere, but I hold onto the thought that my daughter still needs me more than I need him dead.

Parents in Turmoil
Jane and Mark

Thank you for participating in this interview. I know it's not easy to talk about what happened to your daughter. Keep in mind the idea behind this book is to connect and to share stories, in order to help other people with what they are going through.

Mark: Understood.

The first question is related to your names. I think you mentioned that you would like to remain anonymous.

Mark: Yes, we'll use the pseudonyms *Mark* and *Jane*.

Mark and Jane it is. I'd like to begin the interview with one or both of you telling the story of what happened to your daughter.

Jane: I'll start because I was the one who figured it out. It started when my daughter, Erin, told my mom that Devin (her cousin) had showed her his really silly string or something to that effect. Mom called me at work and I said Erin must be talking about the drawstring in his pants or something that's hanging out of his pants. My mom asked my daughter what colour it was and she said it was the colour of his skin.

That raised questions so we needed to do some more digging. When I got home from work, I called Janice (my sister-in-law) and I said, "Look, I don't think there's anything to this but this is what my mom said." Janice talked to Devin and, after she confronted him, he confessed. He said he had touched my daughter inappropriately and had realized what he was doing was wrong and stopped. Janice called us back and was upset and crying and told us the details. When I told my mom she got really upset and called the police. The police went to Janice's house to discuss what had happened and a few weeks later a social worker came to our house. She interviewed Erin to make sure the level of abuse was what Devin had said and that it didn't go beyond that. Devin and Erin's stories matched.

The Special Victims Unit wanted to come in and talk to us but after talking to my therapist from work I said no. I had gone to see a therapist through my employee assistance program and she said that given that Devin was twelve years old this could just be considered sexual exploration. For Erin's sake she recommended to not make a big issue out of it because doing so would probably make it worse psychologically. She told me I should just monitor the situation quietly.

I didn't want to get the Special Victims Unit involved or anything like that. After that whole thing Janice called us back. She had contacted a therapist for Devin since we had insisted on it. We told her that if she didn't get a therapist we were going to the police to charge him. She got a therapist and from what I know he has been in therapy ever since. We're waiting until the point where this therapist says it's okay for him to have a conversation with us about what happened so we can move forward as a family. That hasn't happened yet.

How old was your daughter at the time?

Jane: She was three and a half. It happened Easter weekend.

Were just the two of them involved when it happened?

Jane: Yes. Janice told me that Devin said he got Rebecca (Erin's younger sister) to go to her room and close the door so he could be alone with Erin.

Were there other people around?

Jane: There were eleven people in the house.

Mark: Sharon (Jane's mother) made the call to the police and they called and let us know they were coming.

How did you feel when your mom contacted the police?

Jane: I was conflicted. I was upset at her but at the same time I felt like we needed to do something. Yet it was still the wrong move. I felt more like it should have been my call and not hers because they're my kids. How did you feel?

Mark: I was upset. I didn't feel it was her place to decide on a course of action, although her motives and intentions were understandable. Although she was the initial point of contact in terms of the story coming to light, I thought that it was not her place to involve others.

How did you two express your feelings to her and what kind of feelings did she have after hearing your response?

Mark: I had a very direct conversation with her. I didn't mince any words. She explained her side; I explained mine. There was no resolution because, as with many arguments, we both felt we were right. It was never resolved; we just agreed to disagree.

Jane: Maybe my mom was being over protective because she felt like someone had hurt *her kid*. But she didn't take into consideration Devin's age or concern for him or the family dynamic. We wanted to make sure the resolution wasn't based on anger, resentment and punishment. We wanted to figure out something that would help everyone involved recover. My mom going to the police created an extra level of stress. I tried to explain, saying, "Look, Devin understands he did the wrong thing and he's in therapy," but she wanted revenge. I was thinking about everyone's perspective and how to best come at this so we didn't tear the families apart.

I absolutely understand both positions. When this sort of thing happens, there is such an outpouring of emotion from everybody involved that you need to just take a breath before reacting. Somebody who is the protector, the grandmother and matriarch here, feels she needs to do something and punishing is somehow useful.

Jane: Yeah, I get it. I understood that too.

How did you resolve it and how has it affected family relationships?

Mark: We haven't seen Devin since. It has caused logistical difficulties since we were a family that got together for every special event. Every holiday, every birthday, every long weekend was always a major family event and this situation has created a divide between family members. The adults have had polite conversations and we've resolved things to the point where we spend time together. We talk to each other but there's still that white elephant in the room.

It's still unresolved. Devin and Erin have not seen each other.

Jane: We do bring it up once in a while by asking "How is therapy going?" But we don't know what the next step should be.

Mark: In the beginning the difficulty was that the therapist didn't want anybody, even Devin's mom (my sister), involved in the therapy. He didn't want Devin to be distracted from what he was trying to accomplish. This doctor was keeping things private between him and Devin so Janice didn't have a lot of information to provide for a long time. Now we don't talk about it because everyone is unclear how to start the next process, which is reintegration. This is not an everyday situation that we know how to handle. We're trying to move forward and figure out what's right for everyone. I think enough time has passed now and we're ready to move on.

Jane: Yeah. For the last six months or so Erin has been asking why Devin isn't around. She now senses that something is wrong. I just say he's very busy with hockey, soccer and basketball, or that his mom and dad are divorced and he's with his dad. She's a smart kid and she's getting suspicious. She said, "Why don't I ever see Devin?" She sees her other cousin often and hasn't seen Devin since that Easter. She's smart enough to put two and two together and know that what happened the last time they were together is related to why she isn't seeing Devin. I'm worried about that. I have been talking a little to Janice and her husband about it and although the therapist said Erin's too young to remember, she has a photographic memory. She's a smart kid. We're going to have to find a way to reintegrate that relationship in a positive way. But I can tell you I'm never ever going to trust Devin again or leave him in a room alone with my kids.

Mark: I think that's a given.

I wonder about the therapy with Devin and his mother not being involved in the process and not having any idea what's going on. Where is the family dynamic of healing? If the mom's not even involved, how do you get to where the cousins and you two are?

Mark: Both of Devin's parents were part of the process and went to Devin's therapist separately. I think, in terms of Devin, they were given a synopsis of what the therapist and Devin worked on and accomplished.

Looking back, were there any red flags with Devin?

Mark: None that we could have anticipated.

Jane: When it came to the girls, he was like their older step-brother was; he was very attentive, always liked to play with them, and had fun with them. Their step-brother was always so good with the girls and I just thought Devin was the same. I never imagined this would happen.

Mark: There was nothing we could see, in hindsight that would point to anything like this. We could not say, "That makes sense because of this or that." It was as if someone had placed a different Devin in the house.

Jane: I blame myself a bit because I went up to check on them and our younger daughter wasn't in the room with Erin and Devin. I asked what they were doing and Devin said, "Oh we're playing doctor," and Erin said, "Yeah, we're playing doctor." They had all the toy doctor equipment out I'd bought them to play with. I thought it was fine, that everyone was happy, playing and having fun. I went back downstairs to deal with dinner. I never thought that playing doctor would turn into *playing the doctor*. It just never occurred to me. I didn't see anything that was suspicious. I often think, "If only I was just a little bit more aware." But there were no signs. I mean Devin was always so good. He loved his cousins and always wanted to see them and they wanted to see him. Our family events were always grandiose and always such a good time.

Who do you trust your girls with now?

Mark: The funny thing is that before they were born, I decided that there was going to be very limited exposure in terms of who was going to be with our girls and who would be entrusted with their care or be in their company. That was always in place for me.

Jane: I wouldn't want the girls to go to someone else's house for a sleepover because I don't know what the dad is like. But we never really ever thought about our own family.

Mark: I guess the point I was leading to was that it hasn't changed anything for me. I still feel the same way because I always felt that way before.

Jane: He's always been very, very cautious.

Mark: I'm not in favour of them sleeping somewhere else because

I don't know whose uncle is coming over or whose older brother or sister or mother may do something. There has been no change for me – I'm still very cautious. The kids can be taken care of by Jane's mother, my mother and that's it. We don't have a babysitter who comes into our home when we want our date nights. That has never been an option for me.

Jane: It's because both of our families have experienced sexual abuse and it's caused us to be guarded. We had talked a lot about sexual abuse even before we had kids, how that was never going to happen to our kids because we were going to protect them. But then it happened.

You don't plan these kinds of things, that's for sure. Would you deal with the situation any differently, knowing what you know now?

Mark: Yes, is the short answer. After I was given assurances on the telephone that Devin would be dealt with in a harsh and severe manner, I still didn't feel like he was going to get the punishment deserved for something of this magnitude. So, I took it upon myself to have him understand what he had done wrong. I got in my car and drove to my sister's home. I was not in my right mind, which I think is understandable. When I got there Devin's father was there (Janice's ex-husband) and he tried to physically apprehend me. I managed to get past him and his brother to find that Janice and Devin had fled out a window and made their way to the neighbour's house, where Janice called the police. By the time I went outside to try to find Devin, the police had arrived in the driveway. Very little of the scenario was revealed to them. Again, even in that state of mind, I didn't feel that it was necessary for the police to be involved. The police finally said that if no one was going to say what was going on, they were going to have to leave. My sister chose not to press charges and I got in my car and drove home.

That caused more difficulties with my sister and also her husband, who was not in the country at the time. I had gone into his home when he wasn't there. I had lived there for an extended period of time so it was a place I had called home and they had welcomed me into it. I had come back in a fit of rage and caused a disturbance in his home. That caused some difficulties for a while.

We all got together and had a very candid conversation about what had happened. We had chosen these two people to raise our children if anything ever happened to us. He understood my reaction. He was angry at me for invading his home and causing this disturbance with his wife but he knew that if anything ever happened to my girls under his care that's exactly how he would have reacted. They care about the girls. It was very difficult to know how to feel. After a while, the adults managed to come to terms with what happened and we're still very close and spend genuine time together. I would rather not have seen my sibling flee out a window with her son in a state of fear. Yet I think the severity of what had happened had to be impressed upon him.

Jane: We were very concerned that Devin understood what he did was terribly wrong. When Janice said, "Oh, we're going to make sure he gets punished for this," I couldn't help but think, he would only lose his video games for a while.

Mark: He got yelled at and put to bed, which didn't sit well with me. Regrets? Yeah, for sure.

Jane: It put me in an odd position too because when Mark left and was heading out the driveway, I was the one who called Janice and told her that he was coming so that she could call the police or do whatever she needed to prepare for his arrival. I didn't know what he was going to do. He wasn't in his right frame of mind. It was a strange situation, to be the one to have to warn her to protect her son when her son had just hurt my daughter.

Very complicated.
Both: Yeah.

What would serve as retribution for Devin?
Mark: As upset as I was, I genuinely didn't set out to inflict physical harm upon him but I was certainly going to make him understand the severity of what he had done. It was my intention to put the fear for his life into him in order to make him understand and remember that he had done something that was very real and something that had consequences. I felt like my behaviour was the only way that he was ever going to understand the consequences of his actions.

You are a big strong man and I can certainly understand his parents wanting to escape before you arrived. Did you think your outburst would stop him from acting like that with somebody else?

Mark: It wasn't my intention to just show him that I would protect my little one; I really wanted to impress upon him the wrongness of the action itself. He needed to understand that he had committed a serious wrong.

Jane: When the Special Victims Unit officer was talking to me on the phone, he said they needed to investigate more to find out if Devin had done this to other girls — if he had a history. They wanted to start interviewing his peers. At that point I thought, "He's twelve. They need to keep in mind that he's at the emergence of puberty." An investigation may completely ruin his life. They said they wanted to make sure that Devin was not going to turn into another Paul Bernardo. I told the police officer that if Devin was fourteen then I would be more apt to say that they should do an investigation. But twelve-year-olds are sexually curious. I teach family studies and about kissing cousins and such. It's very common for siblings to look at each other's body parts as they're growing up. But the situation with Devin involved sexual touching — that's the thing that troubled me. Maybe because he doesn't have any siblings himself, he took advantage of the situation. That's how I justified it. I said, "You know he's only twelve, he could be curious, learning, trying to figure things out himself."

Mark: I think we sort of strayed from the question which was: "Was the action I took going to change if he was ever going to do it to anyone else?"

Jane: Right.

Mark: I guess at the time I was being as opened-minded as possible but, if nothing else, I felt like my actions would impress upon him the wrongness of what he had done. Obviously there was going to be follow through afterwards and there was going to be an effort made that whatever happened next had to be for both of the kids to be able to recover and to move on with their lives.

Jane: As a teacher, I was looking out for the welfare of all the kids involved. My mom on the other hand acted like Devin was going to do it again — like he was going to be a sexual molester for the rest of his life. I think that's coming from her personal experiences and not so much what actually happened between the kids. I hope I won't feel like I did the wrong thing in the future. In the situation at the time and what we've done since, I feel that we have been working in the best interest of everybody involved.

Mark: Afterwards I did speak to legal counsel and I was advised that we don't necessarily have to press charges or anything of that nature. Everything was documented with the police and can be used in the future as evidence against him. At least there is something on record that shows a pattern if he offends in the future.

Jane: Maybe it's a good thing the police were involved.

Mark: It's a good thing the police have documentation.

I'm glad you mentioned this because I was going to ask what recommendations were made by the various people involved.

Jane: The Special Victims Unit wanted go after him full on, but the social workers, counsellors and lawyers advised that, because of the age of the children, it was best to deal with it in therapy rather than a criminal investigation. My instinct, after speaking with the social workers, was to choose a healing route rather than a punishment one.

What has Erin's healing involved?

Jane: The therapists all said it was best to leave it alone. New feelings will probably surface when she hits puberty and she starts to better understand the violation that occurred. As of right now she thinks she was just playing doctor with Devin. I told the therapist that Erin is not an average child. I know whenever a parent says that therapists think, "Yeah, yeah, all the kids are the same," but she really isn't. She remembers everything and now she's starting to ask questions about Devin and I don't know what to do. Do we reintegrate them or do we take her to therapy and start to explore what happened. I don't know what the next step should be.

Mark: The adults now have to coordinate things and make sure we do things right going forward.

Jane: Janice did say that the first step should be for Devin to approach Mark and I and for the three of us to try to heal together. So, in order for Erin to heal, we have to heal first.

How and where do you learn the language and method to best approach this issue with Devin?

Mark: I think we're going to have to speak to his counsellors and understand what they've tried to do so that we can be part of the process and stay on the track they've started. They've set out a plan and have worked with him for the better part of two years. We need to be just another step in the process.

It seems like two years is a long time for a twelve-year-old to be in therapy?

Jane: There are other issues and I think that's why he's still in therapy.

Mark: Once they started digging they discovered there was a lot of stuff to deal with. In light of these other issues, it made sense, where he ended up. There were a lot of identity issues and some genuine concerns about his place in the world. It has been a long road because there were a lot of things they had to work through. I'm not even sure if he's finished or if it might be an on-going thing.

Jane: I was very frustrated for the first six months or so. I wanted to make sure the therapy was continuing because if it wasn't I was going to call the police and tell them to do the investigation. Then I thought, "Let's just forget about it and just move on with our lives." But for the last few months Erin has been bringing it up and we need to have some resolution. It has gone on long enough and we all need to move forward. I don't want to do anything to rip the Band-Aid off the wound, but something needs to happen.

It must be difficult not knowing what to do next or what's going on with Devin, and still having to answer Erin's questions as honestly as possible.

Mark: We had a very candid conversation with Erin at the time about appropriate and inappropriate behaviour and we answered her questions as they came, but there weren't many because she was very small and didn't totally understand. We don't hide from her questions. We deal with everything as openly as we can, considering her age. But now she is starting to ask more questions and it's hard to know what the right thing to do is.

Jane: My employee assistance program isn't really designed to deal with this or support us through it. I spoke to them but I don't think they're really concerned about how Erin is adjusting.

Mark: They may not be equipped to help.

Is anybody advising you about services available for the family?

Jane: No, it was always about Erin and Devin; it was never about the family as a whole. It was never mentioned.

Mark: To be perfectly honest, for the most part we've dealt with it and moved forward. This is now a matter of reintegrating the two young ones back into the family together.

Jane: Mark's family have overcome a lot of abuse — not necessarily sexual abuse, but I think they have a different perspective from many people because of these experiences. I think that has influenced how our whole family has dealt with this situation. They've been in abusive relationships and they've overcome them. It's the one thing that binds the family together and makes them so close.

Mark: Hmm.

What advice would you give to other couples with young daughters?

Mark: Wow, that's a pretty big question.

Jane: I would like to say watch your kids all the time, but you can't, and you can't predict something like this happening.

Mark: I would suggest being aware and paying attention. You can't watch your kids like a hawk and if you live your life in mistrust of everyone and everything, then you will worry yourself to death. Know where your children are and what they're doing. At the end of day you have to feel okay with where they are and what they're doing.

Jane: I think a lot of people in my position, when I first got that call from my mom, might have just shrugged it off. Don't shrug off their words; really listen to them, even if they're small kids and they say strange things. It's important to follow up. I never would have known anything if I hadn't called Janice and asked her to speak with Devin.

Mark: Kids tend to exhibit what they're saying physically because they might not be able to express themselves well verbally. Listen to what they're saying and make sure you're approachable. Keep the lines of communication open even if children are very small, since they have to be able to feel they can approach you if something's wrong.

Jane: Or approach somebody else in the family who they trust and who will then report back to you.

Good advice. That's a gem for people reading this; listen and follow up. You have both really thought out each step of the way and have positive healing mentalities. My last question is, how do you two feel when you think about the situation?

Mark: Honestly, I made peace with it some time ago — I had to in order to function. There was a long period of time where it preoccupied my thoughts. Now I don't feel as if I'm owed anything — I don't feel as if I'm waiting for retribution. I'm not pining for the day that I get to confront him. What I want most is for my family to be whole again and for everyone to be able to spend time together and be as close as we once were.

Jane: Devin is not my flesh and blood and, to be completely honest, I don't care if I ever see him again. But I know what he means to my husband and what he means to his family; I would like to resolve this so his family can heal.

Mark: I respect Jane's opinion and her feelings in that regard and I don't expect her to knit him a sweater for Christmas. I don't. I would never expect her to force herself to be anything other than genuine in how she feels about him but I spent the first twelve years of his life being his *Uncle Mark*. I was a large part of his life given that his birth father is not exactly what you would call a good role model. I tried to be a very positive and influential male figure in his life so he had someone who he could look up to. This has not been an easy thing for me to deal with. Given everything that's happened, I'm never going to be his friend. I'm never going to be his close Uncle Mark again, but at least I would like to be able to see him and have our families be together without animosity or fear. Everything won't be okay or go back to normal, but I would like to have the difficulty and the discomfort minimized for everybody involved.

Jane: When Erin asks about her cousin it gives me more motivation to find a way to really solve this. Honestly, I don't know how I'll feel until I see him in the room.

It's been a long time.

Mark: Yes.

Thank you so much for speaking with me. Do you have any last comments or anything you'd like to share?

Jane: One last piece of advice. People react very differently to a situation like this. I know it's very difficult at the time but it is important to realize that everyone's trying to do what they think is right. For instance, we were very upset with my mom calling the police right away because we felt violated, but we've come to realize that people react differently. We have all been trying to do what we think is right.

Mark: Yes. I guess the other piece is to remember to keep the focus on the two children who were in the room — not the parents or aunts and uncles and cousins and everyone else. The focus has to remain on the two people who were involved. Everyone else's interests are secondary. People may start to fight with each other and blame and point fingers, but it is necessary to keep your eyes on what's most important.

Another piece of great advice. You both have great attitudes and I wish you and your family all the best moving forward with this situation. Thank you so much for contributing to this book.

Both: Thanks Deb.

Jane: Bye, bye.

Become totally empty. Let your heart be at peace. Amidst the rush of worldly coming and goings, observe how endings become beginnings.
The Tao

My Father's House: a Memoir of Incest and of Healing
Sylvia Fraser

It's nice to finally meet you. I have a copy of your book from the library and it appears that a lot of people have read it.
Wow, thank you. I sell it on Amazon's Kindle also.

Fabulous. I found your book chilling and intriguing. I got a big brother kind of feeling while reading it and I really enjoyed the way you presented your story. At the end I was wondering about a sequel?

The sequel would be much worse. I remembered a lot of the rougher sexually abusive stuff after I'd finished writing My Father's House. For example, I wrote a piece about my father taking me to a child's brothel, which was later published in *Toronto Life*, and which is now also available on Kindle as *Maggie and the Pedophiles*.

Please tell me about writing *My Father's House*.
When my memories of incest started to return, I didn't necessarily think I was going to write about the abuse. I was instantly aware that these repressed memories had been the unconscious material that, unbeknownst to me, had fuelled all of the novels I'd already written. When I look back at my other books, particularly *Pandora*, but also *Berlin Solstice*, the story of my abuse was encoded in their narratives. For example, in *The Emperor's Virgin* I write about a vestal virgin who was buried alive for breaking her vow of chastity. Who forced her to break her vow? The emperor – i.e., daddy. It became so clear to me after my memories had returned that in everything I had written I had unconsciously been telling and retelling this story of incest, with no idea I was doing so. I wouldn't start out to write a novel about sex and violence, but whether the story was set in Rome or my hometown of Hamilton, I'd end up writing about these dark things. This surprised me. I didn't know where in my psyche all this stuff was coming from. Critics were beginning to accuse me of writing about sex in order to sell books. I

wasn't. I was embarrassed by it, but somehow it just kept happening. So, anyway, when I understood the meaning of all that unconscious material, I didn't know if I would ever write again because my voyage of discovery was over. I moved to Los Angeles at that time. I wanted to go away. I needed to reassess who I was. I would tell people about my discoveries – I mean, boy would I tell people! I was like the Ancient Mariner with burning eyes, obsessively telling my childhood story as I now knew it to have unfolded, but that was too much for most people to absorb. My friends would treat me as if I were the same person they had known last week, whereas in my own mind I was definitely not that person. I was somebody else entirely, but I wasn't sure who.

I went to Los Angeles in 1984 and I lived there for a couple of years. It wasn't until after about a year that I started to write *My Father's House*. Though I was trying to write it as a book of fiction, the truth kept bleeding through. I began to find it more and more offensive that I was covering up once again a story that it had taken me all these decades to uncover. The closer I came to the end of the book, the more I realized it had to be a book of truth. However, I had put in place a number of fictional devices I felt still worked. I'm referring to things like combining characters that weren't vital to the main story and perhaps altering the time frame. I decided that it was all right to keep these devices so long as I explained them in an Author's Note (which I did). In other words, everything about the incest itself and our family was as honest as I could make it at that time, which meant that everything that happened inside my father's house really did take place. However, for incidents that happened outside of my father's house, say in the neighbourhood or at school, I combined or deliberately disguised characters. I mean, just because somebody happens to be in the same class as me, did they want to find themselves named in a book about incest for some small incident that meant nothing to them but meant everything to me? So, there were all those decisions to be made and dilemmas to be resolved. Would I have done that now? No, I'd write it straight out now and I'd take away the fictional devices, but at the time I was writing about people who were still alive and the climate for the shocking story I had to tell was very much different from today. The book was published in 1987, when incest, or even child abuse, was not known to be commonplace in our culture. It was not on anyone's radar screen. Many of my friends were telling me that to publish this memoir would be both personal and professional suicide.

You started writing your book in 1985. Is that when you first started to remember?
My memories began to come back before then, I forget exactly the date, and they didn't come back all at once. At first, I thought the last person I would tell would be my mother, but then I began to feel this compulsion to tell her – the way I as a child yearned to be able to tell my mommy. I did so just before going to Los Angeles, which was in 1984. Up to that time, I still thought the abuse had happened only before I started school when I was five years old. That was all my memory had presented at that point. It was really another shock when I realized that the abuse had continued into my teenage years and that my psyche had divided so that one part of me knew the truth about what had happened to me (my Other Self) while part of me continued to go to school and live my life as if nothing was wrong. So, the full story of my past came to me in a kind of growing awareness. Even after I'd finished writing *My Father's House*, I still had a big gap in my memory regarding what had happened in high school.

One of the things I find most compelling is the process by which my memories returned. Despite the fact that the lid was on for so long, when they wanted to come back, there was no way I could prevent them from doing so. I felt *compelled* to remember, and when I tried to turn away, I would become ill or otherwise forced to pay attention. This is one of the elements I wrote about in my memoir *Flying Higher*. The process of recollection itself seems unbelievable because often it would involve a string of unlikely coincidences that led me not only to specific revelations but also to factual evidence supporting their truth. The power of the secrets to reveal themselves seemed able to impact the environment around me. At times, I wanted just to be done with the past, to be bored with it, but the part of myself who held the memories – my Other Self – wouldn't let me.

Did you ever seek help?
After I published *My Father's House*, I suddenly became an expert. I

was on all the talk shows and I was even being consulted by therapists. I wanted to believe that I at least knew everything about my own case and all this memory retrieval stuff was behind me, but after about a year or so I began to get chronic laryngitis, especially when I was going to speak publicly about my experiences. That was when I began to suspect there were still memories of important events I was repressing. I very reluctantly went into therapy, which I had not done before – at least, not for anything remotely connected with incest. In the seventies, many new kinds of therapy were being introduced by psychologists who were rejecting psychiatry based on the Freudian model. People who didn't think they had any serious psychological problems but were curious about the workings of the human psyche began going to these therapists, often as part of a group. This was called the Human Potential Movement. Participating in it was almost a form of recreation with the goal being self-improvement or what was being called *self-actualization*. I was one of those people. I didn't think I had a problem for which I needed therapy, but as a journalist, I thought it was part of my beat. I went to a massage therapist for a few sessions. I went with a group on a primal therapy weekend. I became interested in Jungian therapy. Looking back, I can see that I was likely preparing myself on some unconscious level to remember. Call it inner wisdom. I have no other explanation beyond that; some part of me understood that before I allowed my conscious self to remember the incest, I had better build a very solid container around myself so that I wasn't going to explode. I think that's why I was forty-eight before I allowed myself to remember. As I've already said, our whole society was in denial about child sexual abuse — not just me. Unlike today, there weren't a lot of therapists trained to deal with the issue so I knew on some unconscious level that if I was going to remember, I would have to be able to take care of myself.

While dabbling in these seventies therapies, no one ever mentioned incest, including the therapists. With one exception. During the primal therapy weekend, one young woman talked about her grandfather who had orally raped her. The grandfather was the only one she believed loved her, and the only person she loved, which is typically part of the seduction. This young woman was round like a barrel, with no breasts or waist to speak of, and with a very short broad throat, out of which came a beautiful singing voice. I remember thinking that it was as if she had physically turned into a container for her grandfather's sperm and her beautiful voice sang a song of love and protest. I was fascinated with her story, but I certainly didn't identify with it at all. In fact, I felt it was the worst, most pathetic and far-out story I'd heard all weekend, which seemed to be the feeling of the rest of the group as well. In hearing these stories and attending these group sessions I guess I was learning that it was possible to have these terrible things happen to you and to survive them. Then, after my memories began to return, writing about them became a need and an obsession, whether I published a book or not. That was always up in the air and, in fact, I write every book that way. I never start out by asking who's going to publish it and who's going to read it. I just write it, and if it's publishable and I find a publisher then that's great.

When *My Father's House* came out, I was quite surprised by the reaction. There was some debate about if I was telling the truth. Some people questioned whether I really had forgotten about the abuse – they thought that I may have actually remembered all along. It was a very difficult story for people to get their thinking and emotions around – however, child sexual abuse, including incest, was an issue that had begun to gain attention. Mostly, I was very surprised by the positive way I was embraced. For a few years, I became the poster child for incest. At the same time, dozens and dozens of other survivors were coming forward with their stories. It was as if the floodgates had opened. Though I've written twelve other books, *My Father's House* is still the book for which I'm best known.

It's a huge part of who you are.
It's interesting to me that so many people who have been abused want to go public. It's as if, because they have kept the secret for so long, that just telling family and friends isn't enough. They want to tell the world as well. This process was more natural for me because I was already a writer and a public figure who was very used to the media.

That's something I want to ask you about. What I find is that people either don't want to approach the topic of sexual abuse and don't want to talk about what happened to them or they really want or need to reveal the deepest secret that has been buried, typically for years. Currently, there is an explosion of people coming forth with stories of sexual abuse and that is a huge change from when you wrote *My Father's House*. When your book first came out, it must have been shocking to the public. Can you tell me what the reaction was?

The timing was exactly right to create a sudden explosion of interest and awareness. Before my book, incest was a topic you might find in a Tennessee Williams' play or it was believed to be a perversion that was way, way off on the far edges of society, like something that might happen in families where no one paid their bills and everyone was always drunk. Now, suddenly, there were many women like me who came from apparently *respectable* families who were claiming to have been sexually abused. After that came a wave of boys who were declaring they had been sexually abused, and often the abusers were people in authority, such as doctors and teachers and boy scout leaders and coaches. Now we have an explosion of sexual abuse allegations involving Catholic priests. And it wasn't just the abusers who were at fault, but also those in authority who were covering up for them – the principals and the bishops and politicians. Since my book was one of the first sexual abuse memoirs to find a large readership, I was suddenly being accused of having inspired an hysteria of false memories in people who had merely read my book and now thought they had been abused.

Leading this backlash was an organization calling itself the False Memory Syndrome Foundation (FMSF). By now, quite a few therapists were devoting their practices to the treatment of sexual abuse survivors, and the premise of the FMSF was that these therapists were, through suggestion, *implanting* false memories of abuse in their patients, who were then accusing innocent fathers and uncles and brothers and boy scout leaders of abuse. The FMSF received a lot of publicity because, by now, the media were growing bored with all the stories of sexual abuse. It's an old adage that if you tell a story one day and then deny it the next, you have two stories, so at first journalists were on the side of the victims of sexual abuse and then many of them switched over to debunking the victims.

You're a writer and you're creative so if you were going to come up with a story, why would you choose something like incest? Why would anybody draw that kind of attention to themselves? You could write about your adventures in Africa. Why write about incest?

Well, you'd have to ask the False Memory Syndrome Foundation that question. The story of sexual abuse is an ugly one, and a lot of people would prefer to believe such things didn't happen. Of course, sexual abusers have a very strong reason for trying to undermine the credibility of their accusers. My family was unusual in a very positive way. My father had died before my memories of abuse returned, but when I told my mother and my sister and my other relatives about the abuse, they believed and supported me. It was such an incredible story at that time in our culture's history that I was prepared to risk alienation from my own family. I was not a favourite among relatives. As a child, I was full of rage. My father was also an angry man, and nobody liked him either, which was lucky for me. He wasn't one of those charming people who could easily deceive others about his behaviour. I can feel sorry for him now. He made his own life as miserable as he made my life. He was a fat man who could not control his eating. He was a terrible bully at home while being effusively polite to others in a way that made them shy away from him since he seemed inauthentic and boring. He spent his life working shifts at a steel company, which was not easy or satisfying. He dutifully supported his family. It is because of all of this that I can no longer remain angry with him. Perhaps he kept his misery at bay a little bit longer by giving his misery to me and my sister. I doubt that he was ever happy or felt fulfilled or loved.

My parents were never invited anywhere. The only friends they had were church friends. My mother was popular at church, but my father was only tolerated because of her. Perhaps by faithfully going to church he tried, in his way, to be a good man or tried to convince himself that he was a good man. Or perhaps the church-going stuff was just a cover.

Unfortunately, when I was growing up, I was always raging at my mother, who functioned as a kind of doormat for my father because she was an easy target and I was so full of the fury that helped me to survive. She was a good woman, very dutiful, absolutely moral and upstanding. So, what relatives saw when they looked at me was a little brat who was always having temper tantrums. I certainly expected no sympathy from anybody.

The first person I told was my sister, who instantly believed me. Now that was unusual. That was a real gift and, years later, on her deathbed, she also had memories of having been abused by my father. Presumably, he had switched to me because I was more vulnerable, being the youngest child, which is what you often see in abusive families. Predators choose the most vulnerable one, who is easiest to control. Also, I believe my sister was more protected by my mother, as well as by my grandmother, who was still alive when these events first happened. When I told my mother about the abuse, I didn't expect her to believe me, but she said, "Of course I believe you. You're my daughter." That was another gift. Later she went back on that a little bit. She asked my sister if she thought it had really happened; when my sister said yes, my mother never broached the subject again.

As more memories returned after writing and publishing *My Father's House*, I realized my mother was much more involved as an enabler than I had imagined, and much more culpable, but I also came to believe that her consciousness was as split as mine. There was a mommy who was in complete denial and didn't know, and a mommy who did. That caused me to do some ancestral research because it made me suspect there might have been incest in her family. From my research, I came to believe her grandfather, my great grandfather, had abused my grandmother, and possibly my mother and her sisters. It's interesting that no matter how old these secrets are – in this case seventy years – they can still be brought to light. I found a couple of old relatives who remembered incidents and conversations that had aroused their suspicions even though they were just children themselves. When I started asking the right questions, they put two and two together in a way that was enlightening.

When most people reveal to their families their stories of abuse, they are more likely to be given a hard time, especially if there are a number of siblings. People have their own version of the past and they may ostracize those who have different memories. They may also feel pressured to take sides in a bitter dispute about what did or did not happen. I think partly that didn't happen to me because I didn't go to my family looking for corroboration or sympathy. As soon as I was old enough, I had emotionally separated myself from them. I wasn't estranged or anything, but I was emotionally independent. When I told them my truth – as I had come to understand it – and I received their support, it was an unexpected gift for which I was grateful. Maybe they had started to remember; maybe they hadn't entirely forgotten; maybe they had been suspicious. It's hard for many people today to understand how sexually repressive the fifties were. Divorce carried a taint and virginity before marriage was considered a woman's most prized possession. What was my mother to do with the whole concept of incest? It was better not to see it or acknowledge it. If my story had come to light at that time, my life would have been ruined. I would have been considered no better than a prostitute even though what happened to me wasn't my fault. Forgetting was the survival tactic of the women in my family – including me. Perhaps just as astonishing was the inner wisdom that let me know when it was safe for me to recall the past, so that my story became conscious to me, piece by piece, allowing me to absorb it slowly, instead of being overwhelmed. I don't know where this inner wisdom came from. You can call it the soul, if you wish. Hypnotherapists sometimes find evidence for what they refer to as *the caretaker personality* when they hypnotize patients. Whatever it is, it's not anything I can take credit for, but it is something I can feel grateful for.

Early on you didn't have memories but it seems as though you had symptoms.
Oh, I had a lot of symptoms. I was probably close to being bipolar throughout high school. I experienced mood swings and I had a lot of difficulty dating. I was expected to be attractive and alluring and lots of guys were interested but I couldn't stand to go out with anyone more than once. I think it was the part of me that dealt with sex – with my father – that shut down. I was afraid on a subconscious level of getting into a situation with a teenage boy where sex might be expected, so I just froze over and went through the motions of dating and being popular.

In the fifties it was socially dangerous for girls to be sexy because other girls would turn on them. I was sexy in my appearance though not in my behaviour. Nevertheless, I was always protected by my female friends. They never criticized or judged me and I don't know why that is. I still have close friends from that era in my life.

I think there must have been some kind of shield of protection around me. Maybe people sensed my vulnerability on some level. I don't know what it was. I was getting a bad reputation with boys, not because I was putting out, but because I wasn't. I was considered a tease. The ugly term used at the time was a *cockteaser*. I recognized that I had a lot of fear and confusion around dating, but I had no reason to believe I was any different than other teenagers.

What did your friends think about your memoir?
I don't really know. They were surprised, of course, but they remained loyal to me. If they were judgmental, I never heard about it. I didn't go to them or to anyone asking for corroboration or support or understanding. I just told my story and was grateful when people were supportive. There's a difference between vulnerability and neediness. It's when people are needy that others are likely to bully them or be critical. As I said, I've always felt protected in ways I don't really understand. In my travel book, *The Rope in the Water: a Pilgrimage to India*, I relate the story of how I was carried by a riptide way out in the Arabian Sea, and when I thought I was going to drown, suddenly I felt a rope slap my thigh and I pulled myself to shore by that rope. Where did it come from? I don't know. There was no reason for a rope to be in the water.

It's the same with my bicycle. Every once in a while I'm careless and I hit a curb or a slippery streetcar track and I flip over the handle bars. The spectators think I'm going to be badly hurt but I usually end up just being embarrassed. The accident seems to take a long time to happen, during which I decide that I don't want to be injured and I'm not. Also, when I jumped off a moving train in India after missing my stop, I seemed to spend a lot of time in the air and all I could think of was, "Nobody knows I'm in India. I can't be hurt." I was so badly shaken up that I was too crippled to walk for a while. Yet my injuries went away quickly and I didn't even have any bruises to show for it.

If you've been through trauma, does time slow down?
I haven't any idea. It's just something that seems to happen to me that I am puzzled about. I would say the only reason I survived as a child is because my survival instincts were really, really strong. If

not, I would have been broken in some way – either I would have gone crazy, been schizophrenic, ended up being attracted to abusive men, or become an alcoholic or a drug addict, as so many abused women do. For some reason, none of that happened and I don't know why. I was always able to keep the damaged and abused part of myself hidden even from myself, while maintaining some form of normalcy with my cover-up personality, even to the extent of being able to attract a lot of friends and to achieve a certain amount of success. I don't know how I managed to do that. I sometimes feel that I must have come into this life with some money in the bank, that is, some kind of psychological reserve or strength. I don't necessarily believe in reincarnation, but maybe I did have another life or two in which I dealt with this issue.

The memory loss was, in a sense, a survival mechanism. Did you ever get to the point where you thought, "I don't want to remember any more?"
I wanted to remember everything, but then I'd get to these plateaus and I'd think, "Oh, let's get on with my real life – my present life." It really bothered me when my throat was sore with chronic laryngitis and I began to feel that this symptom meant I still had other memories I was covering up. I didn't want to go into therapy; I didn't want to spend good time going after bad time. Why was it necessary for me to learn all of the various ways in which I had suffered? I was bored with the idea of going over and over the past yet again, but the chronic laryngitis gave me no choice. Once I had reluctantly decided to go into therapy and I was working with a wonderful therapist, then I really did become excited all over again in my determination to uncover all the information and prove that I could remember. The simple truth is that the hidden memories would not leave me alone until I uncovered all of them. The chronic laryngitis was like being hit on the head with a block of wood and being told, "Wake up! There's more." It's hard to explain, because the clues I received sometimes defied the usual world of cause and effect. For example, I would experience a series of weird coincidences that would lead me not only to valuable information about the past but also to prove that the information I was uncovering was factual. My psychic powers seemed to be heightened. They would lead me to information that was meaningful and useful in ways that are hard to explain.

As a result of this process, I became very interested in quantum physics because the weird ways in which particles behave has created a new paradigm for describing reality that is supported by leading physicists. The weirdness of quantum physics allowed me to understand my rather strange experiences in scientific terms.

How did you feel when you first began to remember the abuse?
It was a big shock, especially since I prided myself on my very detailed memory of my early school years. I'd remember all kinds of things that my peers had forgotten, like the names of the milk monitors in my grade three class and who played which roles in the school play, *Hansel and Gretel,* including the understudies, even though I wasn't in the play. If I could remember all that, how could I have forgotten anything as important as my father sexually abusing me? I came to see that these memories are what psychiatrists call *screen memories* because they hide the larger truths hidden behind them; the intense detail of these memories makes it seem that this is the full story and that nothing has been hidden or forgotten. I knew my memories of the abuse were real because *my body* remembered. It remembered what had been done to it and all the emotions that were connected with the abuse. It wasn't a matter of thoughts just popping into my head. My body would go into a series of convulsions that acted out the abuse and I would relive the experiences emotionally as well as physically. My body knew. It was my head that had to catch up. I felt I was actually going back in time, by reliving the events as they had happened to me as a child. The physical and emotional experience was so powerful that it became impossible for me *not* to believe myself.

Were the travels that you took a number of years after the book part of the search to find all of yourself?
That journey began in college when I chose to study philosophy. The basic question philosophers ask themselves is; *What is reality?* While Aristotle argued that the basic reality was the material world that we experience with our senses, Plato argued that the material world was just a poor reflection of an abstract reality that we could not experience directly through our senses, but only intuit very imperfectly with our minds. In other words, consciousness, or the

non-material world, was more real than the material world. In college, my prejudice was to accept all the philosophers like Aristotle that believed in the world of the senses – those who believed in what was concrete and material. However, when my abuse memories exploded into my conscious awareness, I no longer even knew who I was. I had to admit that the world was much more mysterious than I had ever imagined, and my experiences since then have made that even clearer to me.

When I went to India, I visited ashrams and spent time with Hindu gurus and Buddhists, and the Eastern view of reality became very convincing to me. Similar to Plato, Hindus and Buddhists consider the material world to be an illusion. Reality resides in a higher consciousness that can be perceived through meditation. When I nearly drowned in the Arabian Sea, and a rope suddenly appeared in the water, allowing me to pull myself to shore, it certainly seemed that my desire for the rope and the need for it had somehow materialized it. That appeared to be dramatic evidence that consciousness alone could create events in the material world. That was *my experience* of what happened. While I don't have a set of beliefs, there are ideas and theories that I prefer to others. For example, I like the idea of reincarnation because I like the idea of a soul continuing after death, but that certainly doesn't mean it's true. I'm a quester. I look for evidence on life's big questions, but the jury is always still out. I wrote *The Rope in the Water* because of that trip to India.

There are many people who are struggling with issues related to sexual abuse. You have been through a tremendous amount and have taken a very interesting path of survival. What can you say to people who are really struggling, those whose emotions are all over the place and are trying to understand and deal with everything?
You don't often have much choice as to which issues you must deal with. There are a lot of experiences I would prefer not to have had and there are others that I'm glad that I avoided, like being born physically disabled or into conditions of war. If sexual abuse is your issue, then I believe that it's best to go as deeply into it as you can, to the extent that you can. That may mean stopping your ordinary life for a while, perhaps keeping it on hold while you take time to

investigate what might have happened to you. That may mean allowing yourself space to remember by physically returning to the places where you think the abuse might have occurred, looking through old photograph albums as an aid to memory, or seeking help through intensive therapy. There are now a lot of therapists who are skilled in treating sexual abuse survivors. I didn't have a therapist until my throat was causing me difficulties, and that was after I had published *My Father's House*. Therapy can be very absorbing and it can feel very selfish to spend time on yourself in that way, but abuse creates deep wounds and you've got to recognize that emotional healing can take as long as, or much longer than, physical healing. Sometimes writing things out can be wonderful therapy – not with the goal of publication – but just writing whatever comes into your head for yourself, putting your emotions on paper without judgment, letting your notebook bear witness to your grief, your anger, your hurt, your confusion. It's often difficult for people who have children and other responsibilities to make time to go on the necessary inner journey, but not doing so will almost always end up being more debilitating in the long run.

I think it's dangerous to expect friends and relatives to understand what you're going through or to corroborate or justify how you feel. You can send out a few test feelers and you may find some people who are supportive and have useful information. Yet the road you have embarked on may be a long and difficult one, and you can't expect other people to stop their lives for you. Be responsible for your own healing, at the same time as you explore your environment for resources that can help you – therapists, survivor groups, the many books written by other sexual abuse victims, and writing groups. Don't look for escape routes such as drugs or alcohol or abusive love affairs. Male abuse victims tend to give into anger more than women. They are more likely to try to make others suffer for their own repressed pain and may abuse others. Women are more inclined to self-punish through guilt, which may lead to addictive behaviours of all kinds, promiscuity, prostitution, and so on. It's very important for sexual abuse victims to learn to understand these behaviours in themselves or to seek out professionals who will help them to recognize the dangers. Women victims are also more inclined than men to fall into depression. Depression is usually a mix of conflicting emotions that need to be sorted out and traced to their source.

I believe it's a waste of time to feel sorry for yourself or to engage in a lot of wishful thinking about what you may have missed out on or how things should have been. I realized right from the beginning that even to wish the abuse hadn't happened to me would be like wishing for my own death because I wouldn't know who that other little girl would have been. She would exist and I would not. When I look at my life, I realize I that I have learned a great deal that I value from my difficult experiences, including the strength to survive the abuse. There's an old Arab proverb that says, "The poison that does not kill makes strong."

Many people who have been abused want to give to others the early happiness that they themselves missed out on. Some become wonderful parents, and in giving to their children, they recoup some of their own childhood losses. That's a very healing choice to make. Others turn their suffering into compassion for others. They become therapists and help other survivors, or they take up other worthwhile causes. That's also a fabulous way to heal the past. When I was growing up, as a kid, my best friend was my cat. As an adult, I have spent twelve years fostering homeless cats and kittens until they are adopted. I'm now working to bring awareness to the wretched way that many humans treat other animals, including the ones we raise to eat: the abominable way in which we crowd them into pens and cruelly transport and slaughter them.

Now, if you ask me what damage I still carry in my psyche from the abuse, I would say that I often find it easier to empathize with the suffering of other animals as a species, rather than the suffering of other humans as a species. Also, I don't think it's accidental that I work and live alone. I have a lot of friends but some part of me likes to have a little margin of separateness. I had a wonderful marriage to a very loving man – I left him before I understood the abuse in my background. I realized afterwards that my abuse figured very directly into the reasons why I left. That caused both of us a great deal of pain, and I still carry a lot of guilt about that. That's a regret I have never been able to get rid of. So, am I damaged? Do I carry scars? Of course I do. Do I have strength as a result? I would say yes. The advice I would give people, which I don't necessarily follow myself, is to get rid of these kinds of regrets. Forgive yourself and get over the guilt by finding some way of helping others or bettering your own circumstances.

Another product of my past is that I don't have children and I've never wanted children. I don't regret that. I've lived an interesting and adventurous life, and I've never believed that it was possible for me to do everything without living in a state of acute exhaustion. Almost everyone has to makes choices. We all possess many unlived lives and unused potential.

Your father sexually violated you for years. What do you think about some of the laws regarding sentences for pedophiles and other sexual offenders?
I can feel sorry for my father but it doesn't mean that there shouldn't be some payment for wrongdoing – not necessarily as a form of revenge, but in order to require that person to take responsibility for their actions and get them out of circulation for the protection of others. What has happened in the Catholic Church over the years around the issue of abuse is an abomination. The policy has been to pass around pedophile priests from parish to parish, allowing them to do the maximum damage in order to save the reputation of the Church through this massive cover-up. The same has happened with some teachers. Instead of being exposed for the perverts they are, they have merely been recirculated.

I think it's the rare pedophile who understands or is willing to admit to the damage he or she does. They usually have a really strong set of defences that allow them to think that they're making their victims feel special if they show them affection and take them to ball games or give them candy. A number of studies have shown that therapy often makes pedophiles *better* pedophiles in that they learn to become more skilled in covering up their crimes and more manipulative in grooming and attracting victims. I personally believe that pedophiles should be sent to prison to prevent them from abusing more children and to demonstrate to other pedophiles that this is a crime for which there will be serious consequences.

Do you think the punishment for pedophiles is too lax?
Yes, I do. For sure. What is the price of a lost childhood that perhaps leads to a life of addiction? I also believe that the cover-ups must be

dealt with in a clear way that sends the message that this will not be tolerated. As a society, we are moving in that direction. What used to be acceptable no longer is. Many pedophiles have gone on for years being protected by those in authority, and even when they are caught, people who should know better still want to make excuses for them, especially for so-called charismatic abusers. "Oh, but he was just so wonderful. He was the best choir leader we ever had!"

You're referring to a case in a book by Judy Steed, *Our Little Secret*.
Yeah.

I read that recently. I was surprised to see your name in it. It includes a story about a choir master, from Kingston, Ontario, where I grew up. When I was in grade six a friend of mine told me about a boy, Henrick Helmer, who had committed suicide. He was one of the kids Judy referred to in her book. He was fifteen when he hung himself. At the time, I heard he had a terminal brain tumour so he decided to hang himself. The sexual abuse story came out about twenty-five years later and I happened to see it on TV. I was shocked. He took his life because he had been molested at the church. He was one of many choirboys there, and the abuse went on for years. The perpetrator was protected by his circle.
Wow. I knew the basic story. I didn't know about the brain tumour cover-up.

That's what I heard. What's so heart wrenching is that some people must have known, on one level or another, what was going on and didn't connect the dots.
Abusers like that provide a cover-up service and they're charismatic, so even if people suspect them, they think maybe their value still outweighs what they're doing on the side. But it doesn't. There was also a choir leader in Toronto who was charismatic. He took his high school choir to various places in Europe where they performed and won prizes. Even after he was found out, a Toronto writer wrote an apology of sorts that said, "But he was such a good choir leader!" People like that guy, and the one from Kingston, have a very strong motivation to appear wonderful because they know damn well what they're covering up. They express all their negativity by screwing around and abusing and bullying and playing power games, but they have a protective mask that makes them seem like good people. You can't say, "He was a wonderful man but he had this problem..." You

have to put the two sides together and say, "He was able to pretend to be wonderful because he was getting rid of all his anger and narcissism and cruelty and negativity through abusing his innocent victims."

You're making me think of Deepak Chopra's book *The Shadow Effect*. We have more than one side. We too often hear, "I never would have guessed." Once in a while we hear, "There was something about him."

I had a widowed friend who was always telling me what a fabulous guy her husband had been except that sometimes he'd beat her up and break her bones. She described this as his "illness" as if it was not really him who was responsible for this abusive behaviour. Once again, of course, he could appear like a saint to the rest of the world because he was getting rid of all his underlying fury by breaking her bones and beating her bloody when he felt like it.

Before my memories came back, I was also two people, and I feel now that a lot of things that I did before then were quite shallow in that they were geared to my own survival and don't reflect how I would act now. Even though I didn't have access to my real emotions at the time, I still feel that I have to take responsibility for all my actions and for my whole life, not just the parts that were conscious to me or the ones that I like. In fact, I'm more inclined to be judgmental about myself instead of empathizing with myself as a child who had few choices. I think it's important for victims of abuse to strike the right balance – to empathize with their damaged selves and be self-forgiving at the same time as they take responsibility for their whole selves. I think women perhaps have a harder time with that equation and are more inclined to blame themselves, to feel guilty and to punish themselves for things that were done to them that they couldn't help. However, when you hear about male abuse victims who commit suicide, you know that it is not just women who struggle with the aftermath of abuse.

I have heard and read a lot of comments about forgiveness from women, while men tend to make statements about wanting to kill their abusers or themselves.

I had been an angry child and I became an angry adult. Small things would make me furious; for instance, a blouse would come back from the cleaners with the buttons ripped off and I'd explode. As I wrote in *My Father's House*, when I realized my anger had a genuine cause, I wasn't angry anymore in that uncontrolled, inappropriate way because I knew that my anger had been part of my survival mechanism and was no longer necessary. I found myself very ready to get rid of my anger and to move to forgiveness. Some readers thought that was the best part of my memoir, while some abuse victims became indignant with me because they felt I had trivialized the abuse by forgiving my father.

My final position on the subject is that I believe that if you're angry with your abuser, then you're still in that person's grip. If you forgive your abuser, you are also still in a relationship with that person, but with the power reversed in that now you are the one in control. At this stage in my life, I'm not angry at my father and I don't forgive my father. I don't blame him and I don't think about him. I would describe my attitude as the Buddhist one of benign indifference. But, let me go back and say that I think every emotional stage that an abuse victim goes through is right and useful for that person. Probably, the most important thing is not to get stuck. Because I was so angry growing up, I was very ready to give up that emotion. It had become a burden. People who have repressed their rage all their lives will likely find it very therapeutic to release it, to feel it fully, and even to wallow in it. Furthermore, I have respect for the wisdom of children who, when given a set of bad choices, are able to take the least damaging one. I think every abused person's circumstances are completely unique, despite some terrible similarities.

Thank you so much for sharing your wisdom. You have made a lot of very interesting points. I could sit here all evening thinking about the important information you have shared with me, but I don't want to keep you any longer than we agreed.

It was interesting for me too. It's lovely to meet you and I'm sure that you'll do a nice job of whatever this evolves into. I also hope that you'll be able to live your life in a way that pleases you. So there we are.

The person is at the center of all troubles.
Dalai Lama

My Brother
Jenni

Where do I begin? To start from the beginning is a bit tough because I can't remember when it began. In my mind it started out as childish curiosity: "You show me yours and I'll show you mine."

But nonetheless, I'll start with my family.

I come from a traditional nuclear family: mom, dad, sister, brother and dog. I am the youngest of the three. My sister is six years older so, as much as I would like to say we had a good relationship, it was kind of hard for us to relate to each other growing up. She was the protector, but was very involved in school and most nights she was away at band practice, karate or baseball.

My mom is one of the kindest, most loving people I know, and at the same time she is extremely clingy, emotional and always looking to fit the social norm. She comes from a home of adultery and divorce. Her mother neglected her and at the age of sixteen moved into her boyfriend's house, taking everything with her except the kitchen table and my mother's bedroom furniture – leaving my mother alone in the big house. My mom loves her kids very much and would do anything for us – however, she is also a *guilt-tripper* and doesn't like to admit when her kids aren't *normal*. When I told her I made myself throw up, she said, "Oh, I'm sure that was just a one-time thing." Thanks for the support. When my sister told our parents she is gay my mother didn't say a single word to anyone else in our family for fear of what they would think. Way to be there.

Then there is Dad: loving, amazing, and the one who is always there for me. I didn't see much of him as a kid because he often travelled out of the country for work. Despite that, he and I have always managed to have a special daddy-daughter relationship, for which I am very grateful. He's the one who said, "Let's get you some help, you need to get better." Where I would be without him?

Then there is *him*. My brother. Four years older than me, the brat of the family, the one who always got in trouble and was picked on as a kid because he tried so hard to be the class clown. He would chase me around singing, "Barney's dead," knowing all too well that this would hurt me.

Then there's me, the youngest. My brother and sister, being two years apart in age, played together all the time and had friends that they could hang out with together while I was stuck by myself. They would sit in the captain's chairs in the van and play cards – two-player games so I couldn't join in.

I was picked on at school. My mom made me have a mushroom haircut even though I wanted to grow my hair long. She would give me the hand-me-down clothes, or when she did buy me new clothes, she picked them out and not me. For example, I was sent to school wearing a purple turtleneck and matching purple tights in *sixth grade* despite crying and saying I didn't want to. Guess who got made fun of that day?

So, from the very beginning my self-esteem was the equivalent of shit on a brick. I felt ugly, I was picked on, and everyone laughed at my freckles and stupid haircut.

Cue, my brother and the only times he wanted to play with me. When my brother played these games with me, I felt important, like, *he is actually playing with ME!* It was the best thing ever, finally feeling included! The abuse goes back as far as I can remember. Most memories from when I was younger I can't recall. I'm sure they are suppressed. The times I do recall haunt me. The games he used to play, "Let's pretend we're aliens and if you die the only way I can bring you back to life is by doing unspeakable things, but only I can do it to you." Or the deadly "Let's play Truth or Dare." *Truth or Dare.* What a twisted, fucked-up way to play. I would always pick Truth. Always. I said Truth, but in my mind I screamed no, no, no, no, NO!" I never said it out loud. His truths always led to dares without me knowing. The things he did he should not have asked his sister to do. They were nasty. It seems like there were millions of times I would lie on my back focused on the shelf of teddy bears praying to God for it to be over. I froze – my mind escaping to keep me sane. I remember asking him if this was normal and why we did it and he said, "Sure it is, a lot of my friends do it too." Loving that I was included, I accepted his stupid answer. I am being *abnormal* if I don't do it.

He would ask me if I wanted to talk if I was upset, making me feel like he cared. Did we ever talk? Barely. But I always went. Truth or Dare followed. I prayed each time it would be different. I knew if I didn't go, I'd lie in bed feeling guilty for him, embarrassed. So I went.

Then there was Saskatchewan. We went for my aunt's wedding and stayed at a hotel with a great, giant waterslide! So fun … oh, wait, no it wasn't. The time he and I went, he went down first. I waited twenty seconds then went, like you're supposed to. But less than halfway down, there he was, sitting sideways to stop me from going down. He wanted me to touch him. Let's play a game. I couldn't get past him. I was so scared. What if someone saw? What if there are cameras? I couldn't push past him.

Let's play a game. Let's play a game. Fuck your stupid games. But I always played. Why? How could I? Throughout puberty I continued to get picked on, called ugly, and no one liked me. Where did the attention come from … him.

It happened every weekend until I was fifteen and he went away to college. At Christmas when he was home from school he asked me if I wanted to talk. I stayed in my bed sweaty and anxious with my mind spinning with emotion. I didn't go.

I had three friends in high school, hated my life, and tried to kill myself. I had a boyfriend who cheated on me five times, but I stayed with him. He told me I was fat. I was bulimic, anorexic, and obsessed with the gym. Thank God I never got into drugs and alcohol. I didn't give two shits about my life. I didn't belong anywhere. Most of my best friends in high school were one year younger than me. That's how I felt important – being older. The kids my age never let me live that down. I was laughed at and mocked for being friends with younger girls. I never ate lunch in the cafe.

A week before I turned sixteen I had a yelling match with one of the popular girls at school. My brother was going to be home the following week and my emotions were shot. I went to school crying. One of my friends asked me what was wrong. "Nothing," I said. She persisted. "I am thinking about a friend of mine, her father raped her." Thinking it would be an "oh shit, that sucks," and we would move on. Nope. She took me to the guidance counsellor's office despite my attempts to avoid it. I repeated the same story and they said they needed to get the police involved. Shit.

Waiting for the officer I tried to figure out how to get out of the mess. I couldn't leave without going past the counsellor's or the principal's office. And even if I could, where would I go? I was screwed. The officer came in and said, "Tell me what's going on." Here it goes. "I lied about what happened with my friend." I revealed what was happening with my brother and how he was coming home the following week and I was scared.

Police report. I wasn't sixteen yet, so the Children's Aid Society got involved. Did my parents know? Of course not, so they found out when the police called. This was just amazing ... I wanted to fall off the face of the earth.

The week of my birthday was filled with victim impact statements, court dates, and going to watch my brother get fingerprinted. Sweet sixteen – it actually could have been if my mom didn't insist on making me feel guilty. We went for walks and she said, "Why did you do this like this? Do you know how expensive lawyers are?" Lawyers? How expensive lawyers are?! Are you fucking kidding me? What about my life? What about my childhood? What price tag do you want to put on that?

The next four years were spent suppressing my anger, my feelings, everything. We did one family counselling session in which my mom urged me to forgive my brother. So I did. Nothing was said after, other than, "Get over it."

I went away to school to break free from the hellhole I called home and to create new memories. My high school boyfriend proposed in February before I left because he wanted me to himself. I said yes because I would have felt bad for him if I said no. I broke up with him in June. Thank God.

Clean slate. School. I screwed around with a guy who made me feel important – then another, and another. I didn't understand why they would tell me they were falling for me, and then when we slept together they'd cut ties with me. I just wanted to feel loved. I went home for Christmas and reconnected with some guys from high school, in particular one guy. I always had a thing for him but he was one of the cool guys, so he barely gave me the time of day when we were in school. We started hanging out and sleeping together. I met his family. The day before I went back to school we were at a friend's house and he picked me up, took me to the bedroom, asked me if I was on the pill (I was and said yes), pulled my pants off and raped me. He left and I didn't hear from him again.

I became numb. I wanted to die.

I went back to school the next day to start a new semester and then finally met Jason. I needed a ride home and hated taking the subway. I knew he had a car and when I asked for a ride he said he would drive me to the train station. We went on a road trip to pick up his friend in Barrie and I ended up missing my train. He drove me to Brantford, an extra hour's drive for him. We started dating a month later. He came to my cheerleading games, competitions, took me out for dinner and cared about me. He wasn't the type I typically went for. He was a nice guy. I didn't go for the nice guys. Ever.

After two years of dating, something inside me started to break – the anxiety was rising. I felt worthless. Clingy. We were dealing with misogynistic roommates, which sent me into a triggered spiral of anxiety. I would throw things, break things, yell and scream, and hit myself.

Cut.

I began cutting again. I experienced a sheer release of emotions seeing my arm bleed. At the time I did not know why this was all happening. It was because of *him* – the suppressed abuse and the fact that I had never dealt with it.

Finally, Jason and I got our own place, but my emotions remained a mess. I felt fat, ugly, and worthless. I hated sex and touching, and I didn't want Jason to hold me. We started seeing a therapist together, so we could both learn how to deal with my emotions. When she introduced me to *The Courage to Heal* I connected everything: the eating disorders, the self–loathing, the obsessive–compulsive behaviour, and the need to busy myself. It all made sense.

Even after understanding where the emotions came from, I didn't know how to get out of the spiral of depression. I cut. Again. Then I took ibuprofen, about fifteen to be exact, and Jason rushed me to the hospital crying and screaming at me that I was his best friend and he hated that he had to do this. He loved me. I was numb. I didn't care. I spent the night at the hospital and they made me drink charcoal, to make me puke up the pills.

Jason has been my saviour and my rock. He saved my life by working with me day after day and putting his needs second to my well–being. He's gone to hell and back with me.

It has taken time and counselling to understand why I felt the way I did, and do, and how to embrace love again: how to embrace Jason and be physically involved with him again. I've learned how to fight flashbacks and recognize my experience for what it was: traumatic.

Two years ago my brother tried to apologize to me. He picked me up from work and wanted to talk to me. I was terrified. On the way home he said, "I noticed you were being really distant last weekend at home and I wasn't sure if it was because of what happened. I just wanted to tell you that I'm sorry, but I thought you liked it."

I yearn to email him and to scream at him saying, "I am your fucking sister, how could I like it?" He told his ex-girlfriend when everything with the cops was going on. She got mad at me. Figure that one out. He told his fiancé, she talks to me and is still marrying him. Figure that one out. I don't know if I'll go to the wedding. I'm not in the wedding party – big shocker there.

I try to believe in forgiveness and pray to God that it will come. Only time will tell. For now, I'm trying to learn how to move on. I try to look to the future with a bright mind and with one of the strongest support systems I have had in my life. I have come so far in the last ten months, and the journey's not over. Still not over – and it won't be, for a long time.

The Emotions of Not Feeling
Tabitha

As a teenager I discovered romance books and was very much into the whole notion of love and the idea that the *first time* should be very special and happen with the one you love. However, all my expectations could not have been further from what actually happened. It was really weird because I didn't even understand what really happened. It was confusing. It was not until years later I understood.

I'd gone out with friends doing the typical teenage things, including drinking, and I'd bumped into two boys I knew. One of them was in my grade at school and his friend was a couple of years older than me. I vaguely remember talking to them and acting quite stupid. I was aware that I was very drunk. After that my memory gets really, really hazy. I know I ended up way down an alley with the older guy touching and caressing me. I was thinking, God, how on earth did I get here with him?

I remember trying to push him away and that he asked me if I was a virgin. I said no, since I didn't want him to know that I was. I just wanted him to stay away from me. Next my memory shifts again and all I recollect is lying farther down the alley with my trousers around my ankles and no concept of what had happened to me.

When you're drunk, I mean severely drunk, it takes so much effort to fight back. I actually got to the stage where it was easier to give up rather than continue to fight. I can remember this detail because it's a bit embarrassing. At the time I remember thinking, "Oh my goodness, what's happened?" I remember sitting at a bus stop talking to somebody, having no idea what had happened. I was so confused immediately afterwards that I was not able to say if I'd had sex or not.

Later, I bumped into the group of friends I had been with and told them, "I think I might have just had sex with somebody but I'm not actually sure." I was obviously distraught. One friend took me back to her house and by the time we got home and I took off my trousers there was blood everywhere. I said, "Oh my God, I have." I didn't even know what to call what had happened. It took me a long time to actually put the label of *statutory rape* on it. I didn't know any better. I was sixteen and it happened sixteen years ago. It was a time before things like this were really talked about.

I wrote a letter to him afterwards trying to gain some insight into the evening, but I never received a response. I can remember having a confrontation with him sometime later after realizing what he had done was statutory rape, but nothing came of that. After the rape it changed my perceptions of sex and I started drinking often and heavily. I really didn't want to think I'd been raped because I felt so cheap and so worthless. I was a naive teenage girl with dreams of meeting somebody and falling in love and sharing something special – that was sure discarded fast. I tried to laugh it off but I felt so cheap and so worthless that I actually ended up sleeping around. For some strange reason, it felt like I was getting back at him. You've done that to me so I'll do this to you. I didn't realize I was only hurting myself.

For a long time the rape really affected who I was. To this day I am not comfortable having sex with drunk men. It's very difficult for me to have sex, even within a long-term relationship, with someone who is drunk. I don't want that at all.

That rape also compounded the abuse within my family. My stepfather was very abusive toward my mom and there was a lot of stuff that wasn't right while I was growing up. I didn't know what to do about it, but I knew it felt wrong. Every time I would go into the bathroom my stepfather would come in and he'd watch me. We had a mirror and if the mirror was one way you could see into the bathroom. I would always change the mirror around so he couldn't see, but I wasn't allowed to lock the door. I was told there would be trouble for that. He would always come in and stand and watch me in the mirror. There was one time he kissed me to see if I cleaned my teeth.

There was weird stuff going on, but I didn't know what to do, nor did I understand. It took me a long time to fully grasp the memories because I blocked out a lot of my childhood. It was only after my brother Peter died I realized I had no memories of him. When I opened that door many other memories returned, but they were surrounded by blank spots. I don't think anything awful happened, but I don't know for sure. I've reached the stage where I don't particularly want to know because it's not going to accomplish anything. I do remember, after my mom left my stepdad, that one of her boyfriends made a pass at me that wasn't just talking and joking. I remember telling my mom about it and she said, "Oh yeah, I can believe he did that, but if you said that about your stepdad, I could never believe that." I remember thinking, "Oh, okay. I better not tell you about the other stuff."

I ended up talking about my stepfather to my mom later, after Peter died. I had memories of the kissing and I knew stepfathers shouldn't do that to their stepdaughters. I can't imagine any situation where that would be considered normal. I've tried to justify what he did and pretend it didn't happen, but I can't. There was no need for him to ban me from locking the bathroom door or to come in and look at me. It was so uncomfortable. It's so bad I'm laughing. I did eventually tell my mom about him and she believed me. After all, there was some other stuff that was a bit weird about him that came out later.

There's a backdrop to this story. When I lost my virginity, I didn't talk about it much. Then, when I was twenty-two, I told one of my friends and she said, "Yeah, he had a reputation for doing that." I thought, "Holy crap! You knew he had a reputation for doing that? Why didn't I know about it? Why didn't anybody say or do anything about it?" That man is now married with children, which makes me wonder, "Did he ever think what he did was wrong?"

This makes me think of another story. A friend and I were out on one of my drinking binges, celebrating down in London (England). We were really, really drunk. We went to a guy's house and I had sex with him. I don't even remember how he talked us into going to his place. Once there I thought, "Okay, well, I'll just go along with it." When you're drunk inhibitions are down and stuff happens. After we had sex he kept talking about my friend. He wanted to have a threesome and I was completely freaked out. He went to the bathroom and I ran downstairs to try to wake her so we could leave, but she was passed out, completely unconscious and I couldn't wake her. All of a sudden I felt really vulnerable, but didn't know what to do. At that moment he came down and asked what I was doing and I replied, "I'm just getting a cigarette." I didn't want him to know that I was freaked out because I knew, from past experiences with men in such situations, you don't want to antagonize them. I went back upstairs and told him I was really tired and kind of pushed him away and fell asleep. The next thing I knew, my friend was screaming because he'd raped her.

We left immediately and I told her we needed to go to the police station. I felt what he had done to her was definitely wrong. She kept saying she didn't want to go to the police, she just wanted to go home. I tried to reason with her. I said if she went home, that was fine, but if she had a shower she might regret it, since the evidence would be gone and if she wanted to go to the police later, it would be twice as hard to prove anything. So we went and told them what happened. I was mortified because I had been with him and felt I had to tell them so they could swab me too. I sat there thinking, "God, why do I put myself in these situations?"

They took us individually to identify the house. When it was my turn, he walked out of the house and in front of the police car. He ended up getting arrested and it went to trial. We found out later that they only take a rape case to trial if they believe that it has a fifty-one per cent chance or more of actually winning. Apparently my friend's case was really strong and the man was convicted. That incident brought everything about my rape to the forefront.

Those unpleasant experiences are something I'm still dealing with sixteen years later. I've had relationships in which I won't give the full intimacy I want or need because I feel there's a barrier. As much as I would like to say my past experiences of sexual abuse don't affect me, I know they do because I'm still not completely comfortable with my sexuality. It's something I'm constantly working on and aware of. I need to let go of the past because it negatively impacts my current relationships. To be honest, I'm still quite wary of men, even though probably ninety-five per cent of them are okay.

Thank you for sharing. Have you talked this freely before?
No. I would say I'm a little bit more open about it now, but you're probably the only person that knows the entire story. I have shared a little bit before but not everything all in one go, and certainly never as openly as what I've just done.

I appreciate your sharing it with me and with the people who will read this book. Before we continue, I want to clarify if you're going to share your name.

At first I wanted to remain anonymous and then I thought I could actually reveal my name. I'm still not sure. I'm oscillating between staying anonymous or revealing my identity because I know there's more strength in being open and honest. I'm just not sure if that could potentially open a can of worms that I don't want opened. I will get back to you on that one.

Okay, take your time and think about it. Who would you definitely not want to know about your story?

My mom.

Can you tell me why?

Why? That's a really good question because she knows about my friend's rape and what happened to me that night but she doesn't know how I lost my virginity and for some reason I don't want to tell her. I don't know if I'm protecting her or protecting myself. I'm not quite sure. I don't think my sister knows and I wouldn't be comfortable with that either. She's only twenty-two years old, ten years younger than me. I'm more comfortable telling somebody I know less well than my family. It seems more intimate to share this with family.

I totally understand. Do you think there's something a twenty-two-year-old can learn from your experience?

Oh God. Well, my sister is in an abusive relationship of her own, or was. I don't know if they're still together. We don't talk about that. Yes, there is something my sister could potentially learn if she'd heard my story as a teenager. I don't know if she would have been open to listening, but there's definitely something she could learn. In fact, I wanted to talk to you because I'm aware that only by sharing stories will the stigma subside. Maybe I don't want this stigma attached to my family.

Would your mom or sister acknowledge their abusive relationships?

Well, my mom knows she was in an abusive relationship when she was with my stepdad and we've talked about that quite openly and discussed the implications of it all. I only know about the full extent of my sister's abusive relationship through my mom. The way our family works is that my mom tells me what the situation is with my sister, but I can't tell my sister what I've learned because then my sister may feel that my mom has betrayed her confidence. My sister and I don't talk about things like her boyfriend because she knows if I find out that he's hurting her I would want do something about it. So, she has shut down and doesn't talk about it with me.

Our family is not really good at being open and honest. I grew up in an abusive household. My mom left my stepdad when my sister was two. My sister never saw any of the abuse; therefore she can't really understand what I told her. She didn't want to believe I was talking about her dad – she can't imagine it. She didn't see the things I saw him do to my mom. She says she's glad she didn't see any of it, so she can pretend it didn't happen.

But, we still don't talk nearly enough about abuse and that's really silly. By not talking, we have created an environment that's wrong. I met up with an old friend I knew as a teenager who works in an office that deals with sex offenders. She was talking about kids and asked if I remembered my mom's boyfriend — the one who was grooming us to be his sexual toys. I replied, "Oh, it wasn't just me then." "Right," she said. She also talked about another friend of ours who was fourteen and had a twenty-seven-year-old boyfriend. She said, all of this is unfortunate because a lot of things were happening to us, as children, and nobody was saying or doing anything about it. Years later, we found out that just about everybody we knew experienced some type of sexual abuse. She named two other girls we went to school with who were being abused. So much abuse in various ways and nobody said anything.

I hear this over and over again. If more people talked openly they would realize that they are not alone. They may also reduce the number of people violated if they talked about the offender and he or she would get a reputation which would precede them. If we talked about abuse as soon as something happened, if we went and told all our friends, then they would hopefully stay away from that individual. We should never take on guilt or shame when abuse happens and we can't articulate the experience. Still, there must be some sort of correlation between nobody knowing and these people having the opportunity to surprise someone who isn't aware of their behaviour.

A situation where a fourteen-year-old girl has a twenty-seven-year-old boyfriend should alert someone. No one I knew said anything. It began because he was babysitting her. That was how he befriended her and her mom didn't even know what was going on. He hung around with her outside school and we all knew that he was her boyfriend.

Too often people don't say anything. You've reminded me of another situation. When I was about eight or nine years old I went swimming. There was a guy who was in charge of cutting off the tickets as the kids went down the flume. He'd give free rides to attractive kids. The guy sat there with holes in his shorts, with no underwear on, and was playing with himself. At the time I thought, "That's so funny." He's touching himself. He doesn't know we can see. Oh my goodness, what an idiot. He's giving us free rides, *Woohoo!* Now, looking back, that was strategic and manipulative on his part. It wasn't a, *ha, ha, ha, that's funny* type of situation. It was actually, *Oh my God!* But, as a kid you have different perceptions of things. Even when you do you wonder about off behaviours, who are you going to tell? Like when my mom said she wouldn't believe my stepdad could be sexually abusive I thought, "Okay, I guess I shouldn't broach that topic."

Tabitha, you're talking pretty rapidly here. How are you feeling about sharing your experiences?
Once I start sharing, I get a stronger sense of other stories I want to share because it really makes me angry that in today's society women and children are still not safe and we are not doing enough about it. There is still a stigma, disbelief, people saying, "She asked for it." How can they say that? Nobody deserves sexual abuse.

I remember hearing that one in three women and children are abused. As long as there's a threat of violence toward women and children, we're never going to have true equality. In the United Kingdom, I am actually quite privileged and I do have many freedoms. Yet we go on about the fact that this is an equal society, while there are women who are being subjugated to abuse. It's widely considered normal and even accepted within our seemingly advanced civilization. It's also still hidden away. Survivors are often left alone to struggle and wonder, "Did I do something wrong? Did I ask for it? Did that really happen? Maybe it's all in my head. Maybe I'm just overreacting." We start to downplay the abuse. Why do we do that? It's because we are taught to downplay it by society.

What can we do to change that?
That's a very good question. It starts with being aware of the problem. We have to talk about it and we have to show what is acceptable and what is not acceptable.

Where do we talk about it?
Within our families, at the grassroots level and at the governmental level. They have statistics. People know how bad it is, so why are we not doing more? Why is it we actually have a society where somebody can kill or abuse another person and get a lesser sentence than if they steal money from a corporation? Many levels of society have to talk about abuse. Real change has to come as a grassroots movement.

There has to be more of a legislative process and more dialogue about the implications of what happens as a result of abuse. There also have to be more resources to support survivors. I was absolutely horrified to find out that until around 1975, in the UK it was acceptable for a man to rape his wife. Come on, seriously! That wasn't that long ago. There is no way women and men are equal now – that was such a short time ago. In a grassroots movement, people come together to talk and take action. Education does not necessarily have to take place at a home or at school. Let's create some kind of community awareness and community dialogue to help educate people. Education needs to take place beyond schools because they are controlled by the government. Community programs have the ability to educate more people.

As a community we need to come together and say, "We do not tolerate abuse. It's not acceptable. If I heard about something I considered abuse I would report it to the police." We need to develop a strong sense that women and children are not objects to be used. The media has given this impression for too long. Legislation to discourage this view needs to be created. It's time to change societal attitudes. When I was in Spain I noticed that they have a macho culture where abuse has been acceptable for a long time. Now they're trying to change the whole culture, but it's very difficult. Change is difficult because fathers pass attitudes down to sons. That's why change has to come from a variety of sources.

It's a difficult topic and there is a lot of work to be done. In terms of what happened to you, was there something that you could have done to change the situation and any type of advice you would give to young people when they're out and in similar situations?

My biggest piece of advice would be, don't drink, because you put yourself in a vulnerable situation, often with consequences that are particularly unpleasant. There are studies in the UK that point out that a lot of young people, especially young girls, engage in more sexual behaviour than they would have otherwise due to the influence of alcohol. Keep yourself safe by keeping your wits about you. That is the best advice I can give. Also, trust yourself. If something doesn't feel right and something feels uncomfortable, if possible, get yourself out of the situation as quickly and as smoothly as possible. Don't doubt yourself – just do it and then find somebody you trust so you can talk about what happened to you. When I say find somebody you can trust, I don't mean your best friend. Find somebody you can trust who is an adult and can do something about it. It's a case of finding the best person to go to, someone who will give you the support you need, be non-judgmental and unbiased.

Very good advice. What do you think your mom would have said if you had gone to her about the first incident you experienced? Also, if not her, who could you have gone to?

That's a very good question because had I said anything to her, I don't know if she would have believed me. She was being abused herself, so I don't know if she could have actually heard what I was revealing. I don't know who else I trusted, maybe my grandmother or a teacher.

And if you had gone to them, what would you have wanted them to do for

you?
First of all, I would have wanted them to listen to me and then support me in what I wanted to do. I think the issue is that as an adult, when you hear something like this, you have a duty to report it. It is important to support the young person first and help him or her feel comfortable taking action and being in control. Don't say, "This has happened, I have to report it." Actually give them the space to make that decision for themselves.

Thank you. What's the biggest impact sexual abuse has had on your life?
I think it's the experience of *not feeling*. There's a sense of frustration because the abuse still affects me. I haven't been able to let it go. In effect, I've let this man continue to have power over me because I'm still letting him affect my life. I've not been able to fully make peace with the sexual abuse.

I appreciate you sharing your feelings, stories and advice. Is there anything else that you'd like to say?
No. I mean, I'm feeling pretty good. I was little bit nervous about how to put everything on paper when you mentioned I could write my chapter. I'm glad we've done it in this interview format. I've actually enjoyed the opportunity to talk about it. So, thank you.

You're very welcome. Silence is what we get used to, even as it chokes us. The anxiety around talking about abuse is very real. You have a lot of courage.
I look forward to seeing the chapter. I'm actually quite excited to be part of your project, Deb. Thank you again.

My Husband Raped Me
Laurie

The first experience I remember with sexual abuse is when I was four or five years old. Keep in mind that although I feel there are different levels of abuse and I don't think some are as terrible as others – regardless, it all affects you. Anyway, a few neighbourhood boys took me in a tent and wanted to see what was under my panties. Before anything really happened my sister went to tell my mother and she arrived and diffused the situation.

I have another memory when I was young. We were at someone's house for a function. I needed to go into the house and there was a person I didn't want to walk by. I had to walk around the back of the house and come up the side, close to a fence, to get to the other door. I could never understand that memory and I have always felt there was something more that I don't remember or have blocked – there has to be a reason for that happening in my mind.

The next time, I was sixteen years old and working at a flagging job. One of the truckers would drive another girl and I back near our homes and drop us off. One day he dropped her off first and continued to take me closer to my place. I was sitting in the centre part because it was a dump truck. After he dropped her off he put his hands between my legs and rubbed me and tried to get my zipper down. My mother had always told me that if something doesn't feel right or if you know it's wrong, get out – do whatever you can to get away. I was scared because we were alone in the truck. The only thing I could do was move over to where the other girl had been sitting and say, "No, I'm not doing this. Stop and I'll get out." He stopped and I got out. The next day I quit my job. Up to that point I had only heard stories about that type of thing. It really scared me to be in the situation.

You were lucky that your mom had prepared you. I remember her from our high school days and I thought she was a really cool lady.

I think parents should start talking about this type of situation when their children are at a very young age. They know they aren't supposed to talk to strangers, but they also need to know that if somebody makes them uncomfortable or tries to get them to do something they don't want to do, they need to scream, get out of there, say no, and do whatever they can to get out of the situation. It doesn't matter if it is a family member or a stranger – especially a family member. Even if they threaten your family, kids, go talk to someone you trust – a parent, someone you know. Too often it's someone in a position of trust or authority that you would not question.

If the perpetrator is a parent and you leave the responsibility to the parents to educate the child about sexual assault, the abusive parent will not share the information.
True. Where else will you get it? Sexual abuse education should be in the schools. There should be somewhere kids know they can go for support, like the Kids Help Phone.

Did you tell anybody about your situation?
No.

Looking back, do you recall why you didn't disclose the abuse to somebody?
Honestly, I have no idea. I don't think anything happened – seriously. It wasn't like he raped me or anything. It wasn't serious in my mind at that time. I just quit my job to avoid him.

Did anything happen with the other girl that was riding with you?
I don't know. She started working there before I did.

What happened with your mom's boyfriend?
My mom started to go out with a new boyfriend. I was smitten with him – he was a trucker. When I was seventeen my mom would let me go for rides with him and he got close with me and tried things. I stopped that too because in my head I thought, "I can't do this because he is my mom's boyfriend," and I had never had a sexual relationship before. I knew the relationship was wrong because of my mom, but he was always there and we spent

time together. It continued until I moved away from home and got married. You can tell this one flusters me. I think I always felt it was my fault because I had a crush on him. But he was the adult – still I shouldn't have done anything.

I shouldn't have gone for rides in his truck. Some were long rides – some overnight and we would have to sleep in the cab. We would cuddle and he would kiss me. Later on in his relationship with my mom, he got an apartment and I would go there at times – after school or whatever – and be there at night. One night it went too far and we almost went all the way. At seventeen, as I said, I had never done anything and all I could think of was my mother. I couldn't do it – he stopped. He wasn't forceful. I felt like it was my fault – like I had a part in it. So I guess it wasn't abuse other than the fact that he was the adult. He was in his late twenties when it started.

That's an interesting point you make. Where's the line in that situation? What makes it abuse versus not abuse?
I think the age difference versus the age of consent. I wasn't mature enough to know much. I had a crush on a guy who was very good looking – who was around me and in my life. He should have known better and kept his distance from me.

Let me play devil's advocate. Some people would say, "Come on, what were you thinking going on those trips?" or "What was your mom thinking by letting you go?" People are very judgmental in this area.
Yeah. But the thing with mom was that he was her boyfriend and she trusted him. I'm her daughter and she knew that if anyone tried to do anything to me he would kill them. He would not allow it. He never forced me to do anything, there was no violence, he was trying to have relations with a seventeen-year-old immature girl. What guy doesn't want to? All of this has made me not trust men at all.

It's very common, you are not alone.
It goes on. When I was twenty I ran into my mom's ex-boyfriend, who was a father figure to me. He was in his forties and owned the bar where my boyfriend worked as a bouncer. He asked me if I wanted to dance and I said sure because we were still friends. As

we were dancing he said he wanted to touch my breast. It shocked me – he went ahead and did it. My boyfriend saw it. I stopped dancing and told him I had to go. It made me think that all men were the same and not to be trusted. You know what, I'm just sick of guys. At twenty years old that never should have happened. When he said it I thought, he's not serious – he's joking.

At that point you'd had about four or five experiences. You told me earlier that there is another situation you want to share.
It was with my first husband. Throughout the whole marriage he was emotionally and physically abusive from time to time. It got to where he would say, "You're my wife, I want sex, and I want it now." He would be forceful and take it. Did I say anything to anybody? No. He was my husband. Who was going to believe me? I never said anything to anybody. I knew it was wrong, but I had two little kids. If I didn't have the kids I don't know if it would have been different, but I had kids and it was hard to separate from him. I didn't have anywhere to go. I could have gone home, but I didn't want my family to know. My family never knew, which was weird because I grew up in an abusive family situation. I swore I would never get married but I ended up doing it.

I've read that women who grow up in abusive homes often attract an abusive man.
My mother knew what he was like before I even married him. She had experienced abuse and recognized the signs in him.

How old were you when you were married and how long did that marriage last?
I got married when I was twenty-two and left him New Year's 1999, when I was thirty-five. We were together for thirteen years.

That's a pretty long time. Was there sexual abuse from the beginning of the relationship?
No, it was more later on, probably the last year we were together. I didn't love him anymore. Previously I had. When he was emotionally abusive that was one thing, but when he became physically abusive I would leave. Then he would say the same old thing, "I won't do it again." So, we would get back together and

then it would all start again. Also, there was infidelity throughout the marriage. Later on, of course, I wasn't as forthcoming sexually as he would have liked, so he just took me sexually. I was afraid of him; he could be quite violent.

Where you able to talk to anyone about what was happening at the time?
No.

Out of all of these abusive situations and their effect on you, what would you say was the biggest emotional impact?
I'm not a very trusting person. I don't trust men very easily.

How old are your daughters? You must have been very protective of them?
Twenty-three and twenty-one. Yes, I was. I would never have a boy babysit my kids. I would never put my daughters in a position like that. I made them aware of the fact that sexual abuse could happen and that they could tell me if somebody tried something.

Clear communication is a huge part of education. Are there any other big impacts, besides the lack of trust?
I was emotionally hurt; people that I looked up to, like my mom's boyfriends, took advantage of me. They didn't treat me with respect or like I was the daughter of someone they were dating. They thought of me in a totally different capacity – as someone they could also treat in a sexual manner.

Knowing what you know about them now would you do something different or recommend some different behaviour to a young person reading this?
When I had a crush on my mom's boyfriend, it was tricky – I wanted him to like me. I was also very lucky that he did not force me to have sex or do anything I didn't want to do. To me, having sex with my mom's boyfriend would have been disgusting. He should have known better than to put me in that position. At fifteen or sixteen girls are pretty vulnerable, especially when they have a crush on someone. If I could do it again, I would not have placed myself in those situations.

When we were talking *pre-interview*, you mentioned that you had gaps in your memory.

I don't remember a lot of my childhood and family life and I never had therapy to help deal with all the emotional things. My doctor asked if I wanted antidepressants, but I'm not depressed because I know what's wrong. I just have to learn how to deal with it. If there's somebody that can help me learn how to deal with it, I welcome the advice. My doctor is afraid that if my depression goes on longer it will become chemical, but it won't – I know what's wrong. I know why I am upset, and why I am the way I am, and why I feel the way I do. I did see someone about my marriage and difficulties with my children.

Can you make some comments about the counselling or your healing?
As far as I'm concerned, my emotions are healed. All the abuse is in the past and I can't change it. The only thing that's lasting is the lack of trust. That has stayed with me and I don't think it will ever change. To be truthful, I don't know if it's a good or bad thing. It's a good thing in certain ways, but it's a bad thing when it comes to my present marriage. I dissect every little thing and it's not that I have a reason to mistrust him – but I'm always a detective wondering where he is and what he's doing.

How does he react to that?
Not very well, even though he knows why I'm this way. When he tells me I can trust him, I repeat why I am the way I am. For example, he'll tell me he's going to the store. I know how long it takes to get into town, get something, and get home. When he's not back in a reasonable amount of time, because he hangs around doing other things for hours, which he does often, I get upset. He should call me to say what he's doing and when he'll be back. I've told him to phone me and say, "I've stopped at my cousin's for a bit and I'll be home in a little while." Then I'd say, "Fine, no problem." If I had a problem with that, that would be my problem, but if he doesn't phone me that's his problem. I'll be on his back when he gets home.

I'm laughing because I totally understand.
Yeah. Don't tell me one thing and then do another and expect me not to react.

And are you accountable in the same way to him?
I have to be because of my medical situation. There was one time when I went to a show by myself and he didn't know. When I got out of the show there were ten calls on my phone from him. He was furious when I got home. I said, "Now you know how I feel." He didn't think it was the same and I disagreed. But he's learning; we've been married nine years – it's a guy thing. Takes a lot of training and some men are *untrainable.*

That's cute. Interviewing you, my mind is seeing you as a seventeen-year-old, the kid I remember from high school. I'm sure your mind is doing the same thing with me – two innocent kids.
Yeah, we were.

Yet, we had some pretty serious things happen to us at such a young age.
Sports took us away from that, that's the only time I forgot everything. That was also when I got to spend time with my father.

Yeah, we spent a lot of time driving from place to place in that big old truck of yours.
It was awesome. When I had my kids and got back into playing, I loved it – except I had to take my kids with me. My ex-husband wouldn't look after them, but I still went. It was my getaway. It was important to have an outlet.

It's helpful to establish a place to feel safe and get away from the stressful environment of abuse. Did any of our teammates know about what was going on with you?
No.

I wonder what it would have been like if we had shared stories as kids.
It's easier now; we have things like email and Facebook to keep in touch. What did we have then? You had to do it in person, which is harder.

Kids these days ask more questions and speak out about more things than we did. Would your ex-husband's circle of friends have believed he was assaulting you?
Probably not, it would have been his word against mine. He was totally different with other people. Everybody knew him as a nice

guy – nobody would have ever thought anything different. He was my husband, I had two little kids – what was I going to do?

Should a man be charged with rape within a marriage?
Of course.

Did you consider it?
He threatened to kill me quite a few times, which is another reason why I didn't leave him. I had to protect my children and my life over the years – reporting the abuse could have pushed him over the edge. I was finally able to leave him because he hit me in public. He typically made sure not to leave a mark when he was abusive in private, so there was no proof. When he hit me in public, I had one of my kids on one side and the other kid on the other side. I left the next day. I couldn't leave when it happened because he took the keys to the truck. The next day I left and his sister took me to the hospital. The incident was recorded. I thought he broke my jaw and I had a bloody nose. After that, I had proof if I needed it.

When he was out one night I went home to get more stuff for the kids – I was worried about my dog too. I phoned him and he asked if I was home and if I was staying. I said no. He wanted to know why. I said, "Because I'm scared." He said, "You should be." He always threatened if I ever left there would be consequences. Until he hit me in front of people I was stuck; afterwards I had the proof and my out. That's what I call it, my out. It was important to have proof of the physical abuse because I couldn't prove the emotional or sexual abuse.

It took a lot of courage to leave. Is there anything else that you want to share about your story or any advice you'd like to give?
Sexual abuse is becoming more common to talk about – with all the problems in the church, for example, people are speaking out. There was a big case locally and gradually people told their stories. People need to know that it's okay to tell somebody. It's hard to do that. I know that we learn not to trust because of the abuse, so we are afraid to tell somebody. As far as my ex-husband sexually assaulting me – it wasn't right. Women need to know that it's not right. If you say no, it means no, whether it's your husband, your

boyfriend, or whoever. That's my advice: find someone to talk to and know that what happened to me happens to other women and it's not right. Overall I feel the sexual abuse when I was young was minor compared to what others go through.

Minor or not would be based on different people's perceptions. To me it was pretty significant. I think you avoided something more serious because you were courageous enough to say no.

Yeah, I was lucky when I was young. There's one other thing I haven't mentioned that is very important to me. I think that everything I went through is why I love animals so much. I haven't been without an animal since I was young. They have kept me going through everything I've been through – emotional and medical. There are times I didn't want to get out of bed in the morning but I had to because I had to feed my horses. And my dogs, well, they give and get unconditional love. I remember whenever I was really upset as a teenager I would visit my horse. It was heaven, riding through the woods with my dog following. It was an escape and still is today. They always listen and never judge, maybe nibble, but never judge. I will never be without an animal of some sort!

Thank you for talking to me today and sharing your story. We haven't talked in over thirty years –let's stay in touch, okay.

Yes, and thank you for listening.

Never let anyone tell you who you are, hold your head up high, look them in the eye and Tell them who you are.
Sonya Parks

Why Me?
Dorothy

My abuse began at the age of five when my mother's cousin, who was mentally challenged, was babysitting my brother, who was nine, and me. He would make us touch him and do things that were not appropriate. Later, when I was six, another brother who was thirteen, took me to a park and would hide me in different places and fondle and touch me. Then for two years, starting when I was nine, my brother-in-law would come into my room and molest me. He would tell me he loved me, and I was so scared. I wouldn't tell him I loved him – it was very awkward. When I was twelve I was sleeping and my brother, who had just gotten out of jail, came into my room and began to touch me and then raped me. When I asked him to stop he told me he was almost done and to let him finish.

When I finally had the courage to tell my mother and my older sister what was happening with my brother-in-law (my sister's husband), I was told I was a whore, I dressed like a little slut, and I deserved what I got. From that point on I didn't get Christmas gifts, birthday gifts, or anything like that from them. It made me feel like it was my fault, so when my brother raped me I kept it quiet. My other sister who was supposed to be babysitting us at the time also told me to keep my mouth shut or I would be in big trouble. It was devastating. I've carried this for a lot of years. I remembered some things that happened at the age of five and six with my mom's cousin, but I didn't really absorb them until after my brother raped me. Things started popping in my head and I could actually see myself as that little girl – what he was doing, what I was wearing, where he would take me, and things that were said. It was awful, it was just awful.

Clearly there were several people who violated you.
There were four: a cousin of my mother's, a brother-in-law and two brothers.

Statistics show that most sexual abuse occurs within families and with people you know, yet the public generally fears the stranger. I always say be aware of strange behaviours, not necessarily strangers.

Yes. It was very difficult. At one point I had my little sister sleep with me so he wouldn't touch me. He basically went around her and afterwards I was devastated because I put her in harm's way. I carried that with me until a few months ago when I finally asked her to forgive me. She said "There's no need for forgiveness, I would do it again in a heartbeat." I hung on to those thoughts for so long. I've carried this stuff for forty years and I finally broke. I have been through deep depressions and have anxiety attacks that continue to totally paralyze me. I can't go to the dentist because as soon as he's hovering over me, anxiety kicks in, and I can't breathe. I feel like he has his hands around my throat. I can't seem to get over what happened.

I hear the emotion in your voice; this has affected you deeply.

Yes. I think a lot of it's because two of my abusers died very violently. I was always told God would get them for what they did, that I didn't have to worry. When they died suddenly, I took that on. *It's my fault, oh my God.* At that time my anxiety escalated. It was as though I'd killed them. Through counselling I'm just starting to see it's not my fault, that it's nothing I did.

How did they die, if you don't mind my asking?

My brother's liver exploded without warning. He thought he had the flu and went to the hospital – six hours later he was dead. My brother-in-law was killed in a tragic drunk driving accident. The car fell on top of him. He was basically ripped opened from head to toe. I couldn't attend the funeral. I just thought, he's dead, it's done, and it's over. He can't hurt me anymore. When my brother died I went to the funeral but I was like a zombie. I felt nothing; I was dead inside. It was really strange.

These are tragic deaths, but you in no way had anything to do with them.

It was just that people who knew what happened would say, "Don't worry girl, God will get them for what they did." When it happened, my response was, "Oh, my God, did I wish this on them? Did I want this for them? Is that why it happened?"

Did you wish that?
I didn't want them dead. I don't want anybody dead, but I did want them to feel the pain I've felt for forty years.

Can you describe what you wanted them to feel?
I wanted someone to invade their private space and for them to see how it feels when someone hurts them the way they hurt me. I wanted them to understand the pain inside my heart. I was five years old when my uncle told me to touch him down there – I had no idea what that area even was. Then my brother said, "I'm going to take you to the park, let's go to the park." I was so excited. "Oh I'm going to the park, I get to go to the swings." But he didn't take me to the park; he took me to some tunnel and then he ripped my shorts off.

You trusted him. How are you now with trust?
Not so good. I don't like having anybody behind me. I don't like anybody too close. For the first twenty years of my marriage, I wanted the lights off when I changed. Sometimes even during intimate times with my husband, I slip back and I can hear him saying, "Tell me you love me, tell me how much you like this." I could just about die. I feel like I want to die.

Have you spoken in depth about these violations in the past?
I never told anybody about some of this until recently – probably the last six months. The incident at twelve, I told my other sister, who was babysitting me, and she told me to shut my mouth or I was going to be in big trouble. She said she would make sure I got grounded. With my brother-in-law, I finally got to the point I couldn't stand it anymore. I told my mom, and my older sister totally tore me apart. She ripped my heart out of my chest. She blamed it all on me and said I was flirting. I was just a young child.

How old is she now?
I'm forty-six, I think she's fifty-eight.

Pretty cruel words to hear from your older sister. Have you spoken since?

I've wanted to many times, but I keep being told to just let the past be the past. Don't dredge that up. Every day I think about writing a letter or talking to her to tell her how much she hurt me. She is my sister and I hate her.

What could be accomplished, from your perspective, if you had a conversation with her?
I want to understand why she thought it was my fault. I was only ten years old. How did I deserve what I got from her husband who was twice as old as I? How could he touch me, intrude on my body like that? Why did she think it was my fault? She stayed with the man – she went home with him. I felt like I was nobody when she said what she said. I had two younger sisters and at Christmas and Easter and birthdays there would be gifts for them. I was left out because I was bad. I was the bad girl.

What was the situation like with your brother-in-law when you were older?
When I got older I was very careful. I didn't get close. I didn't stay overnight at their house. I always made sure there were a lot of people around. When I went to the washroom somebody went with me.

You must have been frightened of him.
Very. He was very mean. When he was angry, you could see his face turning so red. I also know he was abusive to my sister.

I was just going to ask if you knew of other people who were being abused?
I found out years later he molested two of my nieces. Who else did he hurt? One of my nieces goes through the same thing I do. She has anxiety and depression, and all of that because he was so scary.

Have you spoken to her about your sexual abuse?
Yes, we've talked about it. We have the same abuser and feel the same fear. Even though he's been gone over twenty years, we're still terrified of him.

He's controlling you beyond the grave.
Yes.

Are you doing okay with this type of dialogue?

I've never spoken about it this much – how I really feel. I've never talked to anybody like this.

How are you feeling about talking? How are you doing?

I'm okay. I'm okay.

Share as much as you are comfortable with – most people actually feel a little bit better after talking. But I want make sure that you're okay at the same time. Just let me know.

I'm sure I will be okay. I'm okay. I sent my husband out for now because his brother was the guy who did it to me and I didn't want him to listen. (Dorothy married the brother of her sister's husband – the brother-in-law who abused her.)

I understand. That is one question I would like to ask. How did you end up with your husband, considering ...

I was twelve when my sister and brother-in-law were married. I was at the wedding and so was my husband. We talked and started to like each other at that point.

So the abuse had already happened with your brother-in-law?

Yes. I wonder if, at least partly, I latched on to my husband because I thought he could save me from his brother. I don't know if that's logical, but that's how I think I felt.

When did you tell your soon-to-be-husband about his brother?

It was probably five or ten years into the relationship.

He had no idea?

No.

That must have created a very intense dynamic when he wanted to spend time with his brother – he must have assumed you didn't want to be near the brother?

Exactly. Before I told him, he couldn't figure out what was going on and wanted to know why I didn't want to go to things. Parties were the hardest for me. I still fear them because that's where I was attacked. When there were parties at my parent's house he would say he was going to the washroom then come to my bedroom. Today if I go to parties, the anxiety is so bad I have to leave.

I can understand how parties would be a reminder of what happened. Even though you're probably safe at the parties you attend now, you're probably very selective.

I know that in my head but I still can't go. I can't even go on vacation. I can get in the car and go a short distance, but then the anxiety is so bad, I make my husband take me home. I don't feel safe.

What is it you're afraid of?

I have yet to figure that out. I think it's totally subconscious. My husband and I went out with another couple for a birthday dinner a while ago. We were having a beautiful dinner and then suddenly my anxiety surfaced and I had my husband take me home. I was up for hours. I was sick. I was vomiting. I felt paralyzed. It was terrible, and I have no idea why.

During those periods how does your husband react?

He's having a really hard time because he doesn't understand. He thinks it's just me being crazy – like I am smart enough to make it stop. This is not the life I chose. I didn't choose to be stuck in my apartment, but the world scares me.

Have you had any type of counselling for the anxiety?

I did until my counsellor became sick about a year ago. I'm attending a group and it has been going really well except for the last couple of meetings. I've been very anxious and I wonder if it's because I know it's coming to an end. I'm not sure if that's it but I'm having a hard time right now.

What would make you feel better during difficult times?

I want to be a voice for other people. Don't be afraid to speak – open your mouth and tell somebody. Don't carry it like I have, because this isn't a life. I have no life. Children need to open up and tell somebody – don't be afraid.

When you spoke, you didn't get support.
No, I didn't, but I verbalized it and at least it stopped. You know what I mean? Even though I got threatened and criticized, the abuse stopped. We need to have a voice. We need to know that somebody out there cares. Somebody will help you. When I finally told my mother that my brother raped me she said, "Oh, well you know it's just brothers and sisters experimenting." I said, "No mom, I was twelve years old. He was married and had a child. That's not experimenting, that's rape." I don't think she could handle it – that was her way of dealing with it.

Did your mom believe he raped you?
She believed me but she tried to pretend it was okay – brothers and sisters experimenting. Okay? When we're five we experiment, not when we're twelve and twenty-two. He was released from jail that very day and I woke up with him on top of me. He felt like a ton of bricks and I couldn't move. He would not listen to me telling him to stop. When I finally told people, I was told to be quiet or I would get in trouble. You have to believe that won't happen to you. You're not going to be in trouble. You need to keep telling somebody until you get help.

For a twelve-year-old to not have the support of a parent is quite unimaginable. Was your father aware of what happened?
My father never had any idea what happened to me. He now has Alzheimer's. Every time I look at him, I think, "God, I wish I had told you." He would have been out for blood. It would have stopped a lot quicker. My father was a strong, powerful military man. If the TV was on and there was a woman taking her top off, he would immediately turn the channel or turn the TV off. Even if a couple were kissing, he would turn it off. I never saw my parents kiss when I was little. Those things were private. I think things would have been really bad had he known.

There wasn't affection between your parents but there was a lot of sexual abuse in the house.
Yes, I think my father felt adult affection wasn't for children to see. He was adamant that way. At the time he didn't want his children to be exposed to any kind of sexuality at all.

It wasn't uncommon for that generation I suppose.

Yes. Today he's very affectionate with my mother. He tells her he loves her. He smiles at her all the time and he kisses her on the cheek. He's comfortable now but when we were children he didn't want us to see any of that. I often look at him and I think, "Dad, what would you do if I told you? If I had told you, what would have happened?" I replay that in my head, but I know I can't tell him now – he wouldn't even remember.

I took care of my parents for eight years. The hardest part of this is they now live with my brother, who was one of my predators. When I go there, I see him and pictures of my other brother who was killed – his urn rests on the mantle with a big picture of him. That just makes me want to be sick. It's so hard because they're my family and I think I should feel something. The brother who's alive is currently being tested for leukemia and I'm like, "Okay, whatever." Should I feel like that? I think I need to feel something but I don't. I don't feel anything.

How do you think he feels about you? Was he concerned about you, when you needed him to care about you?

I doubt it. I always wondered. I think I suppressed the memories because I didn't see them until a few years ago. I started getting images of me walking with him to the park and what happened there. Prior to that we were close, growing up. I always wondered why he was so close to me. I couldn't figure out why he, with all the sisters he had, seemed to pick me as the one he cared for and kind of *took* to. When I started remembering, I thought it was sick. It was almost like he was grooming me and making sure I stayed close. It was an awful feeling. I was going through a family photo album one time and I noticed some of my childhood pictures were missing. I mentioned it to my mom and she thought he had taken them. It caused me to wonder what he was doing with those pictures.

Do you remember much about your mother's cousin?

I don't remember a whole lot about him. I just remember my mom going out and he would babysit my brother and me. He would do inappropriate things to both of us. Those are the only memories I have of him until I was old enough to say, "Get lost."

Do you think the abuse affected any of your sexual behaviours?
Maybe. I was promiscuous at a very young age.

Do you think that was related to the sexual abuse?
I don't know. I'm still trying to figure that out. When I was twelve I started dating a boy and it was serious. We were together for two and half years and we were having sex. At about fifteen I recall having a conversation with my girlfriend about a boy. She said something to me like, "I wonder what he's like in bed?" Me being who I was, I had to go and find out. Afterwards I felt sick. I asked myself, "What are you doing?" I always went for the older guys.

Do you think being promiscuous had anything to do with you having control?
I think so. Like I said, I'm just learning about that. I'm trying to figure out what happened in my life. My biggest question is why they zoned in on me? I have five sisters; why me? What did I do? Was it just because I was there? I don't know.

Do you really think it was just you?
As far as I know, it was just me. I've talked to my other siblings and they said no one touched them. Are they lying? I don't know.

Were you close in age?
Two younger sisters, three older. Maybe that's why, maybe the two were too young and the others were older and they would tell.

Can we ever really know or understand the reasons? This is the disturbing thing for me, when people continue to try to figure out the *why's* ... when there aren't any answers to be found.
I think that's one of my biggest problems: Why?

But you never know the *why's* because it's not within you. It has to do with other people, two of whom are dead. Can the *why's* ever be resolved?
No. My husband finds that hard. He feels I should be able to get over it. In fact, I find a lot of people are saying that to me: "Why can't you just get over it? It's in the past, leave it alone, let it go." No, no. They don't know the pain I've carried for forty years – that I was a bad girl, that I shouldn't tell anyone, that I was going to get in trouble, and that I dressed like a little whore. I deserved it. I

carried that! I'm tired of people telling me to get over it. To look at somebody who has carried this stuff for forty years and say, "Get over it, just move on and enjoy your life." How do I enjoy my life?

If there was an option for you to finally get rid of your story, would you let go?
I would, because I hate living like I live. I go to meetings on Tuesday night and I make my husband stay close in case I have an anxiety attack. What a way to live. Not only am I holding myself back, I'm holding him back.

What would your life look like without the anxiety?
Happiness, because that's all I ever pray for – to just be happy. I want to be able to let go. I want them to take it, wherever they've gone, to take it from me. I don't want to carry this anymore. I just want the burden to be lifted. No anxiety, no fear. That would make me so happy.

Your perpetrators are dead or out of your life. Why the fear? Where do you think that comes from?
You know what, Deb, I don't know. I wish I could answer. Am I afraid because this has been part of me all these years and I'm afraid to let it go? Is it who I am?

I wonder what your world would look like in the absence of anxiety and fear, because I see a good person.
Thank you.

It would be amazing if you could walk away and leave that baggage.
Yes, it would be a miracle.

Do you believe in miracles?
I do, and I pray one day I will get my miracle – I hope it's soon.

Not to simplify this, but how about an affirmation every night and morning, something like, "I am so thankful that I am blessed with happiness and a carefree day."
Yeah, that would be just what I want. I want to be carefree. My fear is so instilled in me that I packed on pounds after pounds after pounds so I couldn't breathe.

And now, you have been changing that right?

Yes, I'm losing weight. I'm taking better care of myself. I'm walking, taking Zumba classes, working out at the gym, and doing Zumba at home with my Wii. I have it in my head now that I deserve to look good. I deserve to be healthy. Packing on pounds won't keep men from looking at me because they're not looking at me in a sexual way. I think the larger I got the more looks I received. They were not nice looks yet I felt better inside because they didn't like me. They called me fat. They called me gross. "Why don't you lose some weight." I knew there was nothing sexual about the looks, which is why the weight went on. But now I'm learning that I need to be healthy and that's why I've made changes. I'm taking steps and have been losing weight and feeling better.

How do you feel when you're out on your walk or participating in Zumba?

I feel good. It's a release and believe it or not those are times when the anxiety is not even present because I don't have time to think about it. I'm busy and I find as long as I'm busy the anxiety is not as bad. Not like when I get overwhelmed in a room full of people. I'm a Christian and I go to church every Sunday, but the last two weeks I haven't been able to go. Between the noise of the instruments and all of the people around me talking, I'm totally overwhelmed. I think a lot of that is also because when I was a child the party music would go on and be loud. I'm not sure if I'm connecting the two; I don't know.

You seem to be moving in the right direction for you. The exercise has strengthened both your body and mind. When you're physically working hard it's pretty tough to put your mind in another place.

I'm feeling better. I can walk farther. I can run up the stairs – I don't use elevators as that's another one of my anxieties. I'm very claustrophobic. I live on the third floor and I'm up and down those stairs probably twenty times a day. Fortunately, now I can do it without getting to the top and feeling like I'm going to have a heart attack and die. I know I'm getting healthier.

Wow, you are motivated. That's amazing and I hope you continue on that journey.

Oh, I definitely will. I've just signed up for an eight kilometre walk to raise money for Africa. That's going to be a lot but I will take it one step at a time. If it takes six hours, it takes six hours. I'm doing the walk and it's as simple as that.

You'll be awesome and successful no matter how far you walk – just focusing on other people and their issues for a while gets us away from our own stuff.

Exactly. My biggest problem in the last year has been that I've been idle. I took care of my parents for eight years, which was a 24/7 job; then they moved and I stopped. I also took care of my mother-in-law for eight months prior to her passing and also my best girlfriend who passed away after an eight-month battle with a brain tumour. I was always on the go; I was always busy. In the last year I've been very idle. I have no one to take care of.

Seems like there may be a message there.

I need to find someone to take care of.

Maybe.

It's hard to take care of myself right now.

You are first of course.

It's time to take care of me. I'm trying to take care of me.

Yes, I understand. I have one more question I'd like to ask. A couple of months ago you said you had a hard time looking at yourself in the mirror. In those two months you have done a lot of work on yourself. Who do you see when you look in the mirror these days?

Who do I see? I'm trying to see me, but I see a big, fat lady.

And if that big, fat lady stands aside and you do see the "me," what would she say to you?

I'm not sure. I look in the mirror sometimes and I say to myself, "Dorothy, you're not ugly, you're not fat – you're beautiful." But then the next time I look I think, "Oh my God, I'm so fat. I'm such a cow." People always say, "You're not fat Dorothy. You're not fat. What's your problem?" But I don't see that and I want to see that. I want to see what they see.

Keep looking; you will see her more and more.
Oh, thank you.

I want to thank you for participating. Is there anything else that you would like to share?
I hope my story helps others out there to have a voice. I want my story to help somebody – even if it's only one person I'll know I've done the right thing. I've been very, very open with you, more than I've ever been with anybody.

Thank you. I appreciate how difficult this can be.
You are welcome.

I'm sure more than one person who reads this will take away something that helps them.
Yeah, I already have people on my list saying they want to read the book so let me know when it comes out. I told them to slow down; it's just an interview. I want to thank you for doing this. I think it's really awesome. Like I said, if it helps one person, then I know I've done my job. I've done what I needed to do.

As I am so I see.
Ralph Waldo Emerson

Thought I Could Trust Him

Jamie

Podcast: http://menhealing.libsyn.com

My abuser was my uncle. The abuse began when I was ten years old. I remember my age because the summer Olympics were on the television the weekend the abuse first happened. I was sexually abused for two and a half to three years before I told my mother. Since that time I have confronted my uncle twice but didn't get a good reaction either time. I don't really feel it was worth my while to have confronted him.

It has been a couple of years since I started my healing process. I didn't realize how much the sexual abuse affected my life. I've heard other men say it affects everything, including your ability to trust people. I would say that's the way it's been for me too. I have had difficulty trusting people, difficulty with authority figures, self-confidence issues and feelings of fear. I recently realized that anger has prevented me from reaching the goals and dreams I had when I was young. I didn't finish my degree, I haven't travelled or done other things I wanted to do, and I don't own my own home. I believe that if I had not had that trauma and if it had not affected me the way it did, I'd be in a much better place today. I have a lot of regret as a result of the impact that sexual abuse has had on my life.

I started my healing recovery journey when I was coming out of a bad relationship and was considering starting another. I was surprised to see myself expressing behavioural patterns I thought I had rid myself of when I was in college. I realized I needed to take more time and deal with my childhood sexual abuse. I contacted a local community centre to inquire if they had any programs, and they directed me to Lynne MacDonell who was running a men's support group. That was in 2010. I joined and shortly afterwards I became a co-facilitator with her. I've also attended a weekend recovery retreat with the organization Male Survivor which was an incredible experience. My partner and I also went to a couple's retreat for survivors and their partners. I'm going again to another men's retreat this summer.

I started a podcast called Men Healing in October of 2011. I interview men and give them the opportunity to tell their stories. We usually talk about a specific topic related to their experience. I'm also interviewing professionals in certain fields who can provide tools and advice to men, so it's not just a show where each episode contains a story that might trigger or depress some people and provide no help. After all, the reason I started it was I realized there are a lot of men who are isolated and don't have access to help. I make sure each episode provides some tools for the listeners. Through the Internet, with a podcast like this, I have been able to serve many isolated areas that do not have access to in-person programs. It has been quite an experience and has already reached a lot farther than I expected. For example, the farthest geographical distance is New Zealand. The show has reached fifty-five countries, with number four being Egypt — which is a big surprise for me. My podcasts have had over five thousand downloads.

Wow, that's great Jamie.
Yes. It's actually quite shocking for me. I didn't expect it to go where it has gone, that's for sure!

That's the point Jamie. There's a huge movement going on right now and it's really picking up steam. You are a part of that, clearly!
Yeah it is, and you're right. When Oprah did her two-hundred men episode, where she had two hundred men who had been abused, on her stage, she helped to create the snowball effect that's happening. It certainly seems that sexual abuse is being talked about more, recently. It's in the media because of Sandusky (Penn State football coach charged with sexual abuse) and many things like that. It has gone from a silent epidemic to something that is more commonly talked about. At least now many people realize it's going on and needs to stop.

We are coming of age. We are more receptive to listening and more open to seeking therapy. Many people realize having a therapist doesn't mean we are completely crazy. It just means we need to talk to somebody in a professional setting who has a different education, philosophy and methodology that can provide a new perspective.

I've been saying that for years. Everybody should have a therapist, even therapists.

I definitely want to talk more about the podcast and I would appreciate it if you would expand a little bit about what happened to you, in terms of the abuse itself. For example, you said you waited about two to three years to tell your mother? Why was that?

At the time, in my pre-teen years, there was a small city nearby and when I went there I would go to a variety store to look at magazines. The two guys that owned it were gay. I didn't really clue into that so much in the beginning because I was young. They would let me buy gay porn magazines even though I was only about twelve years old. My mom found one and when she asked me about it I didn't know what to do, so I spilled the news about my sexual abuse. It didn't go over well.

In fact, it was really bad. I remember my dad yelling because he realized that my uncle had been *grooming* me at holiday gatherings. He recalled inappropriate touching. He had mentioned it at the time but my aunts and uncles would say, "Oh, you don't know what you're talking about." I guess they didn't want to believe it was true. I'm not sure.

My sister and I would go into the city where my uncle and my aunt (his sister) lived. My sister would stay at my aunt's and I would stay at my uncle's. We would go to the movies together and do stuff like that. It was our weekend adventure in the city. My dad never liked it. When I finally came out with this news, he said to my mother, "I told you he shouldn't have gone." He was very upset at my mom. It didn't go over well. My mom didn't talk to my uncle for about ten years after that.

Your parents supported you by keeping distance between you and your uncle?

Well, not necessarily. I had a therapist who I mentioned the situation to and his reaction kind of shocked me. I hadn't really thought much about it. He said I was basically a victim of abuse a second time around, because of how my family reacted to it. That included having the pastor of the church come over and sit at the dinner table with my family and ask me questions about what I was thinking, if I had looked at more gay porn, and if I had fantasies about men. I had to answer these questions in front of my mom, dad and sister. A couple years ago, I connected those visits to the fact that I eat really slowly. I took so long to finish my dinner because I knew the interrogation was coming afterwards — I never wanted the pastor to come over.

The pastor kept coming over?
Yeah.

Your parents went to him for advice? Why was he quizzing you about the abuse?
I don't think my parents knew any better. It was a small town and it was a topic a lot of people didn't, and still don't, know what to do with. I guess they were seeking help. I'm not sure my dad was involved. It was probably my mom who went and talked to the pastor. He wasn't skilled or trained in sexual abuse counselling because he didn't handle it properly. The way I look at it now is that I was basically punished for the abuse that happened to me. This was a second trauma. Instead of being supported and hearing, "It must have been terrible for you" and "It wasn't your fault" and "You shouldn't feel ashamed" and "It was your uncle's fault," I had to listen to the pastor. I started feeling guilty because of how I was treated. I felt punished for how I was dealing with the effects of the abuse.

How could they have dealt with the scenario better?
The number one thing is that they could have listened better and not made me feel responsible for the abuse. I was already feeling ashamed. People need to really listen and tell the person who was abused that it wasn't their fault. This will reduce their shame. We need to put the shame and responsibility on the perpetrator. A lot of men remain silent for a long time because they think it was their fault. I kind of felt like it was my fault. It was bad, so why was I doing it? Why did I like it? Why did I allow it to happen more than once? At that age I just didn't know any different. Do you know what I mean?

Exactly. It's very confusing. You're trying to sort out your own world and it's hard to know what to do with the sexual attention at that age. You just don't understand.

And your idea of trust gets messed up. I trusted my uncle. He was an adult and I thought I could trust him and look up to him and listen to him. Once it came out that it was wrong and I felt blamed, there was guilt and punishment and I was left wondering who I could trust. I trusted that person and look what happened. I trusted my parents and they didn't protect me. They had sent me to stay the weekend with him. Trust is difficult for me. How do I figure out who I can trust and who not to trust? I think a lot of survivors have a similar reaction. They either trust too easily or don't trust people at all and there's usually not much in between.

Trust is always an issue.
Yeah. I'm driving my partner nuts with that for sure.

I always say, I give everybody the same amount of trust in the beginning, which isn't a whole lot, and their actions will either add to it or take it away.
Yeah, it's hard for me to know whether I should be trusting more or taking my trust away. I developed bad coping mechanisms that helped me survive.

Such as?
The porn was a kind of an escape. I didn't get involved with alcohol or drugs or anything like that. But I became kind of a hermit when I'm not doing well. I cut off communication with people and disappear for a while. The silent treatment is something I've done a lot in relationships when there's a confrontation or a difficult issue between my partner and me. Even with my family, I would clam up — I wouldn't talk things through. I felt like I wouldn't be believed so it wouldn't be worth me saying my side of the story. So, I just didn't talk and of course that doesn't help.

What was the result of withholding your thoughts and feelings?
It's never a good result because you can't have a discussion when one person isn't talking. I always frustrated people, which made the situation worse and I also felt frustrated because I was unable to break through the silence. I sat there thinking, "Why am I not

talking? Why am I doing this? Why am I doing the avoidance thing?" I can't put my finger on it sometimes and then that frustrates me and I feel ashamed and then guilty, which starts the cycle once again.

I get it. Tell me, what happened to your uncle?
I don't know where he is right now. I think he's still teaching and that he's had the same boyfriend for a number of years but I'm not sure since I don't have any contact with him. People have asked if I would ever go to court and I just don't see the point now. I have some friends who are doing that with their perpetrators but I'm not really interested in pursuing that. There's enough on my plate to overwhelm me and I don't need to add to it. I don't really see what difference it would make. I'd rather put my energy into things like my podcast and the support groups where I'm helping people, rather than trying to punish or get revenge for what he did to me.

Were there any other boys around him at the time that you think he could have possibly violated?
Probably. I worry about that sometimes. When I told my mom, she confronted my aunts and uncles and told them. She told them they should have a conversation with their sons, which they all did. Apparently I was the only one of the cousins who was molested. I'm not sure that's true. There could have been other kids affected. I hate to think that there are more but there probably are. I know that's sometimes why people report the abuse but it's just not something I want to do right now.

You're doing a lot of good work, Jamie. You mentioned the professionals you are interviewing; what kind of advice or tools are they recommending?
The one thing we talk about quite a bit is the fact that nobody can recover from abuse on their own. You need a healing community of other survivors to talk to. If you can't do it in person with a support group, there are Internet discussion forums, such as Skype and Microsoft Network, and people can be connected through various avenues. I think it's impossible to heal on your own.
I know a couple of men who have been abused and do not want to deal with it. Another guy I know said he went to therapy for a while and it's all behind him now. When I hear that I think, "I hope

so," but I really don't think that's possible. It takes so much effort and you need other men in the same situation to be able to talk to and support you and hold you accountable. When I go to my support group or talk to my friends it is like I am looking into a mirror when other people talk about the struggles they are having. A lot of times I think, "Yeah, I do that too, and I wouldn't have realized it, if I hadn't heard that conversation."

I think that when people are trying to deal with abuse by themselves and *just* get over it so to speak, they're not recognizing the impact the abuse has had on their life. They might deal with a few issues and sort of move on, but I think you have to dig pretty deep to heal. I'm not really sure it's possible to do that on your own or with one therapist. In every show, we discuss the importance of healing and connecting with other men within the community who have been through the same thing.

I also talk a lot about mindfulness and self-awareness. Today I tweeted for people to take a couple of steps back and just breathe and be mindful — to step away from whatever they're doing and just be in the moment. To realize who they are and where they are and how they're feeling. This type of practice makes people more self-aware. The best thing that's happened to me over the last two years is gaining more self-awareness — being aware of who I am, why I do the things I do, and why I think the way I think. Also, I've tried to change the aspects of me that are not helpful or healthy.

You are certainly correct about group work. Sometimes we just aren't aware of something until we hear it from someone else. It is like the saying, "It's easier to see the tick on the shoulder of the person across the room than the elephant on your own shoulder." There's nothing like a person sitting across the room from you to help you see your elephants when they are talking about their own experience.

Yes. That's true. Quite a few times in group when someone started talking about something I would think, "Oh my God, that's totally what happens to me too." It really makes me think about behaviours that I hadn't really recognized before. Sometimes I'd come home after having an aha moment in group and I'd say to my partner, "Oh my God we talked about (whatever scenario or reaction or behaviour or feeling) tonight and I realized I do certain things for the same reasons as the other men," and he would just look and me and say, "Yup, I'm glad you realize that." Your mind naturally protects you when you're at a young age and experiencing trauma. People who have experienced sexual abuse develop coping mechanisms such as blocking stuff out in order to survive. Our coping skills kept us alive in the past but now they're killing us, so we need to change them by creating healthier strategies. I think if you're trying to heal on your own it is hard to recognize what those mechanisms are, let alone change them.

Yes, as a child and young adult coping mechanisms may literally keep you alive. However, eventually they begin to hurt you.
Yeah, that's true.

I've asked myself many times, "Have I actually dealt with the experience or am I suppressing it so I just think I'm okay? Is the fear of possibly wakening a giant stopping me from exploring my childhood sexual abuse?"
There is a lot of fear and oftentimes denial. My partner Dave and I talked about that when we went to the weekend retreat in Pennsylvania. I remember him saying, "I wish there were more couples that could experience what we just experienced because it was transformational." We saw couples leaving Sunday morning who were completely different people than when they arrived less than forty-eight hours earlier. It was great to finally have a support system in place and it's important to keep in touch. I know I was afraid when I started looking into myself. I recall thinking, this is the Jamie I've known for years; I know I'm not great and I make mistakes — I do the silent thing and I'm immature sometimes — but I don't really know anything else. You begin to wonder if you start looking deeper and changing, what's the new person going to be like? There is also fear because this won't just impact me. I'm in a relationship so that means there's going to be something different happening in my relationship too. A lot of relationships don't survive the recovery process.

That makes a lot of sense. It's an important topic because if only one person is doing the transformational work it can tear the relationship apart.
Most of the guys I know have been fortunate that their partner has stuck with them through the healing process. But some people are

not so lucky. I really can't imagine what it must be like for spouses and partners. I was glad that Dave and I went to the retreat together. One of the biggest reasons I wanted to go was for him to finally meet some other spouses and partners he could relate to. It's important to be in an environment without judgment.

Many people are afraid of the effort it takes to heal and recover from sexual abuse and what the new *them* is going to be like. Everybody I've talked to has said pretty much the same thing. It's a journey that you start and once you're in it, and you see how hard and painful it can be, you may wish you'd never started it. But because of the successes, life becomes more meaningful and you develop self-awareness. All of the men I have talked to say, "I'd never go back to the way I was."

What gave you the strength to begin your healing?
Like one guy in my group said, "I'm sick and tired of being sick and tired." That's how I felt. I couldn't stand it anymore. I could see that there were things in me like my thinking patterns, behaviours and feelings that were preventing me from moving forward, succeeding and being happy. I wanted to be more relaxed and stop pushing people away. I was really lucky I had Dave around at the time I decided to start this and that he has stayed beside me the whole time. He's my biggest supporter. I told him that last week and he said, "Oh, you're so courageous," and I said, "Well, a lot of the courage comes from the fact that I know you're here." Some people don't have that. Many people around us seem like happy-go-lucky couples but I think the reason they appear that way is because they're basically living on the surface.

The safety of not digging deep. The people listening to your show obviously are ready to begin exploring. What type of people listen to the podcast?
The feedback I've received has all been from survivors. I got a couple of letters this week — one from Texas and one from Ireland. Both of these men have agreed to be interviewed, which is great. I would imagine most of the people who listen are male survivors but I know I've had some therapists and people working in the field listening as well.

How do people find you and your show?
I'm using Liberated Syndication for the host and it's on iTunes.

Help the less techie readers here – they go to iTunes and they type in …
On iTunes you would search for Men Healing Podcast. I think once you type in Men Healing it comes up. Liberated Syndication is the place where a lot of the guys I know, who are not tech people, go to listen to it, so you can just Google that.

Is it free?
Yes it's free. Liberated Syndication is a place to listen online. You can also download the show and put it on your iPhone.
http://menhealing.libsyn.com/webpage and
http://itunes.apple.com/ca/podcast/men-healing-podcast/id477162195

Does it air live?
Not yet. Right now it's always pre-recorded. I'm probably going to change the format a little bit in the next while. I haven't been doing the show on a regular basis, but there are currently about sixteen episodes completed.

It's good to know women can listen if they want to. There are some differences between male and female survivors, but they also have many of the same symptoms. Everyone can learn from listening.
Yeah. That reminds me actually, at the couples retreat I expected to see all male survivors and their partners but there was actually a woman there with her husband who had been abused. As she dug into her anger she said that she was afraid of what she would feel next but she was glad to be able to tap into, whatever it was, so she could deal with it. That's exactly how I felt.

How did she end up there? I thought you said it was a male retreat?
Well, I thought it was but I didn't read the description fully because it said for male survivors and their partners, regardless of sexual orientation. She was very brave to spend the weekend with all those men. The retreat was run by Michael Lew, who has written a book called, *Victims No Longer*. I'm not sure how many years ago Michael wrote his book — there's more than one edition now.

Where did the idea for your podcast originate?
I went to the Male Survivor Weekend of Recovery last summer and met some men there. One guy is living in Northern Canada and he doesn't even have a therapist to talk to, let alone a group. I thought, "Oh my God. I'm in Toronto and have several resources but this guy has nothing." I'm a big fan of podcasts myself and listen to them all the time. I figured that if I made a podcast, then anybody, anywhere, of any age can listen in, as long as they have an Internet connection. So, one of the main reasons I started it is for men who are isolated or too afraid or too ashamed to join a group or tell anyone about what has happened to them. I want to provide the opportunity for them to have a similar experience to what I had when I went to group. I want them to hear other men's stories and realize they're not alone and hopefully that will assist them on their own journey. One guy on iTunes reviewed my podcast and said it was the catalyst to get him started on his road to recovery.

Great feedback.
The other thing I'd like to do, hopefully, is to help young people who are under twenty-five. They are being called *digital natives* because they've grown up with a lot of advanced technology. They have the smartphones, they're always on their computers, and they're really comfortable with the latest technology. I'm really hoping that young men find my podcast because one of the things that always surprises me when I meet survivors and go to retreats is how old the guys are. I really hope male survivors start the process of healing at a younger age so they can avoid years of difficulties and regrets.

Exactly. Hopefully, if we continue to open the channels for discussion there will be less of a taboo surrounding sexual abuse and more people will come forward and share their stories much earlier.
Yeah and since many live their lives on Facebook now, they're already used to sharing with the public.

I believe that is partly why this movement is happening. I think television shows, like the one you mentioned on Oprah, are having a huge impact on viewers and everyone is becoming more aware of the prevalence of sexual abuse and its effects. When other survivors see those men they may think, "If they can do it, so can I" and "I am not alone after all." Those men are paving the way.

Yeah, for sure. When I asked one of my friends if he would like to be interviewed on my show he declined because the recording is available on the Internet and people all over the world could hear him. Sometime later we were talking and he said he realized he needed to push himself to get rid of the shame he felt and instead, place it on his perpetrator. He said it wasn't his fault and to move forward and be stronger he needed to tell his story. I asked if that meant he was volunteering for an episode. He did the show because he realized that telling his story would benefit other men as well as himself. If we speak up, there is less chance of childhood sexual abuse continuing to be a silent epidemic.

I remember watching *Oprah* and thinking it was awesome because there would be tons of women watching and maybe they will ask their sons some questions? Maybe parents will think that they should be more aware of what is going on in their family or with a pastor or priest at church or whatever. That's another reason why men are speaking about sexual abuse more often – the more it's talked about, the less chance that people can get away with it, I hope.

I hope so too. Certainly communication is a first step in creating change. When I saw the show it made me think that sexual abuse toward women is almost expected on some level and its prevalence is pretty well known though not enough has been done to stop it. Most viewers probably found the high number of men and boys on *Oprah* who had experienced sexual abuse shocking. These guys have so much courage to come out and say, "No, it's not just women, it's me too. And we've got to talk about this." With men speaking up more will get done.

There have been some small changes with government regulations; for example, coaches are required to have police clearance. This happened because people are starting to talk.

Yes. I think there could be five hundred podcasts for victims and they'd all be busy. You are doing great work.

Thanks. I find it very rewarding and the interviews provide a chance for me to learn too. I never expected this when I started, but every time I do an interview it feels like going to group.

I can relate a hundred per cent because I've completed several interviews now and I have learned so much by just asking questions and listening to everyone.

Yes, and I'll probably be interviewing you once your book is ready.

That would be fabulous and I would definitely love to be involved, any way I can help you out. Is there anything that you would like to add before we wrap up the interview?

I like what Howard Fradkin, the co-founder of Male Survivor says, "Recovery is possible, absolutely possible." He always wants survivors to know that. I think that's really important because some people don't even want to start the journey. They think it's impossible or it's going to be too much work.

But it's totally possible and I've met guys that are examples of it. I've seen it and I'm experiencing it myself even though it's tough as hell and really frustrating some days. Sometimes you just want to give up, but the work involved is totally worth it. My life is so different now than two years ago or even last summer. I'm more relaxed in social situations and I have more courage. I'm aware if I'm operating in avoidance mode or if I'm giving the silent treatment. I can think it through and know why am I doing this and then actually reach out and call my partner instead of avoiding him. Those things are all huge changes. There are major improvements in terms of my enjoyment of life even though it's very tough sometimes too. It's always necessary to assure people that it is possible to recover — and it's worthwhile.

That's a really good message to end the interview with. Thank you so much for your time and all that you have shared, Jamie.

Thank you.

Only when we let go and indifference overcomes hatred are the bonds broken and we are free of the other person.
Dr. Patricia A. Wiklund

Behind the Bushes
Dorina

My story began as a search for peace. I never felt whole and I never felt complete. I knew there must be some reason, some explanation for the sense of feeling *not quite right*. Throughout my life certain things occurred and I continued to search for a reason. I went as far as working with spiritual healers. Once I even went to a psychic who didn't want to read me, which was disturbing. I was overweight and believed I had some type of mental block preventing me from losing weight.

Determined to find an answer, I asked my doctor if she knew a hypnotist. I thought if I could shift my level of consciousness, maybe I could figure out why I felt the way I did. She didn't know a hypnotist, but said she had a patient who could probably help me. She gave me the lady's number and I went to visit her. She began with numerology. Then she asked me to smell vials with various scents. The first one was okay but the second one was a really, really bad scent. She said to me, "Oh, talk to your mother, something happened to you when you were three or four years old." She said she could help me, but I was a little freaked and I never went back to her. But I remained open-minded and did what she suggested.

I went home and called my mother. I asked her if something happened to me when I was three or four years old. Immediately she asked why. By the tone of her voice I knew the vial lady was onto something. My mother said, "Maybe we dropped you." I wasn't buying it, but she wasn't prepared to reveal anything else.

A little later we were talking about weight loss and she made a comment like, "Oh, why don't you do something about it?" I replied, "You're not getting it. I know how to eat and I know how to diet – it's something mental." I asked again if she was sure something didn't happen to me when I was three or four. She said, "Maybe it was the time you ate the Christmas bulbs from the tree –

too many Christmas bulbs." I still felt she wasn't being quite honest.

More time went by and my parents went to Italy. While they were gone, I was feeling very depressed because my sister hadn't invited me for Thanksgiving. I was feeling alone, so I decided to call the Employee Assistance Program (EAP) to ask about talking to somebody about my depression. When my parents returned, my mom came over and she was talking about a lady she met in Italy. The lady's daughter had gone to a hospital in Torino and lost a lot of weight. Again I said, "You're not getting it mom, there's something here," pointing to my brain. "There's something in my head. Are you sure something didn't happen to me?" She said, "Well I probably shouldn't tell you this." I said, "Well, I wish you would because whatever it is, I'll deal with it. The not knowing is not helping me because I'm forever searching for the answer."

Finally she told me that when we were in Italy, when I was three years old, I went missing for about twenty minutes. When I came out from behind some bushes she knew right away something had happened. She asked me what happened and I took my finger and I pointed below saying, "He put this there." She knew I had been molested by my uncle, my father's brother. I have no memory of it. I remember visiting Italy once and seeing him. We said, "Hello" and then he was gone. I'm sure my mother watched him and gave him a look encouraging him to leave. I had no idea about anything; I was just wondering where he went. I had no idea he had done something to me.

After my mother told me what happened, I went to see the EAP therapist and she said, "Oh, you're here for the depression." I said, "Yes, however there's more." I proceeded to tell her what I had found out. In one hour everything made sense. I knew why I was promiscuous, why I wet my bed and why I couldn't lose the weight. Everything made sense to me and it was such a relief. I didn't feel like I needed to search anymore. Things finally felt okay inside. I felt okay about everything.

When I talked to my mother about those feelings she said, "Maybe we should go to your uncle. I'm going to do something about this." I told her no. I explained she'd had her chance to do something when I was a child. I told her not to worry about it and if I wanted to do something I'd do it.

When I went to Italy, not too many years ago, I told pretty much everybody in the family about the incident. I had family members with symptoms similar to mine and I found myself guessing which ones were also molested by him. So, I decided to tell everybody. I figured, "Okay, everybody knows about it back home and that's enough for me." I went to Homewood Health Centre in Guelph for post-traumatic stress disorder on the recommendation of the EAP therapist. But because I couldn't remember the incident itself, they didn't want to put me into any group sessions for fear my memory might come back. They told me our body has a natural ability to forget, so it's not good to bring it up. It might come up once and it might never come. If it never comes up, that's better. To this day, I don't remember the incident, but I do believe I was victimized because of it.

I want to add something interesting that happened. One day while visiting my father who has Alzheimer's, he overheard my mother say something about this particular uncle. Surprisingly, he blurted out, "Oh, yeah that's my brother, he gave me my asshole." Pardon the language, but we knew right then and there that my father would not say something like that unless he'd been molested as well.

Without knowing you were abused, you had several symptoms of abuse.
When I was in the program in Guelph I noticed the majority of people were either overweight or anorexic. I think when you have been abused you try to make yourself ugly or unattractive so no one will want you or pay attention to you. I still struggle with my weight and I wonder if that is blocking me from losing it.

Once I was coming home from school and a guy chased me with a dog and a knife; other things kept happening to me after school. They say "once a victim, always a victim." I think the assault made me more aware of my surroundings and my intuition was heightened. I always knew deep down something was not right, something had happened. I knew I was not at rest for some reason. I probably would never have found out if my doctor hadn't sent me to the lady with the vials – she obviously knew what had happened.

When you talked about not being at peace inside, what do you mean?

I was never able to relax. Even to this day people think I'm hyper. If there's a day that I don't have anything to do, or I really don't feel like doing chores or work, I feel like I want to crawl out of my skin. I just can't sit still; I have to remain busy. I guess I don't have time for things. Whether it's all related to the abuse, I don't know, but I just don't like to have quiet times. Even when I try to meditate, it has to be a guided meditation. I can't do it in silence by myself.

Some people would question if there's really a relationship between twenty minutes of abuse at three years old, that you can't remember, and the things you described.

I'll tell you, I don't know. But, for example, I used to get really afraid and sick on airplanes. When I learned about the abuse I started to wonder if I was terrified because flying made me think about Italy. After I thought that, I never threw up on planes again. I don't know if the abuse and the sickness were related, but since connecting them, I don't get sick.

I do not want to put words in your mouth, but I get the sense that once you knew what happened it was actually calming?

Oh, yes, because I felt all along that there was something. I never felt normal. I didn't feel like other people and I kept searching and people thought I was crazy. They'd want to know why I was going to a hypnotist or this or that and I'd say, "I don't know." I didn't know why but I knew there was something I needed to know about me. I felt different from my friends. As soon as I found out what had happened to me and learned all the signs of abuse, everything became clear. I wet my bed, and I remember when I was in Italy staying with one of my aunts, I discovered that my cousins also wet the bed. There are pieces all fitting into place – whether that was all because of the abuse, I'll never know, but I think it was.

I'm curious, you mentioned that you had gone to a psychic and the psychic didn't want to read you?

Yes.

Why?

I don't know. She just said, "I won't read you. You're not open to hearing what I have to say." I remember being really upset because my mother had driven us to Hamilton to have it done.

How old were you?
I'd say about sixteen or seventeen.

That's young. The person probably knew what had happened and felt you weren't mature enough to hear it.
Or maybe she felt that my mother didn't want me to know or knew I didn't know. I have no idea. It's so weird. I've never heard of somebody who doesn't want to take your money.

It would have shocked both you and your mother if she had blurted out that you were molested in the bushes.
Yeah. I told my mom I'm not upset about the sexual abuse. I just don't know why she didn't tell me. I had been asked by other therapists if I had been molested; I just wish I had known sooner. I denied being abused because I didn't know – they could obviously see the signs. I had even brought my parents with me to a therapist and they didn't say anything. They had said my childhood was normal, when clearly nothing was normal! I guess they didn't want to admit it or want me to know.

They were protecting you. Why do you think your mom denied it even when you were determined and so close to knowing something had happened?
It's a shame thing. She's Italian. It's taboo to talk about sexual abuse. When I look back at pictures of me and my sister, we have short hair and we are dressed like boys. Even when we're in a dress you'd think we were boys. I guess in order to protect us, our mom didn't want us to look like pretty girls.

How did it affect her when she finally told you?
I think she probably felt relieved because I had a sense of peace and she did not have to hide the story anymore. When I went to the therapist and told her my mom had never trusted my uncle, the therapist thought there was a possibility my mother was also molested. I told my mother what the therapist said and told her it was up to her if she ever wanted to tell me. She never did. There

was an uncle of hers I suspected, when she told me she wet the bed when he babysat her.

There's often more than one family member affected.
A lot of people still don't want to talk about it. I spoke to one of my cousins in Montreal and she told me about other people who had tried to molest her. There were a couple of situations where we believe my uncle isolated my cousins in a barn or bushes. My aunt remembers clearly when my cousins came back in a car after visiting my uncle. She said one of the girls looked really upset, like something had happened to her. That girl is now bulimic. Each time something happened, the event was suspicious to people witnessing it. He lived with his brother and never married. It seems like no one knew what to do.

What's your advice to a younger person who's been abused?
Talk about it, say it. Even though the perpetrator probably terrifies you, say anything because it will repeat itself. Parents must get through to their children so they will talk about it. One time I went to my parents because the neighbours had a party where this man tried to undo my pants. I was sleeping on the couch and he was staying over. During the night I felt him pulling at my zipper. Fortunately, I had a safety pin across it because it was broken. I was terrified and shaking. I was only about thirteen and I had no idea what was happening. That safety pin probably prevented him from raping me. I woke and told my neighbours right away, then went home. Not long afterwards those people moved. I think they felt so bad.

Did you think or act differently after that situation?
When I see a man I feel I can't trust, I'll avoid him as well as the situation. I swear you look them in the eye and they see that you know what they do. When I look at them and they're looking at me, they look the other way because they know that I know what kind of person they are – it's very weird.

You have *sexual assault* intuition?
I swear I do. And when you are no longer a victim, they cannot do it to you anymore. Do you know what I mean? Once you know that

you can control the situation or you're not a three-year-old anymore and you can fight back, you can stand up for yourself. I think that's probably why I was insecure and would never look people straight in the eye when I was a kid. I would always put my head down and be quiet. My mother would tell me to stop making that face. I was probably terrified of everybody and had no idea why.

You've mentioned trust issues, insecurity and victim mentality. Can you expand on those?

I'm no longer a victim. I kept being victimized while I didn't know what had happened to me, but as soon as I knew, that ended. Then if a man tried to make a pass at me, I didn't let him do it if I wasn't comfortable. I would remove myself from the situation. Before, I would be afraid to say no. Before, I wouldn't walk away – I'd freeze. Now I leave and it's totally liberating. Also, I used to have dreams where I'd be running inside a bush. I would grab a tree and try to pull myself out, but I just couldn't get out of the bush. I used to have dreams like that all the time. I used to wonder why. I don't anymore.

Silence flourishes with sexual abuse, you've experienced the opposite. It's ironic that you didn't know the abuse had happened, but when you did you started talking. However, other people remember and remain silent. Why do so many do that?

I have no idea. But it should not be a taboo subject. There are all kinds of groups now for children to get help. They can get help as soon as it happens. They don't have to search their whole life, or try to figure out why they are the way they are. They can get over it. And parents, they don't have to live with the secret, lie, guilt, or the feeling of being responsible – like my parents did.

I'm sure my mother thought, "Oh my God, how did I let her out of my sight? This would never have happened if we had just watched her the whole time." I remember that she never let me out of her sight. When I was growing up she always told me to invite my friends over so she could watch over me. I think she wanted to keep us safe with her. I think she felt guilty even when I tried to reassure her that it wasn't her fault. The guy was sick and it wasn't her fault, but she felt responsible.

I also wonder about the effects of abuse on my family. For example, it always felt very uncomfortable hugging at home. My parents grew up without that type of affection. Maybe they just thought we shouldn't touch. I don't know.

What should happen to someone like your uncle?
They should get help. I don't believe in hanging them like my mother suggested. She said she'd put him in prison and cut a finger off every day. Me, I don't think so. He has to live with it. The fact that he knows I know is enough for me. He has to hide in shame. He's the one who's shamed now, not me. People know and he knows they know. I'm not looking for revenge. I told everybody in town what he did to me and that's enough. One of my therapists suggested I confront him and say, "I know what you did to me." I might have done that, but I haven't seen him. I never really felt the need to do that. I am happy just knowing why I felt the way I did for so long.

Do you think he would feel any regret or remorse?
I doubt it, because he never got any help. He probably never felt there was anything wrong with what he did. If there's somebody who clearly has repeated the offence over and over, I would personally cut something else off so he couldn't do it anymore. Maybe that would send the message out: "If I ever get caught that's what is going to happen to me." Just putting them away in prison, with the rest of us paying for them to stay there, is not doing anything. Cut off the tool that causes the problem and that problem won't recur.

Do you think offenders can be rehabilitated?
Possibly. I think they were sick to start with or somebody did something to them, which made them do something to somebody else. So yes, I guess with therapy anybody may be cured, but the person has to admit to having a problem in order to seek therapy. Generally these people don't go for help. They have this problem and now, with the Internet and everything else, they can see things and get other ideas. It's just bad.

I hear you. It's a fast-moving train. We need everybody combining ideas and working together to find solutions rather than looking only to blame and temporarily incarcerate.

Yeah, maybe public service messages would help: "If you have these issues or these thoughts, go here." So at least they know there's somewhere for them to go for help. If they have those thoughts and want help, they can realize they're not alone. Think about it; we have everything else: Alcoholics Anonymous, Overeaters Anonymous – why not Pedophiles Anonymous? Go get some help!

I also think we should educate kids at home and at school, starting in kindergarten and continuing throughout their education. Remind them constantly. Ask them to repeat the rules back to you about what not to do, say, who not to talk to. Get it ingrained in them so if something ever happens, they will come forward; they will say something. When offenders know children are more educated and know what to do, maybe they'll be less likely to offend because they know the kids are programmed to report abuse. If you educate kids, give them the tools, maybe they can come out of it easier or maybe some will be spared.

Maybe that type of education would help children who are going to become perpetrators.

Yeah, sure. They develop an early awareness that their feelings aren't normal. If it was talked about openly, they would feel more comfortable talking themselves. I remember the first time in health class when they brought in figure drawings of a penis and a vagina. I just remember laughing my head off and being so embarrassed by getting this piece of paper – we just weren't prepared.

Sexual education is behind the times.

Yeah, wow, forget it. Kids are giving blow jobs on the bus these days. I was watching *Oprah* once and they said that's what kids are doing now on the ride to school. I can't believe it, but I imagine it's true.

You're the second person that's mentioned it to me.

Too bad there isn't a pop-up on the Internet saying, "We are watching you," for anyone looking at porn. There are people doing similar work, but more needs to be done to protect kids.

What do you think of the openness of popular social media sites? Many young people are on them.

Some people don't know how to protect their page on these sites. There are probably predators out there looking at girls all day long. Maybe Facebook should spread the message that predators are using the system and advertise that they don't tolerate that behaviour.

That's a good idea.

There are so many different media avenues that could really get the message out. It's like smoking; just expose the dangers. Put pedophile pictures everywhere, or maybe just their names.

Those pictures have been on cigarette boxes for a long time and people continue to smoke. It would be great if there was an easy and quick solution to end sexual abuse. Do you ever feel angry that it happened to you?

No, I never really felt anger towards my mother or my uncle – he's just a sick individual. Maybe something happened to him as a child and that's why he never had a normal relationship and did what he did to me. We'll probably never know that. Maybe I'm not like most people. I don't get mad about it, I don't get even. I just say "Whatever." I released my mom and uncle and whatever their issues were. I have to live my life and try to make it better, though I'm probably still insecure because of the abuse. That's my job – I've got to work on me. Nobody can fix me and being mad at him isn't going to fix me or help me.

You sound like a pretty strong and optimistic person.

I'm definitely optimistic most of the time. People turn out the way they do for different reasons. I feel kind of sorry for negative people and I try to help them. Okay, I think some people will never change but maybe one day they'll hear something I'm saying. I read books like Louise Hay's, *You Can Heal Your Life*. That book really helped me. It's about healing your life, positive affirmations; I hope I can do something similar for others.

I have read it and enjoyed it. Overcoming sexual abuse can be a challenge and books like that can possibly help us move forward.

I think people still roll their eyes when I talk about it, but I'm okay and ready to accept things. I've had people read the book. Some get it and some don't. Many people go their whole lives without ever becoming spiritual; they continue to think everything is black and white. I think there is so much more out there. Maybe if schools spent some time on spirituality, there would be less bullying. Maybe there's a way. It just takes one person at a time.

I agree. Dorina, I want to thank you for sharing your story. Is there anything else that you would like to share, any final comments that you would like to make?
Nothing, all I can think of right now is that I'm really happy you're doing this – you're sharing your story and helping others to get their story out. It's a good thing.

Thank you.
You're welcome.

Ask your heart for guidance, and be guided by its message of comfort or discomfort.
Deepak Chopra

I Am Here Now
Allison

I am here now
In this Truth
In this place called reality
That which is so far from what is actually *real*
I am in my own energy
Refuelling and recharging
Regaining strength and commitment
Reaffirming my love of self
Remembering who I am and what that feels like.
Thank you (me) for your love and understanding
Your support
Your undying need to question
To understand
To interrogate and know
Thank you for your struggle
Thank you for your defiance
Thank you for your fight
Thank you for love
Because that's all it's ever been about...survival
This fight to stay alive
Because I love myself enough to survive
To always uncurl
To reach out
To feel the sun upon my face
Allowing the curve of my smile to emanate from within my Soul
My heart
From my Spirit within
As it is without
I am a Goddess Warrior
One of great strength
With the ability to be and do anything I choose to

I love myself enough
TO LIVE
TO RISK
TO FEEL!
To want to know who I am and why I am here
To know on such a deep level that only I know it as Truth
As I feel it with every fiber of my being
With every essence of Truth that already exists within me
RESONANCE!!
It has only been waiting to be remembered
To be found
To be loved
To be embraced
I am ever changing
Ever knowing
And ever flowing into and out of love
Back and forth
Light and dark
The Dance
I know who I am in moments
And yet in others I can feel so lost
It's as if I've slipped into the abyss that only I could have created
With and within my own mind
The way in which only I know into and out of
And yet somehow
I lose myself every time
The map of the poisoned mind
That which I am coming to learn about and love
The mind that has helped me so much along this unfolding path of
undying Faith and Love
It's about choosing who I want to be now
With all that I have
With all that I am now
Choice
So much power in choice
I choose to always grow
To always choose faith
To take the leap
Never knowing where

Or what lies beneath
Yet always knowing
Always trusting it will be the Love that catches me
My love
Your love
God's love
Humanity's love
The love that we are
The love we were created from
Out of
Into
The love that is
That was
That ever will be
I am Divine Source
I am Divine Creation
I am LOVE!
I am who I am
Because I am
I choose love
I choose me
I am here now
More than I ever have been before
Knowing that I never will be again
Always moving forward
Never back
More...
And more...
Into the love...I am here now

I am happy to say that today I no longer feel like I am surviving. At many points in my life I felt like surviving was all I could do, just to make it through to the next minute, the next second, the next day, the next hour. It's because of all of that and more that I am here today. My will to live, my will to love, my inner knowing that through it all...everything, to hell and back again, even when I couldn't see, feel, hear or taste that inner knowing, when I had to rely on faith (even though I had no idea what faith was) or those around me to keep me going. Sometimes it was a book, a song, a friend, a stranger, a group, a therapist, a sister or nature. At some point I knew there was more to life than what had happened to me, more to life than the life I was choosing to live. Yes, many of my life choices or circumstances were a result of something that had happened to me when I was three or four years old. Yes, I was sexually molested by a man much older than I and I'm sure he did more terrible things than I care to remember or that my body and spirit actually allow me to remember. I have come through all of that and today I am such an amazing person. I love myself and I allow others to love me. I have dreams and aspirations. I have wants and desires, I have a husband-to-be who loves me and who I love back. I am healthy, mind, body and spirit, and I make every attempt to enjoy life to its fullest because life is here to be lived and experienced.

I once felt weak in my vulnerabilities, but today I am strong. I am who I am today because of all that has happened to me and I am grateful.

Searching for a Safe Place
Kelly

My abuse took place daily over a three-month period when I was ten years old. I was being punished for shoplifting some small items from a local bookstore. When my mother and stepfather found my stash of tiny little rainbow pencil crayons and bright pink heart-shaped erasers, I was given a choice of returning them to the store manager, admitting my guilt, and suffering unspecified and therefore terrifying consequences, or getting a spanking a day. I chose what I considered to be the lesser of two evils: the spankings.

Through some convoluted calculation, my mother and stepfather determined that a spanking a day for about seventy-five days would atone for my terrible crime. Sometimes my mother gave me my spanking, but I could tell her heart really wasn't in it. We went through the motions, and it hurt but was tolerable, and sometimes we both laughed through it. More often because he was into it and usually available after school before my mother came home, it was my stepfather who gave me my spankings. With his hand, or his leather belt with the heavy square shiny gold belt buckle, he put his heart into it with such force that I can still recall with vivid clarity the pain of the leather on my skin, and the puffy raised imprint his hand or the belt buckle left on my body. This is how my abuse began – he would soothe me after my spanking, and the soothing turned into rape.

Usually my mother wasn't home when the abuse occurred, but sometimes she was. One day after she had been napping, she woke up and walked past my door. She saw him raping me. I could see her over his shoulder. She let out a little cry like a surprised bird, put her hand to her mouth, and continued walking down the hallway to the dining room. He said, "Oh shit," rolled off me, and followed her down the hall. I was immobilized and didn't know what to do. I sat on the bed and thought, "Oh no, what's happening? What have I done wrong? Is my mother going to love me? Am I going to get in trouble?" I'd been spanked and raped every single day for so many days that I couldn't bear the idea of it continuing. I just wanted my punishment period to be over so I could go back to my life of playing outside with my friends.

I heard my mother crying and him talking. What surprises and saddens me to this day is that my mother never acknowledged what my stepfather did to me. I now understand that I was never her first priority. There was nothing. No "Are you okay?" or "Is anything wrong?" She simply never talked to me about it.

A lock was put on the inside of my bedroom door and I was told I could never be in the apartment alone with my stepfather. Further, even when she was there, I had to lock myself in. I interpreted this as my mother protecting me. Now I look back at that and think, "That's really fucking crazy." From the age of ten to twelve I was basically locked in my room. I went to school, but when I was in the house I had to be in my room with the door locked. We lived on the sixteenth floor of an apartment building and I remember looking out my bedroom window, day after day, at the buildings across the field, trying to see in the windows and wondering what those other families were doing, where they came from, and dreaming what it would be like to be free, to be outside in the world.

While locked in my room I read a lot. I read the Enid Blyton children's adventure series and desperately wanted to be an adventurer too. Over the years I've come to recognize where this desire originated. I've spent so many years locked up since that time – first in my room, and then within myself, and then in a marriage. There are so many choices I have made that I can now trace back to this period in my life. I've finally found the key and have unlocked the door to let myself out.

I spent a lot of time building tents in my room – little fortresses of books and blankets and cardboard. At day care or at school, I did the same thing. I was obsessed with designing cozy spaces. Since leaving home at fifteen, I've moved twenty-one times. For a long time, because of my interest in designing spaces, I thought I wanted to be an interior designer or architect, and I didn't understand my lack of desire to pursue this through formal education. I now understand I had been trying to create or find spaces that made me feel safe and happy.

As a result of my experiences as a child, I've come to realize I've been driven my whole life by two things: the search for peace and safety and the desire for freedom and adventure. After many years of not understanding my needs or my demons, I now understand what I need, and instead of misinterpreting and misdirecting these urges as I did for many years, I've finally taken control of my life. I left a marriage of twenty years and now have a safe place to call home.

My second desire from my past, to *get out there,* is from wanting to be out beyond the confines of my room, to be free and to explore. I now travel frequently, usually alone, from short day trips to longer trips overseas. It can be expensive, but I know that what travelling gives me is priceless. I spent so many years not being aware of who I really was and what I needed, and doing so many other things I thought would (or should) make me happy, but didn't. For the first time in my life, I feel at peace: my desires and my circumstances are aligned.

You left home at a very young age.

By the time I was fifteen things had really started to unravel. In some ways, although this may seem inconceivable, the direct physical abuse was not as bad as the *mind fuck* that happened afterwards. We were living in Toronto when the abuse occurred, and for the next two years I was either at school, at day care or locked in my room. We then moved to Winnipeg, where I no longer had a lock on my door, and that was when some very weird things started to happen. Sometimes I would wake up in the middle of the night and my stepfather would be in my bedroom, crouched at the end of my bed silently watching me sleep. I'd wake up and see him, or I'd wake and he'd have the blankets off and my nightgown up and would be rubbing my body. It absolutely terrified me. It's been about thirty years since this occurred and I still wake up in the middle of the night sometimes and *feel* him at the end of my bed.

My stepfather terrorized me. Even in front of my mother he would make sexual innuendos. He would say awful things, referring to my sexual practices, saying that I was a slut, or that anyone who fucked me would need to wear a body condom. I was between twelve and fourteen years old at the time. He would knowingly rub up against me if he were trying to get past me in the kitchen, or reach to get something and touch my breasts. He would buy me makeup, jewellery, miniskirts, and other age-inappropriate clothing like black lace stockings or revealing shirts. I actually participated and condoned it because my mother and stepfather would give me things all the time: I was a teenager and I thought it was great. They'd dress me up like a Barbie doll, but eventually I started to feel like I was being sexually groomed to be his mistress when I was old enough, maybe after I turned sixteen or eighteen. I remember thinking, "He doesn't treat me like a daughter, my mother doesn't treat me like a daughter, they treat me like a friend, and we have no other family members around." They isolated themselves from their families, maybe so I wouldn't be able to tell anyone what happened to me.

I would often see my stepfather driving around my junior high school at lunch time. I was always hiding and running around the school or down an alley to get away from him. I started getting into drugs, sex and other risky behaviours to escape. We weren't supposed to leave school property, but I would. He would see me on a street I wasn't supposed to be on, but neither of us would tell my mother because he wasn't supposed to be there either. We had this weird little secret between us. Sometimes I would tell my mother I saw him at school, and he would give her some convoluted excuse about where he was and what he was doing. I told her he was in my room at night, and my mother stopped sleeping soundly. She said she would sleep with one eye open. If he got up in the night, she would wake up and listen for where he went. It was an incredibly stressful environment to live in.

I was working full-time at the Royal Winnipeg Ballet (RWB) while I was in high school. I loved it. I didn't go to school as often as I should have because I didn't fit in and my priority was to create a life for myself in which I was happy. The RWB was my home away from home: my lifeline. I spent as much time there as I could. My stepfather would always offer to pick me up and I always said no. Not only did I not want to be alone with him, I also thought it was inconvenient for him to come all the way to get me when I had a colleague who was happy to drop me off on his way. My stepfather would do very bizarre things because he wanted to drive me. One day he became extremely violent when I suggested that I could get a ride home with the neighbour. He was screaming at me, frothing at the mouth, and he pushed me. He was beside himself with anger and I was so afraid of him. I literally had to run out the door half-clothed to a bus stop, in the winter, to finish getting dressed. He was very unpredictable. I always felt he could become violent at any point.

At this time in my life, things were so strained at home that my mother stopped talking to me, thinking that if she didn't talk to me, my stepfather couldn't talk to me either. She tried to protect me by being a role model for him, but it didn't work. Although they didn't actually speak to me, he would continue with insidious violations, like reading my journal. I stopped journalling and have never journalled again because of this extreme violation. I threw out a lot of what I owned, including clothing and the contents of my room because I felt violated by him. When I left home, he was angry. I think my mother was actually happy or at least relieved. She even co-signed the lease on my first apartment because I was too young to have a lease in my name. The day I was supposed to move, he left a little note near the front door: "Cancel all plans to move" and signed his name – like I wouldn't know who it was from.

It was an awful time in my life. I felt so alone and like I was less than human because they wouldn't acknowledge me. I felt like they hated me and yet also like my stepfather was grooming me. I felt I wouldn't be safe at home once I turned sixteen. Their behaviour toward me made me so angry. They would say things like, "You're not good at this" or "You can't do that." I would say, "I want to be a social worker or an arts administrator," and they would always say, "It's not possible."

I was told I could do nothing, was nothing and was worthless. I'd get my hair cut and my mother would say, "You look better with long hair." Or I'd have long hair and my mother would say, "We like you better with short hair." My stepfather would call me fat and expound on how fat people were a drain on our health-care system and should be vilified. It was okay in their eyes to abuse drugs and have an eating disorder, but not to be fat. I was mad at them for all of these things, and more.

I had to find a way to function and not let the anger consume me, so I repressed it. I don't know if I want to access it. I think I've been afraid of going to the place of anger because anger gives them the power again. I still have a hard time accepting them as my parents and understanding what they are. I didn't feel safe with them. One of my first apartments had stairs going up the back from the kitchen and in the middle of the night I came into the kitchen and looked up to find my stepfather crouched on the stairs watching me. It was two or three o'clock in the morning and I was terrified. I was always scared, always felt like I was being watched.

You were being stalked. Frightening! Where are they now?
Living together in Winnipeg. Last year when I was in group counselling we talked about boundaries. I decided to start applying the lesson. I told my mother I wasn't going to call home anymore because he always answers the phone and I have to pretend to be happy to talk to him and I don't want to pretend anymore. The boundary I set for my mother was, "I want you to call me. I don't want to call you." After two months she called. We had a very awkward conversation about inconsequential topics like the cats and my work. At the end of the conversation she asked if I wanted talk to the old man and I said, "No, actually I don't," and she still put him on the line. She wouldn't respect my wishes then and she still won't. She hasn't initiated any form of contact since that conversation over a year ago. She's basically made the same decision she made back then: him over me, at my expense.

The whole scenario isn't congruent when you think about the way a mother typically is. Let's try to justify her behaviour: she got a lock put on your door to keep him out. She was protecting you because she told you to lock the door. That is a child's level of thinking. If she was truly protecting you, she would have taken you away from him and never let him see you again. That's an adult's thinking.
Sure, I agree.

You mentioned boundaries. Can you talk about how you've used boundaries and maybe why it took so long to create them?
I think it comes down to the fact that I never factored in my needs. I never felt worthy of factoring myself in, so I had no boundaries. I don't think I deliberately and consciously went out to set

boundaries, but I started to think about my needs, and then I started to stand up for them.

You weren't taught that you had needs. It must have been difficult living in that environment all those years.

I'm still in therapy and I've learned other pieces of the abuse. My mother and stepfather told me what I thought and felt all the time. So, not only did I get locked in my room without the benefit of communicating with anyone, I also didn't learn how to process what I was feeling. I didn't sit in my room and cry and feel hurt. I sat in my room and wanted out. That's all I wanted.

I lost my voice and my sense of self because they told me what I thought and felt. When we moved to Winnipeg, I lived in a very insular, weird and dysfunctional environment. We didn't even have a TV for a distraction. We read and sat at the dining room table. A typical evening might be, "Oh, Kelly, how was your day?" I'd tell them my stupid child's story and they would tell me what I thought and felt because my views, feelings, and impressions were wrong. If I argued or remained silent, I was a sullen, miserable bitch who was stupid. If I tried to play along with them, then clearly I was patronizing them.

There was no winning. For example, I was very interested in pursuing sociology and psychology at university, and they told me that I didn't like those subjects, that I wanted to go into science and technology. That was what my stepfather was interested in. It was more than them just expressing what they wanted me to do – they wanted to tell me what I felt and thought about it too.

The result is that I hate having my voice taken away. I hate being told what I'm thinking and feeling. But it's also confusing to me because I'm not really in tune with what I'm thinking or feeling. I was never allowed to think or feel. I fucking hated them. I felt so much anger and frustration. The interesting piece for me is that I still haven't accessed my anger. I haven't taken any steps to say to them, "Bye, you're done, I'm done with you," I get an email from my stepfather every single day. I get five beauty packs a year that contain hundreds of dollars worth of expensive makeup. He sends them, not my mother. I don't even think she knows.

Do you want to say bye?

To him? For sure. To her, I don't know. Because I don't know, I choose to wait. Maybe it doesn't have to be bye forever, just for now. I think about it every day. I write a letter to my mother every day, but I don't mail it. In many ways, as weird as it may sound, the more important aspect of my story of abuse is really my relationship with my mother. I'm still working through my feelings about her. I find it hard to direct anger at her, although I am angry, but I'm also very confused and sad. I try to understand and come to terms with her role in my life, in my story of abuse, and it's very hard for me to hold her accountable for her actions and not feel some empathy and compassion for her. In order to have her in my life, I have to have him in my life. As difficult as it is, I'm in the process of letting go of them because I don't have the option of keeping her and not him. She made a decision to be with someone who abused me, and she's chosen him over me time and again. That's her choice; I have choices as well.

In some ways, as sad as I am to let this woman go from my life, I finally feel some peace because the way she's behaving is congruent with what I've always felt. I always had to rationalize her love for me. I told myself she loved me, even though her behaviour made me feel otherwise: like when she was drunk and said I ruined her life or when she wouldn't talk to me or when she supported his decision to not let me see her. I always made excuses: "She's just drunk," "She's just trying to protect me," or "She's just trying to keep the peace." I've finally found peace because I'm letting go of my need for her, letting go of my romanticized idea of who my mother is, and letting go of my expectations of who she should be. It doesn't matter if I understand why she did what she did or does what she does, I just have to accept it and act in a way that supports me.

That is one thing you can control.
Yes, in a way. My stepfather still emails or texts me, often several times a day.

He's really been stalking you your entire life.
Yeah, he actually started stalking me more when I left my husband about two years ago. I sometimes think I hid out in that marriage for twenty years because it was safe, because it kept my stepfather

away and I could focus on someone else's needs. In my marriage we got to a point where my husband was really struggling with a lot of personal issues and needed a lot of my care and support. It was very easy to distract myself from my own stuff by focusing on his stuff, especially since he kept asking for help. Eventually he reached a crisis point and was doing a lot of mindfulness work and group therapy. He realized in his support group that none of the marriages lasted because of the toll it took on the spouses, so he asked if we could attend couples therapy.

I went to my doctor to get a referral for his counsellor and my doctor advised me to have a personal counsellor in addition to his counsellor. There was an administrative error and his counsellor's secretary wouldn't take me on, so I began working with my own private counsellor and never did the couples counselling.

On the first day, my therapist asked why I was there. I explained the whole scenario about my husband and couples therapy. She asked some contextual questions about my family history. I had been in denial so long that I never mentioned the sexual abuse. As far as I was concerned the abuse was a non-issue. I spent two years with her and she kept circling around to the family issues and the abuse. She suggested I needed to kick that door open and I'd think, I don't think so, that door is fine.

So, we dealt with various relationships in my life and I came to understand where my value system and fears came from, and what was playing out in my relationships – fear of abandonment, feeling not good enough and trust issues. All of those things were causing me pain, with my friendships in particular. I didn't understand my own needs and fears. I just thought things that happened in my relationships happened randomly. I tried to make everyone at work happy. I kept feeling responsible for the happiness of my staff until I learned to separate myself from them and understand they were responsible for their own happiness. If they were or weren't happy, it wasn't a reflection of me or my worth.

After about a year in therapy, my therapist asked where I wanted to go next. I said, "I think we need to get to that stuff I've been avoiding." I began kicking open that closed door, and with her encouragement I also began group therapy for adult survivors of childhood sexual abuse. That's where much of my awareness began to really grow.

Did your husband know what your stepfather had done to you?

He did, but couldn't even begin to understand how it impacted me. I think he always accepted there was more to it, but I wasn't willing to talk because I wasn't falling apart. I had a job and was successful. In fact, we moved to Winnipeg for four years so I could be closer to my family. We lived a block away and saw them several times a week. I know my husband wondered how I could go there every Sunday night for dinner and be in the same room as my stepfather. He didn't understand, he was mad and didn't want to go there, but he loved me and wanted to support me. We all just kind of shut it out and played our roles: good daughter, good mother, good father and good husband, even though on the inside, I imagine none of it was working; it wasn't for me anyway. I played that good daughter: visiting, letting them visit me, calling them on the right occasions, sending cards and gifts on the right occasions, but it never felt right. I never felt loved and I never felt recognized or even acknowledged as a human being.

When I started group therapy, I felt completely devoid of feelings. I was a robot who didn't deserve to be on this planet – I was useless and worthless. It's only in the last three years that I've started to find myself and shed some of the roles that had both protected and hurt me. I found my authentic core and am finally starting to feel whole and integrated, rather than someone made up of random pieces and parts masquerading as a real human being.

When we lived near my mother and stepfather, I kept hoping my mother would make the decision to leave my stepfather. I think she too has this internalized hate she's not acting on. I always thought she was in my camp; now I think her foot is maybe half in my camp, emotionally. Some days I feel mad at her; some days I feel compassion for her. The bottom line, however, is this woman made some decisions that I hope I would never make. I wonder what I would gain by confronting her. I'm worried my feelings and experiences would be invalidated once again and I would be re-traumatized – why put myself in that situation again?

Part of my fear is that I think I've been protecting my mother. I am pretty sure my stepfather has a psychotic edge. I think my silence has been protecting her. When I visited them about five years ago he got really drunk and forced us to watch a concert video on his laptop for about three hours. The laptop was on the kitchen table, and he drank so much that he actually fell asleep at the table. He had a gigantic sharp butcher knife beside him and we were wondering if we should move him because it looked uncomfortable and like he might fall on the knife. We were whispering about various things and every once in a while he would wake, grab the knife and look at us, and then fall back to sleep. We were terrified. Part of me has always been really afraid of his unpredictable nature. I've never understood what motivates him. I lived in fear of him all the time and yet I had to find a way to disassociate from the fear because I had to survive.

Over the past year I have tried to set boundaries with him, but he emails me daily. I set up several restrictions, so he can't see anything I do on Facebook or communicate with me, but I didn't stop him from being my Facebook friend. It kind of grounds me because I know where he is, what he's doing, and who he's with. At first, whenever I got an email or message from him, it would trigger me to get the sweats and want to vomit. But now I see his name and it's like any of the other junk mail. I don't even look at it or give it a thought; I just delete it. It's almost like exposure therapy. He doesn't have power over me now.

You mentioned that by the time you got to group therapy you were devoid of feelings. Is that why you were suicidal?
I'm not suicidal anymore and it's not that I didn't or that I don't have feelings. I just have a tendency to think and analyze my feelings in my head, rather than feel and experience them in my heart and body. Sometimes my therapist will ask me what I am feeling, and I tell her, nothing. The only feelings I've ever really been able to access all along are sadness and hopelessness. I still go there sometimes when I go home at night to my peaceful, safe apartment. It's extremely quiet and I think about the big picture, like why are we on this planet? I know I do good work and I've helped a lot of people, but is that really my purpose? I wonder why I struggle with money and work and relationships and coming to terms with childhood sexual abuse. I don't have the answer. Some days it's pretty hard.

I think about the things we do in our lives for distraction. For example, I often see people who use families and work as a distraction. I'm sure there's love, but I see a lot of people who don't actually love their children and their children don't love them. So, why do we pretend? Why do we continue to act out loving, idyllic family scenarios? Are distractions the reason we can't deal with the bigger questions? Maybe we should be looking at the bigger questions and not fluffy questions. It's important not to be distracted by family and work. Sometimes it feels lonely making a choice not to have family or to have my mother in my life.

When my natural father used to tell me he loved me I thought, "Really, you don't know me." He left my mother when I was five. I'm not that little girl. Though it was nice of him to say he loved me, how is it possible? After he and my mother divorced, he lived far away for most of my life and I never really knew him. However, he always remembered me on special occasions and made an effort to visit me once a year. He continued to love me whether I felt love or not – I now really appreciate him. Maybe this is the most important example I have of unconditional love and my lesson is to be open and accept his love and love him back. I've only recently explored the concepts of conditional and unconditional love, and I am starting to allow myself to recognize, feel and let unconditional love into my life.

What love is to one person is not love to another. Your stepfather would probably say he loves you, as would your mother, but define that love. What does it mean in their mind versus your expectations?
My therapist would say expectations can lead to trouble. I wonder what love means, then I think, "Why does it matter that I don't have parents in my life, my mother specifically?" Lots of people don't have their parents in their lives for all kinds of reasons. I think it would be better for some people to let go of the idea of having parents. Their parents don't show love in ways that are healthy, yet they hold onto this idea of parental love and yearn for a relationship that doesn't exist.

I took a course in ancient mythology last semester and it touched on Jungian analysis about relationships and the subconscious. One of the things that struck me was the idea that children can't hate their parents because it's the equivalent to death for that child: they're emotionally and physically dependant on the parent. That course helped me understand how, as children, we continue to love our parents in spite of everything and why it's so hard to try to change that. Maybe I hate my mother or my stepfather and I just can't acknowledge that hatred. I don't know.

You have gone through a lot. Do you get triggered?
I have many triggers. I am often triggered on the street. When someone is walking too close behind me I feel like I am being stalked, and I get very anxious and angry. I am aware of other situations that trigger me, such as having my voice taken away from me and being told what I'm thinking or being told I can't have an opinion about something.

The first time I was conscious of being triggered was at work. I work in financial aid with post-secondary students who face multiple challenges. A student and I were going through a budgeting exercise and he looked up at me and said something about living at home and needing to find a way to leave. I knew part of his story included trauma and childhood sexual abuse, and he was living with one of his abusers. I knew what he was feeling and knew the horror of living with your abuser. The experience caused me to go into a fair amount of crisis. Luckily, I was already in therapy, because I started going back to the emotional place I was when I was fifteen and wanting to do drugs and have high-risk sex. I didn't do any of those things, but I realized I needed to start to deal with my abuse.

May I ask what you suggested he do? Or did you say something like, "Oh I know how you feel"?
I didn't share what I was experiencing or my story with him, but it was an incredibly powerful moment for me and I connected to his situation in a way that really allowed me to understand what might be helpful for him. We were able to get to some core issues, set goals and address some of his financial behaviours. If I had not understood at a deep level what he was experiencing, I don't think I would have been able to help him as much or have as strong of an impact.

It's difficult to know that there are so many young people in that scenario.
Oh, yeah. His situation inspired me to shift some of my focus at work from simply administering financial aid programs to focusing

on the creation of a financial literacy program. I really believe students need financial skills, knowledge and confidence to be successful. For people with a background of trauma, this program was desperately needed and a critical piece in their success.

It's great that you were in a position to help him and do something for many other students.
I hear a lot more than people actually say.

I think positive traits can evolve from sexual abuse, though sometimes it's hard to see them in yourself because you don't want to associate them with the trauma.
Absolutely. After having had therapy, I can see that my abuse shaped me and is a part of my past, but that I am not my abuse: it's not all that I am. Prior to joining group, my abuse was me. It drove me blindly and painfully through my entire life. I made decisions without even understanding why, and I wasn't always making good choices for myself. I consider myself extremely fortunate that people arrived at certain points in my life to help me shift from where I was.

For example, late one night when I was fifteen, extremely depressed, filled with hopelessness, and about to jump off a bridge into the powerful Assiniboine River, I met an old lady. It was probably two in the morning and she walked by me as I leaned over the rail, staring at the river below. She started to talk to me. Was she an angel? I don't know.

There was something about what she said, though we didn't have a long conversation. She didn't say, "Hey dear, are you about to jump off the bridge? You know, you have some other options." She just started talking to me like a human being. We had a brief chat and then she carried on her way. But I was a changed person. What's an old lady doing out at that time? I don't know, but it made me think and I walked away from the bridge. Another time when I was fifteen I was dating a successful professional ballet dancer several years my senior. He was very beautiful and charismatic. One day, after listening to me complain about my circumstances at home, he looked at me and said, "Why should you kill yourself? You can just move out." I was like, oh. It had never occurred to me that moving out was an option. I felt like there were two options, life or no life. All of sudden I started to see life as a continuum with a whole range of options in between these two extremes.

I had a number of people like these two who briefly touched my life at critical moments. I think of them as my life angels delivering messages I needed to hear. I am so grateful for all of them. I still have angels in my life, people I will always be eternally grateful to have met.

When we're faced with something as difficult as sexual abuse, or the memories of it, we don't see the future or the options because we're so stuck in what's happened or happening – the fear keeps us there.
Yeah. Absolutely.

You know that's a huge message because people, kids especially, don't realize there are options. The systems aren't perfect, but you know the Chinese proverb: Knocked down seven times, get up eight. I am not sure it's going to happen the first time or be easy, but there is somebody or something out there, maybe an angel, trying to keep us moving forward.
Yeah, I think about group therapy; for some of the people, facilitators or participants, there are those moments where *we* are the angels. You know when you have the moment and it's life-changing. There's magic.

That moment where there's the separation from the thought that you are alone to knowing you are not. It is freeing, liberating and so incredibly powerful.
Yes.

Thank you, Kelly, for sharing your story. Is there anything else you'd like to say?
My abuse drove me in a lot of ways. Prior to therapy and group I had no awareness or understanding of how. I was thinking about what you said about this book: that by sharing our stories, you want to help and inspire people. When I think about the layers and layers of understanding I have about who I am as a person that I didn't have before, I want to share that. I've gained an awareness of myself that I never had. My abuse shaped me. I wouldn't say I am glad it happened, or would wish my life the same if I could have it to do over, but I also am very aware that my abuse made

me who I am: a pretty interesting person with some incredible strengths. I'm starting to feel more whole and connected instead of just careening my way through life, not understanding the impulses and demons that were driving me. For the first time in my life, I'm happy just being me.

Sleeping with a Stranger
Patricia A. Wiklund, Ph.D
www.marriedtochildmolester.com

Patricia, thank you for taking the time to talk to me today. I appreciate you sharing your experience because it's from a totally different perspective than other people who have contributed. Please go ahead and tell your story.

Thank you. My journey started when I was woken very early one morning by the telephone. The call was from my husband who said he was in jail. He had been a consultant for police departments so I asked what he was doing in jail. He said, "I've been arrested." I asked what he'd been arrested for and he said, "Well, they said I was molesting children." I replied, "You? Don't be ridiculous." He said it was true and then asked me to call a friend, an attorney, to represent him. As I hung up the phone, I had a weird realization that my life had just changed. I didn't know what was going to happen, but I knew it was going to be a real challenge going forward.

As it turned out we went through days, weeks, and months of unbelievable hell. My husband lost his job and didn't have any income, and I was working part-time. The logistics were very difficult. As I talked to more people, I discovered many of his friends believed the charges were true. Originally I felt I had to stick around because I didn't think they were true. I kept thinking, "Not him, he was somebody who helped children."

It was six to eight months later before I was certain he was guilty. I had been trying to get together with a neighbour and she seemed to be avoiding me. Finally I drove across town and went to her shop. She asked me about ten times, "Are you sure you're going to get a divorce?" Each time I reassured her that I was. She finally told me that my husband had molested her child. At that point I knew it was true. She told me they called the day his arrest was published in the newspaper because they wanted to tell me he had molested their child, but both my husband and I picked up the phone at the same time. When they realized he was listening, they didn't come forth with the information.

I had already filed for divorce and was talking to an attorney because my husband was lying and becoming impossible to be around. After visiting my neighbour, I went home and called my attorney and told her I wanted a divorce immediately. Unfortunately, it took almost two years before the divorce was final.

The divorce seemed to take quite a long time, not just to get past all the logistics, but even longer for me personally. It took some time to finally convince myself that *this is something that happened to me; it's not who I am.* It was with that awareness that I remember sitting down on my bed one day with the sun coming through the window and having this *aha* moment. I said, "You idiot, you're a psychologist. You've helped hundreds of people, help yourself, you twit." I wrote myself a treatment plan, and over the next eighteen months I did every single thing on that plan. It changed my life.

You have a course for women, who have been married to a pedophile. Is that the treatment plan you designed for yourself?
The course has evolved since then and I offer it on the Internet. It's about how to take charge and change your life. The course is specifically for women who have been married to child molesters and it's the kind of help I wish I had had available to me. It covers what a child molester is all about, what other people think of women like us who have been married to child molesters, and how to rebuild your life after the experience. Participants need to go through difficult exercises. I send them messages and let them know what to expect next. It takes time to go through everything and I am available to support them on their journey. I've always said that post-traumatic growth, which is a new field of psychology, is a decision, not an event. You have to decide that you're no longer letting somebody else or something else run your life.

You wrote your book called "Sleeping with a Stranger" about your experience. On your site at www.sleepingwithastranger.com it says that you could not *not* write this book anymore. How long ago was the book written and why could you not *not* write it?
The book was published in 1995. There were a couple of things

happening at the time. I had put together the program for myself, and I put some of it in the book, because I didn't want this experience to ruin my life. That was big. I realized it was a decision I had to make. Sitting around waiting for something magical to help me feel better was not going to help. I was in my bedroom and experienced a moment of clarity – I realized what I needed to do. I'm currently writing a book for spouses of child molesters, called "Post-traumatic Growth: A Decision Not an Event." Up until that *aha* moment I had been waiting for something to happen, so I would know it was time to change or that I had gotten over it. I realized I had to decide to change, not wait for change to arrive. I hoped by sharing my story it would help others.

When you had your epiphany, how long had it been since your husband was accused of molesting children?
He was accused in the mid-eighties and passed away in 1991. I knew someday I would write a book but I didn't want to do it while he and his parents were alive.

How was the book received?
It was very interesting. I did tons of television shows. I was on *Oprah, Phil Donahue, Sally Jessie Raphael,* and all of the big shows of that time targeted at women. I did hundreds of radio interviews until I got to the point where I had to stop. One reason I got to that point was I was totally unprepared for how vicious some callers would be, particularly on the radio shows. They often got very angry with me. Eventually I felt I couldn't do it anymore. It was ruining my life. I took a sabbatical and got in my sister's motor home and wandered around the country for about ten months. I just needed to go into a den and recover.

What did they say that was so unsettling?
There were questions like, "How could you not have known what your husband was doing?"

How did you respond?
Oh, the nastiest reply was on a radio station somewhere in the South. I asked a woman through the moderator, "So where is your

husband right now?" She replied that he was at work. The moderator said, "Well, how do you know that?" She said, "I trust him, I know him." I said, "I trusted my husband too and the problem is that sometimes even guys that look like they're trustworthy aren't." I could hear the phones, the buzzing going through the wires, and I knew it was time to stop doing the radio programs. That was the last radio show I did.

You must have had some interesting experiences on the television shows.
Yes. When I was on *The Phil Donahue Show* I was sandbagged. I had no idea who would be on the show or what it would be about. There were seven of us in a row, including a sweet young man and a convicted child molester who was saying things like, "Oh, I've recovered. I had a series of ten lessons while I was in lock-up and I'm fine now." He went on to say he had a special computer club for the boys in his neighbourhood in his bedroom. He was living with his parents.

The young man sitting next to me had been the driver of a car during a convenience store robbery and the audience was on him like *white on rice*. They went on and on asking how he could have done that. I finally blew up. I stood and with dramatic flair and said, "Stop picking on this kid. What about that twit down at the end of the row? He's the one you've got to worry about; he's the one destroying your children's lives." I just went off. I was so angry at the producers because they didn't tell me what the show was about, and at the molester's arrogance and his "I'm fine now, I had some treatment" line. I felt like he was still molesting children twenty years later. I knew he was.

That's what is so frustrating for the people on the victim's side. Even those charged and convicted may only spend a few months in jail – they get out and they're doing the same thing again. Do you feel you achieved something by appearing on those shows?
What it achieved for me is that a lot more people heard about the book I was writing and the information was getting out. On most of the shows, like *Oprah*, it was a different story. She was really thoughtful and caring and was very appropriate in terms of what was going on. Unlike when I was on with another female host; I won't mention which one. Oh my gosh, there was aggressiveness

there. I could sense when she finally realized she couldn't break me. At that point we got along fine.

Break you, meaning what?
It was like she was trying to get me to say something scandalous or to lose my temper. She would just jab, jab, jab, jab – one after another. Her questions were far too graphic. Finally she sat back and said, "Well, you really know what's going on." There's an adversarial aspect, particularly with talk shows, because they want excitement and energy. It's not necessarily exciting to just put forward an accurate picture of what occurred.

Is the lesson here to be prepared if you're going to be on these types of shows?
Absolutely. Get a media coach. I had a wonderful coach and it was a really good idea to hire her. I also had a good support team, which helped. You don't want to walk onto a show unprepared. You need to rehearse the nasty questions you will be asked. At the time it was both exciting and challenging.

Many people like you have done a lot to bring this topic out of the closet, but sexual abuse is still here and doesn't appear to be slowing down. Will it ever vanish? We are sexual beings; will molestation always be present?
Well, of course we're sexual beings. We wouldn't be here if we weren't sexual beings. It's an essential part of life and I think there is a certain mentality that came up from our early founding fathers: "It's not nice to think about it."

I can remember when I was a little girl sixty-five years ago and nobody would talk about anything controversial, at least nobody in a nice family like mine. For example, my mother had breast cancer when I was about ten years old. She had her breast removed and you just didn't talk about it because it was her breast. Plus, cancer was too scary to talk about. Discussing our bodies and particularly our sexuality is something few of us grew up with, and a lot of people still feel very uncomfortable with. A lot of it stems from the idea that *it's not nice to talk about these topics* – particularly with the older generation. I think a lot of people feel unbelievably ashamed if they've been abused, that there's something wrong with them. Therefore, it's hard to admit, especially now.

Isn't that part of the problem – we haven't arrived at a place where we can talk openly about inappropriate touching?

We have to be able to talk about it in a way that's not frightening to children but helps them understand what's okay to do and what's not okay to do. Quite frankly, the web is helping a lot. Many websites define "Good Touch" and "Bad Touch." It's not just about "Stranger Danger"; it's about, "Don't let your neighbour touch you some place your bathing suit covers." At an early age children should know what's okay to do and what's not okay to do. We need to give them clear guidelines. Also, it's important to not freak out if the child says, "I don't want to spend time with Mr. Martin," for example. Hear what the child is saying, think about it really carefully, and do a little gentle probing to find out what's going on.

Right. As we both know, children very rarely make up sexual abuse stories.

Seldom, if ever. They don't have the ability to make up that kind of a story.

So in terms of education, where should it come from?

Education starts in the family, particularly the parents, because they're the ones who are around when the child is young. You can be matter of fact: "No, please put your pants on. We don't run around the house without pants on." "Pick up after yourself." "You finish your dinner." "Please place your plate at the table." "You don't let people touch you beneath your bathing suit." Just common, everyday correcting – it's just another one of the lessons you teach your children and it doesn't become a big deal.

Okay, but what if the abuse is coming from a parent?

Parents need to be really thoughtful and careful about the condition of their child's body. If your child is having continual urinary infections or complains that his "pee pee" hurts, and this is typical with younger children that suffer abuse, it's absolutely crucial that you investigate and take care of it. It's difficult when children are a little older than toddlers because the incestuous parent is typically threatening the child not to tell.

What type of threats?

"I'll hurt your mother if you tell her." "Don't tell your grandma, I'll hurt you, I'll hurt her." Or to a little boy, "I'll hurt your sister if you tell." Or the offender could say, "This is our secret because you're so special to me. I just don't want to share this with anybody."

How do you teach a child to deal with that type of situation?

That one's the hardest. Incest is always harder than being abused by somebody who is not a part of the family. I don't know how to treat it. I wish I did. The person who is right in the middle of all this is often the wife and mother.

That's precisely where you were.

Yes, and I had no idea what my husband was doing. He was a child psychologist working with troubled preteens, eleven through fourteen. He was acclaimed all over town. He was head of the local psychological association, he was on the board of Big Brothers, and he had been active in the YMCA and its camps since he was a kid. He had been an altar boy too, which may have been where he was molested himself.

Maybe. How long had you known him or been married to him before he was arrested?

We were married in 1968 and separated in 1986. We had been in graduate school at the University of Chicago and he was an Honours Graduate from Harvard. He was not a sleaze ball.

There aren't really obvious characteristics of a molester.

You can't go by demographics, how old somebody is, where they've gone to school, their profession and not even what their family is like. He looked like a regular guy. We were introduced by one of my best friends who had known him for three or four years. She said, "I've got the perfect guy for you." I saw her several months ago and she still has a really hard time believing that he molested children. I think there is so much mythology in this kind of a situation that it's really tough to get your head around the scope of what goes on. Abusers are unbelievably secretive about what they do.

Was not knowing where he was, at various times, a clue?

There was always a good reason. Think about the question on the radio, "How do you know your husband is really at work?" Well, because he told me and I trusted him. You have to trust your husband. That's what a marriage is all about; you trust and respect and watch each other's back. You do that even when somebody's not trustworthy, because you don't know.

Did he molest other kids in your neighbourhood?

There were some. I know there were several victims at his work also. We were sued and I was in some of the depositions.

How far back did the accusations go when you found this out?

I'm not sure how long he had been doing it. For example, when he was at Harvard, he ran a boys' group for the kids in the neighbourhood and he would take them on overnight trips. So, my hunch is that there was probably some activity going on back then. When we were living in Chicago, at the University of Chicago, we were involved with one of the local churches and were sponsoring the youth group at the church. Again he had access to children there. I went on a couple of trips with him but most of the time I didn't go. I wouldn't be surprised if he was abusing children both at Harvard and at the University of Chicago.

That wouldn't be surprising. How old was he was when he was convicted?

He was in his early forties when he was arrested. He was never convicted and only spent one day in jail. They took less than a week to come back with findings of "insufficient evidence to indict."

Wow, that's fast.

Right. By then it had hit all the newspapers. He was fired from his job as soon as he was arrested and it became very clear that there was evidence, but not enough to go forward with it. He was never tried. What most people expect from our justice system is justice – what most get is indecision.

Did he ever admit he was guilty?

I saw him the week he died. He was in the hospital and I stopped by to see him. I couldn't believe he was the same person. He was still denying that he had ever hurt any children.

The term hurt *is tricky because pedophiles often don't feel they are hurting the child. Pat, you went through a lot because of his behaviour; do you consider yourself a victim of sexual assault?*
For a long time I referred to women like myself as the *hidden victims of childhood sexual abuse.* It stuck with me for quite a while until my epiphany. I am not going to see myself as a victim. I've got more of a life. I've got more to offer than that. I made a deliberate decision I'd had enough. I did not want to let him run the rest of my life.

When you say you're a victim it's almost like you're giving somebody else power over you. That's why I dislike using the word. Though people understand what we mean by it, we need to come up with some other terminology – even survivor *isn't accurate to me.*
Yeah. I hate the word *survivor* too. I don't want to define myself as a survivor.

How do you then define yourself?
As a wonderful woman. I've got the wrinkles to show it. There have been some hard times and some great times, but I am not letting who he was define my life.

Wonderful. Can you share what you were thinking and feeling when you were told your husband was a child molester?
There was a time when I was not very sane. There was a time when it was really hard. There was one point I clearly had a breakdown. I couldn't find the cheese grater and I realized I had left it a half a mile away in his big beautiful house. I had moved into a small ratty apartment with my son. I couldn't find the cheese grater. I wanted to make tacos for dinner and I didn't have a cheese grater. About that time my girlfriend called and I fell apart crying about the cheese grater. I felt I couldn't do it anymore. She said, "Stay right there." Forty minutes later she showed up at my apartment with a cheese grater and said, "Here, we've got work to do." It was important having people who were that supportive.
My friends and my sisters were particularly helpful. I have four sisters and two of them were just amazing. Some friends were

missing in action and some colleagues were downright nasty. One fellow psychologist said, in a professional meeting, "Well, of course he had to turn to children – look at Pat, who could put up with a woman like that?"

What? How did you and the other professionals respond to that?
It was quiet. I was part of the local psychological association and pretty active on radio and television. I had my own TV show and was known in the community. I think the thing that hurt me the most was the police lieutenant who had been the major investigator in the case. She was on *20/20* with me and the only clip they used, out of hours of interviews, was when she said, "She had to know about this all the time, the whole time. It's her fault these children were hurt."

This was a police officer speaking?
The police lieutenant. Yes, it was a woman who said that. Then, when I was on *Investigation Discovery*, I received an email from the same police lieutenant, through the producer of the show, apologizing for what she had said when she was interviewed. She said it never dawned on her that I was a wife first and then a psychologist. She assumed all psychologists knew all about child molesters. It was a very nice apology, but that was the gist of what she was saying. It didn't connect with her that I could not have known. She was making assumptions and was caught up in the tenor of the times – the reason men molest children is because their wives aren't good enough.

Oh, my. If that's the case they go to another woman possibly, not a child.
Isn't that amazing? You know that and I know that. It was a different time: 1986, over twenty-five years ago. There was a different view around this type of thing.

No Internet back then to do some research.
I can tell you there was nothing available then. There was a women's abuse centre for women who had been raped or abused by their husbands, which a friend of mine ran. I remember talking to another professional about what had happened to me and she didn't want to have anything to do with it. She said, "That's not

my job." ARCH Protective Services was another place where the door was closed. It was really hard and many times I felt alone wondering, What did I do to deserve this? Why did this happen to me?, How could I have been so mistaken? and How did I misread this man and marry him? There was a lot of self-blame. It was a very difficult time.

I knew there were other women in my position. I didn't have any idea as to how many, but I knew there were a lot of them. I remember I was out shopping in Phoenix one day. I got some food at a deli and sat outside on the patio to eat. A woman came up and asked if she could share the table with me – she was obviously not having a good day and we started talking. It turned out that she had also been married to a child molester and we talked for two and half hours. I had never talked to anybody else who'd had the same experience as me. I had no idea what her name was and we went our separate ways. That time together was such a gift because, although I knew intellectually there were other women in my position, at the time it felt like I was the only one. I think that's part of what helps people, the gifts that we don't anticipate: someone delivering a cheese grater or somebody helping you clean up a mess in the kitchen or somebody showing up at a deli who's literally a stranger in the night.

What a coincidence, sitting with her. You know others are there, but ...
It's just finding them; where do you go to find them? It was clear I wasn't going to get much support at the sexual assault program that colleagues of mine were running. Also, there was a lot of criticism of me, from other professionals in my local area, that it was me not him who was responsible for his behaviour. "Of course, he had to do it, look at who she is," was the refrain. Well, I'm the big sister of eight kids – of course I'm a pushy broad; I grew up that way. That was my role.

But still, it's really hard after you've been criticized so many times and people have been really skeptical that you're telling the truth. At that point it's just easier to be quiet. I actually moved to Washington four years ago and, with the exception of one or two friends I felt that I could trust, I haven't shared my past.

Well, sometimes we say children can be cruel, but I guess adults can be cruel as well. Nobody recognized you from your days on the various TV shows?

Well, I was significantly younger then.

Tell me more about the course you've developed.

The course idea had been developing in the back of my mind and when I retired, a colleague suggested I put the program online and create a term membership site on the web. I thought it would be a way to help other women, so I did it. I wanted it to be forward-looking. As a psychologist I had worked with people in therapy and I also did a lot of organizational consulting. I had a lot of written material I was able to adapt and use for the course. In the organizational consulting, I was teaching people how to be more effective with their business, and in developing the course, I took those suggestions and modified them to teach people how to be more effective in their life.

Over the last four or five years post-traumatic growth has become a real focus in psychology. This is thanks to Marty Seligman, who was president of the American Psychological Association a number of years ago. He challenged the organization to stop focusing on why people are having psychological difficulties and start trying to help them grow to be more effective people. The idea has really taken off.

I love the term *post-traumatic growth*. It's optimistic, it's positive, it's moving forward – as opposed to the term *distress*.

Isn't it wonderful? It's so hopeful. The reality is that at least sixty to seventy per cent of people who have been through trauma actually end up feeling better about themselves, being more capable of operating in the world, and having more energy and more enthusiasm for life. We hear so much about post-traumatic stress disorder, but only around thirty per cent of people that go through trauma are deeply affected. We don't think about how many people go through really tough situations and do just fine.

I never thought about it that way. What's the name of your course?

"Take Charge and Move On." The focus is on how you take charge. In fact, my second book was, *Taking Charge When You're Not in Control*. How can you meet a situation, figure out how to get past it in a much more robust and happy way and have a healthier life than what you had in the past? It came together kind of serendipitously as I'm retired and living in this great place. I now have the opportunity to sit down and send email lessons every week to the people taking my class. It's something that, once I get it all set up, works automatically, though I'm still involved and scan the comments participants make. It becomes somewhat of an interactive process. I've also had seminars with participants or special events. For example, we are doing a television show this week on *Investigation Discovery*. I'll let them know what is happening in other areas and include that with the course.

Can anyone take the course?
The course is specifically for women who have been married to a child molester, or what they're sometimes now called in the literature, the *non-offending spouses*. These are women who have gone through a situation similar to mine. Unfortunately, there are still very few resources for women who have been in this position.

It must be so difficult to be in this situation with nowhere to turn.
Some women that write to me say, "I saw you on *Oprah*" or "I was with you on the stage when you were on *Sally Jessie Raphael*." They've connected with me because of the media I did years ago. One woman in particular just broke my heart when she wrote, "I just can't get past this. My life is ruined. There is nothing I can do." I could hear the sigh in her email. So, some of what I do is keep in touch with women like her on a very regular basis. I don't believe there's nothing they can do. I'm not going to let what happened to me ruin my life. I didn't choose what he did. I didn't know it was coming. I certainly didn't do it myself.

Do you feel, as a psychologist, there exists an *always the victim* mentality? I mean, two people can have something similar happen and one somehow takes charge and moves forward, whereas the other lives his or her story over and over and never feels healthy. I don't mean he or she will forget, just move forward. Live, you know?
Have the courage to take the steps needed. There were times that I was so angry and so frustrated and so unhappy and I just wanted it all to be over. I didn't want to have to deal with it; it wasn't fair. I

was screaming, yelling, hollering, "I shouldn't have to do this." Well, yes, but you have two choices, you can take charge of your life and move on or you can let this ruin your life. Are you going to remain a victim all your life? Move on to something that's better. Do the work.

How does one find the strength to come out of this and be productive? Pretend I'm a woman who's just contacted you. I don't know how or where to begin to heal. I can't get rid of the shame and the guilt. I can't eat, I'm depressed and I can't even get off the couch. He ruined my life. What would you say to me?

I would say, "This is something that happened to you, it is not who you are. You're not responsible for what he did."

But I feel responsible.

I can understand that you don't feel like you can get out off the couch. What I want you to do is choose one thing to change today. If you're sitting in front of the television and you're watching show after show after show, take the television schedule out and choose which show you're going watch tomorrow. Choose just one show and then purposefully turn the television on when it's time for that show. When people get depressed or feel ashamed they may only be able to handle one tiny thing at a time. If I told you to join an exercise class, limit your television viewing to two hours a day, choose several shows and put them all on your schedule, eat three meals a day, stop eating candy – you'd be overwhelmed. You have to start with one little thing, and it works.

Okay, so she does that. Then what?

If you miss it today, start tomorrow morning fresh. Which show are you going to watch today? I am an absolute believer in changing one thing.

What is that one action building toward?

That change is one step toward taking charge of how you're living your life. The other thing you need to do is start telling yourself the truth. One of the truths is, *it's not about you*. Another truth is *you did not do anything to make him molest children*. The third truth is *this is his, not yours*. I can go on with truth for a long time, but the bottom line is, we do not know why people molest children. The answer is, it varies, but we don't know for sure. Another truth is the likelihood of him changing his behaviour is somewhere between remote and nil.

Child molesters molest children and they do it over and over and over again. Pedophilia is a drive disorder. It's not volition. It's not a behaviour people choose. There's a great book called *Stop Child Molestation*. It's based on a research project by Gene G. Abel and Nora Harlow. Their website summarizes a lot of their material. One thing that they talk about is how young boys, particularly when they are molested during early and mid-adolescence, may start to develop a sexual attraction to children because their sexual attraction is so robust at that time. It seems to be more of an imprinting of sexuality and what kind of sexual contact is gratifying. Most pedophiles maintain an active and seemingly innocent life with their marriage partners or girlfriends. I have been hearing about a type of therapy called Sex-Specific Therapy that I want to research.

I know someone in Northern California who works with many outpatient sex crime perpetrators who are called *opportunistic* rather than pedophiles. They rape or molest children because they can: "Oh, you're handy." That often happens within the child's family or with somebody close to the family. It's not about stranger danger anymore. That's the other thing we have to really let go of.

I teach, "It's not the stranger, it's the strange behaviour" you watch for.
Yes, great line.

Everybody is a stranger at some point. It's the strange behaviour you need to be aware of and that can be from a parent, sibling, or uncle Bob. It can be anybody.
It can be the guy at the convenience store or your pediatrician. My former husband was a child psychologist. Incidents of stranger danger, although there are headlines on every television station and in newspapers across the country, are very, very, rare. It's not the strangers we have to worry about, it's the people who live next door to us, come to our barbeques, folks that we know at work or health professionals.

This is why we need to talk about healthy sexual behaviours, so children can recognize and speak up when lines are crossed. There are many unclear lines and boundaries today. Just watch a movie and we can see sexual behaviour that wasn't appropriate in the past. I often teach the high school girls to pay more attention to their intuition.

Yes. There's a lot of work that needs to be done. Writing about this is going to be my last *hurrah*, in terms of the psychological area, and there's an enormous amount of work that needs to be done. It's time. I think it's an age-related mission too. I know I wouldn't have been ready to do this when I was much younger, probably because I had a child to support and I had to work. Now, I'm in a new relationship with a great guy and I'm retired. After sitting here for about a year and a half trying to figure what I was going to do with my life, I told myself, "Alright Pat, stop avoiding it – go back and finish up with what you were going to do." At this time of my life I come with a different perspective.

So, what does that perspective say we, as a society, should do with offenders? It seems like they've been allowed to continue. We know they do it, yet most people avoid talking about the problem and hope it's not their child.

I used to think the answer was to lop it off and lock them up, but I don't think the prison system would want to do it. It is sexually driven behaviour and I am interested in speaking to sex-specific therapists about child molesters to see what they think. In terms of somebody who's married to a child molester, you have to insist that they tell you the truth. No fudging at all: "Where were you?" "Oh, I went out." "No, tell me the truth. Where were you?" "I was at the hardware store and I bought these three things." That's the truth.

For women in this situation, you have to tell yourself the truth. The truth I finally came to was very hard. I knew when my former husband and I were talking, particularly about arrangements when our son was flying back and forth across the country to visit, that when he said he would do something, he thought he was telling the truth. Although I knew in my heart that it probably wouldn't happen and I could not count on him to do what he said he would.

Now, here's a sensitive topic for you: people are going to suggest leaving your son with a child molester is risky behaviour. Was he supervised?

My son stayed with his grandma when he went to visit his father. By this time he was sixteen or seventeen so it wasn't as much of a risk as if he had been four or five. The visits were court ordered. I had to give him visitation. I just had to frame the visitation so my son was as safe as possible. As he got older, he made the decision about whether or not it was safe to stay. The last time he saw his father I didn't realize his father was very sick with a type of dementia. My son had gone to visit him and he phoned me and said, "Mom, dad's crazy," and then recounted what his father had done. I told him to get to the airport immediately and there would be a ticket waiting when he arrived. He came home and his father died about two months later.

How old was he when he first knew what his father had done?
He knew when his father was arrested – about ten or eleven.

Wow, that's young to find out something like that.
It's one of the reasons why I took a job across the country. I wanted him out of the area.

How do you tell a ten-year-old his father sexually abused children?
We said some version of, "There are a lot of children who say that your daddy did bad things to them." This was the day after I found out. So it was gruesome, just gruesome. It was the most stressful period of my life.

How did all of this change your life?
I grew up with the belief you got married and you stayed married for life. Sometimes the changes were really cuckoo or almost trivial, but I was really furious that he wasn't around. We had promised each other that we were going to go travelling all over the country in an RV when he retired. Then I was on my own and couldn't do it. However, one day it dawned on me that I could travel all over the country when I was retired. That's when I took a sabbatical and travelled in my RV. What I realized is, you can't stop your life just because you're by yourself – that was a big step for me.

For a long time I was very brittle and very angry. It was hard for a lot of people to be around me because I was wary and watchful, wondering who else was out there. That's a very common feeling after experiencing trauma induced by somebody else. Eventually I figured out how to do a lot of things I otherwise wouldn't have done, like travelling. I did an enormous amount of travelling with my work. I was an organizational consultant and went to Mexico, Canada, England, South Africa and the South of France. I'm grateful I was really busy and had a full life with lots of friends. Yet, I spent a lot of time at home alone too. I became much less social than previously.

How did his family react to all of this and towards you?
I had two mother-in-laws; his stepmother and I were very close. After the sexual abuse came out, it wasn't until he passed away that I saw her again. His mother, who referred to me as "that woman" through my whole experience with her, continued to be an extremely difficulty person. Both of them and their husbands continue to have a good relationship with my son.

Do you think anybody in his family knew what he was doing?
I don't think anybody suspected it. His father was particularly supportive and ended up supporting him. He had a very hard time finding a job and then he got very sick. I'm trying to think about how to say this... I know his father loved him, but I also think he was very conflicted. Like, "How could my son have done that?" and, "What did I do wrong?" That's just my sense of what happened.

I'm going to ask you this question again because I'd like you to go deeper: what should be done to someone who molests children?
Well I am not sure what should be done with them. I think one of the most important things that we can do is to really help the kids that are molested. Young people who have been molested, particularly boys, are much more likely to become pedophiles than children that haven't been molested. So, we need to get a lot of help for young kids who have been molested, particularly if they're in the early preteen years, just after they start going through hormonal changes. This seems to be a crucial development period, particularly in boys. That way we can remediate the process shortly after they've been molested and reduce the chance that they

become pedophiles.

There's a difference between physical abuse or verbal abuse and sexual assault. Children, particularly teens, are developing their own sense of sexuality. If a sexual abuse experience is layered on top of that, it can really muddy the water because they now have a connection between abuse and sexuality. That can be really problematic, especially for boys. Boys have different floods of testosterone at that time, and the testosterone is what triggers their sexual appetite. It's what triggers boys to feel like they're becoming a man and having a sense of sexuality. So, being abused at that time has a tendency to connect the abuse and their sexuality, and they can start to develop a *drive disorder*, which is a really sticky place. It is typically those men who will turn around and abuse younger children, particularly boys.

The other thing parents need to do is be open about sexuality with their children. Help them understand and know their little bodies. Teach them the names of their body parts, help them establish good hygiene habits, and teach them to not be afraid or ashamed of their bodies. Let them know that their bodies are their own, not available to other people. Many families adopt the bathing-suit rule I referred to earlier: don't let other people, children or adults, touch you anywhere that is covered by your bathing suit.

At the same time, it is important not to engender a feeling of shame or naughtiness about the sexual play they will do. All children do that as they come to know about their bodies. Almost all little girls and little boys will fondle or stimulate their genitals. Let them know it isn't *nasty*, but it is private. Being matter of fact is probably the best approach. Just start with the guidelines early and often.

I think the other piece is that we need to inform more people about sexual abuse. That's one of the reasons why I really like the web right now, because there's a lot of information there. Some of it is just opinions and some of it is really solid information.

How do we make it more comfortable to speak out about a topic that has been taboo for years?

I think a part of it is just what you're doing: speaking about it, writing about it. It sounds strange, but there are lot of people who say, "I don't want to talk to you." My neighbour, whose child was molested by my husband, had that approach. "I don't want to talk about anything that's nasty, I don't want to talk about anything that's uncomfortable," and as a result her son was taken advantage of. We owe it to our children to be more comfortable with all of life's hazards and to teach them, not about stranger danger, but about what is okay for adults to do to you.

I think it's so unique that you can speak about this, not only from the perspective of the wife of a child molester, but also as a psychologist. Thank you for sharing your knowledge through radio, television, books and now your course. It's amazing – who better to learn from than someone who has actually gone through it and moved forward in a productive way.

Here's the deal: I don't want him controlling my life. I don't want what happened to me to control my life. I want to be in charge of my own life. It's mine. I get passionate about this sometimes when listening to a woman say she just can't get past it. It's disheartening when I see people who have been crushed by this kind of experience. I just want to grab them and hold them and say, "We'll walk together on this. You don't have to be by yourself." I often have teleseminars with people taking my course and I always reassure them that they can make it. Sometimes you need a coach along the way to answer some questions and give you a different perspective. This experience does not need to ruin your life.

It's wonderful that you have taken a difficult experience and turned things around in your life to help others.

Well, thank you.

Your passion is clear and powerful. The topic is difficult but you keep on going year after year, building up and educating women who have basically nowhere else to turn. Quite frankly, people are probably either drawn to or repulsed by your energy, with regards to this kind of topic.

Yes, exactly. That's a wonderful phrase you used. It tends to repulse people.

You have shared many insights today and I want to thank you for taking the time to speak with me. Any last thoughts?

We keep focusing on the "Ah, this is my awful story." Well yeah, I've got an awful story, you've got an awful story, everybody's got an awful story, but that's not what my life is about now. Build yourself a better story for your life.

Anger is like gasoline. If you use it wisely, it will drive you where you want to go. If you use it unwisely, it will blow up in your face. *Unknown*

Lyrically Speaking – How the Years Burn
Ruth

Speak to me in a language that I understand, preferably without words.
Maybe preferably
with.
Please just help me
to understand.
How to make sense of it all?
Heart and mind looking for the resolution –
how do I integrate,
reconcile this?
Paradoxical heart.
I want to believe, but I also want to remember
and it makes me angry, so angry
at you.

Tuesday nights, in a room full of hyper-awareness
unearthing a lifetime of disassociation
and memories blocked.
A mystery unto myself.
An abandoned well of afflicted waters,
a river of pain I walked away from.
Parts of me I turned my back on,
broken moments I would need to go back to
in order to reclaim her and collect
all of her little
doll parts.

Tuesday nights,
spent unearthing an ancient ache.
So I can be present in the here and now.
And not look to the future with the terrified eyes and broken heart of
a long-forgotten child.

Sharing and claiming a hard-earned wisdom
and chipping away
at the spots of cement that have formed on my heart.

Keeping me away from myself,
standing small behind guardian vines
of a bridge overlooking the distance
from me to you.

Tuesday nights, sisters of spirit.
Speaking my truth and acknowledging that sorrow.
I am clearing my heart for love,
for you.
Cleansing away the mud, but begging to understand,
why? Screaming out, sometimes silently,
other times far from.

He cannot answer me,
though I know on some level, I am loved.
And on some level,
the deepest of answers reside within.
Hidden inside,
engrained in the very seam and fabric –
very essence of my soul.
Predestined, karmic agreement
that we both made.

Maybe I came here just to find my way back to you.
And you, to watch over me and make sure that I did.

Blessed but trying to process it all
kneeling by the hazy river of faith,
sifting for diamonds in a murky bowl.
Reeling at times
from the grip of a shimmering mirage.
My hands shaking,
but I still grip this bowl.
Searching for the diamonds of
absolution and understanding,
crying out for my innocence and trying
to accept the darkest parts
of me
and
where I've been
and
what I've seen.

Yearning for that love I am working so hard to purify my heart for
and be open
to
receiving.

I want to know if you can be alone with yourself and if you truly like the company you keep in the empty moments.
Oriah Mountain Dreamer

Loving My Sinner, Hating His Sin
Charmaine

Thanks for meeting me on this snowy day! Are you revealing your name?
I have changed my mind a few times. My final decision is to only use my first name, out of respect for a family member's request for privacy.

I'm excited as this is the first interview for *Unlock the Door*. How are you feeling about revealing your story?
Oh, very good – very inspired to share with others on this topic.

Are there any people in your life who you would want to know about your story, or any you would particularly not want to know?
I want to share it with everybody.

When did you first make other people aware of your story?
When I was fifteen – prior to that nobody knew.

Who knows about the sexual abuse at this time?
My family and some organizations that I've done charitable work with. I can't even say how many people know – a lot.

How long was it from the time the abuse began until you revealed what was going on?
Ten years. It happened from the time I was five to fifteen years old.

That's a very long time. When did you realize that what was going on might not be right?
At about age nine or ten, I started feeling like it wasn't good. It was scary; it wasn't right. I started wondering if I should tell someone.

Do you recall your feelings at the time when it first began?

Yes. I wasn't really thinking anything – my father just showed me his penis and had me touch it.

That must have been a surprise, as a five-year-old?
No, it wasn't.

No?
Never. It never occurred to me it was anything I was not supposed to do.

Five year olds are very innocent. How and why did the abuse with your father stop?
I started to like boys. It was a different experience away from my dad and I started identifying that what my dad was doing was probably not good or right. At age fifteen, I had a boyfriend and I finally decided to tell my family. I was hoping we could work through it as a family, but it didn't quite happen that way. That's when it stopped.

I can't imagine what was going through your mind.
I had a mixture of feelings because I really loved my dad. He was really funny – the fun parent. He was not the one that disciplined us. We were scared of our mom. I was always special to my dad. The abuse was our secret and he never made me feel bad. He was very gentle and soft about it and I never had a really harsh feeling.

How did he isolate you or have the opportunity to abuse you?
It was usually when we were all sleeping or when we were alone.

Other people in your family were around?
Probably, yeah. I was on a bunk bed when he came in the night before I revealed what was happening. There was a bunk bed in our houseboat and my brother was asleep above me while my dad was there.

How often did the abuse happen?
At least once a month. I'm not sure how many times, but it happened often.

The abuse must have affected you deeply.

Yes, in all areas of my life. When I revealed it to my family, it was very traumatic. I was told to leave the family. I was disowned. From that point on I couldn't trust anyone, not even family. I felt love was just going to break everywhere. I went into survival mode, trying to get a job, working on my own, and taking care of myself. It was a different way of being throughout all areas of my life.

Can you talk about what happened to you and be okay with it now?

I'm totally okay. I've had to work through it. I'm not just what happened to me. The best thing I can do is to first of all be thankful – I expand into who I choose to be from the experience.

I hear you. It's tough, but a good attitude to have. When you were a child, did you have nightmares?

Eventually. While it was going on, I didn't want him to come in at night and eventually I became really numb and really scared. By age fifteen I was done; it made me sick to my stomach.

Do you see him now?

I'm in contact with him and we see each other sometimes. Sometimes I'll go a year without seeing him. I charged him successfully and he showed no remorse and lied about it for years. I didn't speak to him for a long time after the court case. He finally told the family I was telling the truth. A lot of perpetrators never admit their crime, so it's a unique story. When I chose to charge my dad, years after leaving home, I discovered he had actually abused both my siblings and a cousin. We didn't talk about it until I activated the charge.

At the same time he was violating you, he was violating them and you each didn't know about the others?

Right.

What a shame.

Yeah, it is. It really is. I took a lot of responsibility at fifteen. Yet, I didn't know it was happening to all of us. I wanted him to stop touching me. I didn't know it was happening to them too until I was twenty-one.

Was he charged with abusing all of you?
No. Just me, because I was the one who charged him.

Has he admitted guilt with the others?
I don't know. He might have admitted it to my siblings, but I don't know if he's admitted it to other family members.

He was just charged for assaulting you?
Yes.

I can only imagine the emotions you must have felt, finding out about the others.
Yeah, I wasn't alone. We started to share our stories. I was scared to death. I didn't know what lay ahead. It was a relief and it also gave me power. I knew I had to follow through because he was working in a public job. I was very afraid that he might be abusing other people or children.

How often do you think about the assault now?
I don't think about it often. However, I get really angry when patterns show up in my behaviour and I know they are related to the abuse, for example, in the patterns I sometimes show in relationships and how I survive, like making sure my home is safe and sound. I grew up in a household with sexual abuse, physical abuse and bullying. So, the pattern I learned in falling in love with my dad, and the physical abuse in the family, was familiar space for me. It was something I knew I could be dominated by, and it was something I knew I could control. I knew I could lie a little bit and get away with it. I used my sexuality in a way that was familiar to me.

I attract that style of personality that I grew up with, in all of my relationships. Have I had a relationship with anyone who's different? I don't know. I can't answer that question to be honest. There are traces of what's familiar in each of my past relationships. I certainly haven't had that full experience of euphoric safety. I can't even explain it. I feel best when I am home by myself or when my kids are here with me. I can lock the door and I'm in my own space. I find the most comfort with my friends, with my family and with being at home. I'm okay with being alone, too. I'm not alone a lot; I usually have people around me.

Do you know how your father feels about what happened?
He wishes he could be a better grandfather and father and he's remorseful. Is he fully trusted? No, absolutely not. I often compare it to putting a bottle in front of an alcoholic. What's really great about the experience of forgiving, moving on and having him in my life is that I am empowered by setting boundaries. There are always adults around when we're all together as a family. It's not just me alone having to watch him all the time. He'll sit and have a coffee and just relax. He's a very big family guy. There are multiple sides of him that are hard to reconcile. It's really hard to believe that someone who sexually abuses his children has another side.

That's probably one of the greatest challenges – something hard for people to believe.
I didn't speak with my dad for six to eight years, but I learned he became quite remorseful. When he ended up telling the family the truth, it allowed me to start opening up, to see his good side. I decided to talk to him even if it meant arguing and possibly ending our relationship permanently. I didn't want our relationship to be dramatic and filled with anger. I knew if I never spoke to him again and something tragic happened to him, I would regret it. So, I found peace within myself to forgive him, as well as myself.

It took a lot of counselling. When I was able to forgive him I learned that could empower me. I set boundaries that would support us being together and then just moved on. He's in my life. He sees my children. He loves to be the crazy, fun grandpa. The greatest memories I have with my dad are going on Ferris wheels, climbing trees and just doing fun things. I like that side of my dad, but there has to be adult supervision – there can't be alcohol around either. We visit for a couple of hours and then walk away. It feels good to be with him.

Do you love your dad?
I love my dad very, very much.

You love the man, but not what he's done.
Absolutely. That's the book I'm trying to write, remember? "Loving My Sinner, Hating His Sin."

I remember. That's a great title. I wonder about other kids in your situation, not saying something for so long. Why do you think that is?
It's pretty hard to grasp. When you're very young, and you've been living with abuse, you don't know if it's right or wrong. Then as soon as you have the feeling that it's not right, it takes time to get the courage to tell someone.

Who should kids tell?
I don't know. A friend, a friend's parents, your family, a teacher, someone you trust. How do you say it? I don't know – you just have to say it.

What would you say to a youngster reading this who wants to tell, but is afraid of getting into trouble or getting taken out of their home and ending up in a place that's worse?
All of that might happen. Truth can be difficult to face; it's hard to tell someone. But it's the only way to go. For me, my minister helped. My mom was a Sunday school teacher, and one day while she was closing school I asked my minster if it was safe to tell the truth. He didn't know what I was referring to. I asked because every time I'd told the truth, I'd practically been beaten to death. It was never safe to tell the truth, it scared me. He said to me, "You know what? Sometimes it's hard to tell the truth and really hard to deal with it. When that happens, take your right hand and spread your fingers, then take your left hand and spread it really large – this is God. Put them together and hold tight and everything will be okay. The truth will always come out whether we like it or not."

Are you a spiritual person?
Very faithful.

What would you like to share with people who have never told their story, never acknowledged that they were sexually abused?
If they are old enough to actually know what's going on, I would say, "Look at your life and ask yourself if it's really working the

way you want. Are there things in your life that are affected by the sexual abuse or assault? If there are, speak up."

When did you begin therapy?
I was in counselling the moment I was told to leave my house. They actually put me in a psych ward because I became suicidal. I couldn't support myself emotionally. From that point on I was in and out of counselling. When I was on my own in Toronto, I found a good counsellor. The best counselling I've had was with Landmark Education. I've done some pretty heavy transformational work. I had my first orgasms with my dad, so I really had to deal with and learn how to manage my love life. I had to manage sex from a new perspective. I often couldn't have an orgasm but when I did, I would curl up like a little baby. I'd get scared and cry and shake.

That's heavy work for sure.
Recovery is a process, but you know what? Life is a process.

Should we be talking about sexual abuse openly?
I absolutely think it should be talked about. It's not a unique area in life. I think the more we withhold anything that is confrontational, the more we allow resentment to build. We have to keep speaking about it. Any time it comes up, it should be openly discussed. It should be discussed early on with young children. When my little boy was five or six years old, he started to figure out that his privates were working a certain way. So, for me it's very important that kids start to identify what is appropriate and not appropriate right away – what's acceptable, what's loving of yourself, and what's appropriate to do and not to do in public. Also, kids need to learn confidence about their body and learn to ask questions.

How can we bridge the gap between the shame, the guilt, and the anger and healing, and being at peace with who we are, and forgiveness and…
Great. You hit the word. It's the only word. Forgiveness.

How does one find forgiveness when there's so much anger and sadness?
You've got to let go: you've got to let go of the meanings you've

attached to the abuse. Separate yourself from the action. The person did what they did. You identify with being there and you take no responsibility for what they did. Yet, you can take responsibility for what you are and what you do and say, moving forward. Does that make sense?

Yes, complete sense.

When you distinguish what happened and who you are as entirely separate things, you can start to fully forgive yourself. You're the one that made it mean what it has meant to you thus far. If you continue to blame yourself, you give your abuser power for what he or she did. Right? When in fact you can choose to empower yourself around what happened. Forgive yourself, find some peace and resolve it. It's tricky to choose whether to forgive your perpetrator. That's up to each individual. I know it's difficult, not even close to imaginable for some. To me, forgiveness is the only space that identifies that the two, the act and the person, are separate from each other.

We are more the way we respond to events than we are the event itself.

Yeah, that's what I often say. If we could actually see the power in the choice of words that come out of our mouths and the actions we take. That voice in our head makes it all mean something, right? Once we identify that distinction, I think we have the power.

Well it would be wonderful if everybody could grasp that concept. It's so difficult when the pain seems insurmountable. Forgiveness can be a lifelong process or it can be completely absent.

How do you forgive? Prior to my work with Landmark Education I would never have been able to because I would have been clinging to blame and to the belief the abuse was wrong. Heavy emotions. I don't want to be that way all the time. I'm not like that normally; actually I love life. I think it's playful and fun, but I had a hard time finding that out. My counsellor once said to me, "This will never go away. It will show up in little ways."

When my daughter was about eighteen months old and I was changing her diaper, I realized how easy it would be to do something. As soon as the thought came into my mind I asked my husband to come in. I felt faint and like I was going to be sick to my stomach. I was so angry and upset about what was happening between me and my dad. We were in a place of starting to forgive and I was in counselling. My dad said to me, "Whenever you need to say something, you can say just say it, and don't ever think I'm going to hold it against you or that I'm going to defend myself." He gave me that space, which was really great. So, I wrote him a letter when I was really angry. Not that I was going to do anything to my daughter, but it made me so angry at him: that he could violate me like that and think it was all okay. I just didn't get it.

I have a very difficult question to ask. People talk about the cycle of abuse. If you've been abused, you are more likely to abuse your children, particularly if you are a male. As a female, you're more likely to attract the type of people who will abuse you as an adult. What do you think about that? It's quite a burden. It makes sense that people don't want to say they were abused when the perception is that they will also abuse.

Well, it goes around. People often say my dad was abused, though he's never admitted it. I finally asked my grandmother and she said there was a woman that the boys would visit and she wonders if something happened with her. Does it justify what my father did? No. I'm working with a counsellor at Rockwood Psychological Services in Kingston, Ontario, who works with pedophiles inside the federal prison. She's working in the area of healing men. She's trying to help them create a new and better life when they're released.

I was listening to a YouTube recording of *Oprah* recently. She has done so much work in this area. She said when you release the guilt, that's when you truly understand it wasn't your fault. Can you comment on that?

It's ironic you ask that. I was talking to my children on the way to school about taking responsibility for their actions and words. When you actually understand the impact on both sides, it is a phenomenal state. It really takes a superhero to take full responsibility no matter what you've done. If you never take responsibility for things you have done or continue to do and be, it's like karma: it comes around. God has a way with us no matter which way we go. That's why I feel like I'm fully surrounded by faith.

When I think of your situation, I wonder where you would get your strength and guidance if you didn't have faith.

Thankfully, I have been trained to take full responsibility for what I make things mean. It's not a unique idea. People will do and say what they choose – nothing is bad or good; it just is. There's no need to play the blame game. I would love to live in that world. It definitely would make me feel better.

What happened to your father after you charged him?

He was charged with gross indecency and sexual assault with a minor. He went to jail for four months then just went on with his life. He confessed and has gone through a lot of counselling. He eventually went back to work, I think, and is retired now. He's not drinking as much. He has a girlfriend and lives in the Southern United States. I actually don't know what happened with him a lot of those years because nobody would talk to me about his life. I didn't care to talk about his life either.

What happened to your mom through all of this?

At first she was completely lost and confused. She was already dealing with him having affairs inside the marriage before I told her about the abuse. She chose to put me out of the house and trust my dad. I thought she would support me. She was so confused. Imagine marrying a man who did this to your child. Years later, when I had decided to charge my dad, she found out that all of us had been abused and became suicidal. She went missing from work for three days because she had overdosed. If she hadn't been found the following day, she probably would have died. Her blood had coagulated – fortunately, she survived.

It would be an awful shock to learn your child was sexually abused by your husband.

She had no idea. Their relationship ended when I was nineteen.

What was your family's reaction when you told them your dad was abusing you?

My dad had abused me the night before I told them. I woke up to him touching me and pretended to cough just to get it over with. As soon as he fell asleep, I went to my boyfriend's and phoned my mom. I told her to call my dad and bring him home from the boat in the morning. She called him, although she didn't know what was going on. When I came home, my dad was sitting at the table looking nervous. I walked around and stood on the other side. My sister was in the room and my mom was pacing the floor. She was so scared. She didn't know what she would hear – my dad was also an alcoholic so she probably thought other things were happening. When I sat down I said, "Mom, dad has been sexually abusing me," I was hoping for more support than I got.

I think my dad already knew what I was going to say, but maybe he didn't. I don't know. My mom paced back and forth in the kitchen asking, "Is this true, is this not true, is it true?" It was intense. My sister was sitting quietly on the counter looking scared. My dad vehemently denied abusing me. He would not admit it. The first time I heard him deny it, I just stretched over the table in shock. I could imagine how it might have felt for him to tell the truth, but I still couldn't believe he didn't. It seemed to go on the entire day.

I don't remember the transition, but when we moved from the kitchen to the living room it became more intense. My mom was hitting me on the head and asking me if it was true or not. I felt like I was being made out to be the liar. At one point I said, "Okay, it didn't happen." It was brutally intense when I said that. My mom was so confused and freaked out. She told me to get out and said that I was *absolutely* disowned by the family. I left. That moment was so impactful on my life. I began surviving on my own. I went to my boyfriend's mother's house and I started keeping more to myself. I think my whole personality started to shift into dominating, yet I was very innocent – still trying to figure things out.

Like I said, I was having sex with my boyfriend, which made things really confusing. I didn't do drugs, but I was really lost. As I mentioned I became suicidal and was put into a psych ward. I remember the experience clearly. I looked at ink blots and they gave me medicine; I don't know what the medicine was for. Then I left the psych ward and life went on. It was never addressed again throughout high school. It's funny because on Facebook, everyone at my high school saw me as having it together. In reality, I never had many friends and was quite introverted. I had two girlfriends and a boyfriend. I was seen differently by the other students at my school and didn't realize that until much later.

After high school, I went to college and concentrated on my art while also doing a lot of modelling. I had a lot going on as I began my twenties. Then one day my brother visited me with a really pretty girlfriend and I felt compelled to tell him to be a little cautious around dad. I didn't even get to finish before he said, "I know." I said, "What do you mean you know?" He said, "I was sexually abused too." I'll never forget that moment. I felt like a kettle immediately put on high that didn't even have time to boil. I was looking up at my little brother, who was six foot three, knowing he had also been abused by our father. When I was fifteen I was worried sick and had to stop my dad from touching me; now I was learning that he had also been touching my little brother. It didn't make any sense to me. Not that touching a little girl makes sense. You know when parents talk about what they would do if anything ever happened to their children? They go into this serious, protective state; that's what happened to me when my brother told me he had also been abused. I was six when he was born. I was his older sister and in my mind what happened to him was unforgivable. I think I probably took responsibility for what happened to him.

Instantly I became intense and unstoppable. I put on my coat and went straight to the trauma police to report my dad for abusing me. My brother was freaking out. Everybody was freaking out: "Think about this, this might not be a good idea." I just went full force ahead. I wanted the man stopped. I told the police I had to charge my father for sexual abuse and I needed to start *now*. They said, "Okay, are you sure about this?" I said, "I have no thoughts otherwise." My brother was trying to stop me the entire time. He told me to think about it and wondered if it was a good idea. He wasn't telling me not to do it, but just to stop and think about it. That's another pattern of my behaviour – I'm extraordinarily proactive when I adamantly believe in something. It can be good or bad. Sometimes it's better to have more patience.

In this case, it was good because it led me to act right away. I was directed to the police department in the district where the offence occurred. So, things began. However, my quick action also meant that I hadn't taken the time to consider the future. For example, surprise witnesses and all the paperwork from the psych ward that declared I was lying, looking for attention and had a personality disorder. Furthermore, seeing my grandmother upset during the two-day court session was very difficult. Everyone in the family was learning what had happened. Remember, my dad was the fun parent. Everyone was really shocked. He was loved by his family – to have this revealed inside the family was heart-wrenching.

What happened at court?
The first day of court I told my story. My dad sat there looking numb. I looked at him; then I couldn't look at him; then I looked at him again. He just sat there as if he was hollow. For me, it wasn't about charging him because I wanted to see him go to jail. I simply wanted him to stop what he was doing. I didn't know what the outcome would be. When I was told there was a witness on his behalf I had no idea who it would be.

On the second day I was shocked to see my sister come through the door. She was manipulated to support him; she chose to do what she did. She testified about his good side. Later she said she felt terrible about standing up for dad. It was difficult for me to not be supported. Then my dad had to give a statement. He sounded like a tape recorder – he was really rehearsed. Finally, when it was over and the judge was going to reveal the verdict, I asked to speak. Normally they don't allow someone to speak right before the verdict because the decision has already been made, but I was told I could come up and say what I wanted.

I went up and I looked my dad in the eye and said, "Dad, I just want you to stop. I can't believe all of this. That's all I want you to do, stop." I came down from the stand and I fainted. I fainted right there in the courtroom. I was taken out of the room and didn't even hear the verdict. My mom and stepdad were in the courtroom. I remember the judge saying of me, "You know I really believe her. This is sad. I really believe if she didn't have to do this, she wouldn't have." I remember coming out of the washroom when everyone was walking out of the courtroom. All I saw was my grandmother holding my dad because they were taking him away. She said to me, "I hope you're happy." It was the worst feeling in the world. I was really close with my grandmother. It hurt.

Where are you now with everything that has happened?
I'm inspired to share my story and make sure that all those who have suffered sexual abuse know that no matter where they are, if they haven't told, don't know how to tell, if they're thinking about charging their offender, don't know how do to it, or wonder what might happen if they don't charge their offender – it's okay. When I talk to a victim whose offender is dead, I address how to find forgiveness within yourself: whether you go to the grave or speak to your offender in your mind or write a letter and read it out loud – whatever it takes to resolve and forgive. First, take care of *you*. It's the only way to move forward; it's what's going to help you break patterns. Remember what I said about knowing the distinction, that there are two separate worlds. You are not the thing that happened to you. Allow yourself to speak publicly about it. I've had a lot of great experiences empowering women through helping other victims and survivors, by being a mentor. I keep myself quite active. My art is inspired by children. Just live. I use my experience as an empowering context now. That's where I am.

Thank you for sharing your story. I just have one more question. Was four months enough punishment for what he did to you?
I didn't want him to go to jail. What I understood by speaking to a psychologist who treats perpetrators in jail is that they don't get therapy. They don't get treatment to heal from their experiences. I think they should have a fair chance to heal and an opportunity to talk and get support. I think that's one area we all need to acknowledge: as much as we would like to say put them in jail for life, they are human and should get treatment. They need to deal with their situation. It's getting back to the responsibility I mentioned earlier. If they continue to show no remorse, are cold and take no responsibility, then send them to jail. There are so many different levels of sexual assault.

I really appreciate your time.
I acknowledge you. I acknowledge you because it takes a lot to deal with your own experiences. Being touched and moved by all these different stories – it's going to impact you and your own experience.

That's one reason I waited a long time before beginning this book. It was an idea I had years ago. I kept pushing it aside, but now I'm embracing it. I know it's going to be a very interesting journey. Many people are beginning to speak out and seek help, yet many are remaining silent. You're brave sitting here and sharing your story. Many people never even acknowledge what has happened to them. So, I thank you for having the courage to speak out for the people who can't.

I can relate to them. I know what it's like to end up in a numb space where you no longer see the abuse and its impact on you. When you do begin to understand the impact and how numb you've become, it's like an exorcism.

One's dignity may be assaulted, vandalized and cruelly mocked, but it can never be taken away unless it is surrendered.
Michael J. Fox

Naming It to Tame It
Kalin

My mom was raped and I'm the product of that rape. My parents were dating and I had a fantasy that mom had said "Yes – no" rather than "No." But, I know that's not the truth. I wasn't conceived in love and I've asked myself, "Why does it matter to me?"

At a young age I sensed that my mother was keeping something from me. I swayed from being a good student to having suicidal thoughts. She still won't tell me all the details, but I know she was raped and that it was violent and probably at knifepoint. She tried to get away from my birth father by moving, but he followed her. I've asked her if she has any grudges from what happened back then and she said, "Do we have to talk about this?" It would mean a great deal to me if my mother would sit down and tell me the details of how she was violated.

Mom was stressed during her pregnancy. She intended to give me up for adoption and told the nurses she didn't want to hold me, but a nurse gave me to her. It was love at first sight. She put me in foster care for a month, and then got me back. I had the privilege of reading a letter she wrote to her father asking to move back home with me because "I just couldn't give her up." She kept me but still carries the pain from what she went through. She was terrified to have me, but abortion wasn't really an option.

I hired a detective to find my biological father and discovered he was in jail for sixteen years for that rape that caused my conception, as well as multiple charges for breaking and entering and other assaults. In 1993 he was alive, but I haven't heard anything since. He was mentally ill and aggressive. His sister told me that he knew I was a teacher. He was loving and good with animals and children. I continue to wonder why he never came to visit me and I feel the pain from the loss of a man I never met. Yet, I believe that he felt he was doing the right thing by staying away.

Ironically my biological father's name is Kenny and my adoptive father's name is Ken. I liken Kenny to the immature one and Ken to the stable mature influence. Ken and I have never discussed that he is not my biological father. He doesn't like to talk about those things. It's like nobody wants to talk about my past, so I have now made it my mission to talk to people every day as a teacher, friend and counsellor.

I tried not to mention my birth father for a while because I knew it upset my mom. I felt like my father was *missing*. Reflecting back I don't think it was because I was a product of rape – it was more about missing my father. It bothered me and was on my mind, and those feelings typically came out when I was drinking. I was never quite settled. I wondered about him.

I really was upset at my mom for not telling me the truth and all the details about what happened. It has been difficult, but our relationship has improved and grown. I don't push with the same intensity that I used to. I love and accept her. She has created a life she loves – she's independent, volunteers and is fun and unique.

I feel like I got the best out of what happened among the three of us. When my mom wouldn't discuss it anymore, I did an exercise for her where I listed all the benefits of being raped – there are some benefits, like having me, for example. I hoped to free her. She was just as much imprisoned as my biological father. One week later she sent me a picture of her graduating class with my father's picture in it.

When I was younger I was quiet, embarrassed to perform in public, expressionless and didn't share my feelings with others. I listened to music in my room and cried a lot. By grade seven I had written a note to my coach about killing myself. It was during this time I snooped in my parents' private papers and found out Ken had adopted me when I was two years old.

I asked my mom and she told me she had me before they were married and they decided to make it legal with the adoption. The explanation eased the itch, though I felt or instinctively knew there were lies and unspoken truths.

Sometime during this period I found out Ken wasn't my biological father. I can't remember the details. It wasn't until my twenties that I learned my mom was raped. My grandmother told me who my biological father was. When mom confirmed things by saying, "I was raped," she had so much pain, hurt and fear in her voice. She was still afraid that he would come back and kill her. She didn't want me to get in touch with him because she thought he would want money from me. She hadn't even told Ken she was raped.

When I shared my story with an elderly friend, amazingly, she shared that she was raped during the war at seventeen years of age. She'd never told anyone. She shared all the details of location, being held at knifepoint, and her feelings, and how quickly it was over. What an honour that she told me. Her story fulfilled some of my need to know what happened to my mother when she was raped.

As a result of what my mother, birth father and I have been through, I seek to understand human behaviour and emotions. Personally I have come to a balanced perception, and gratitude and love for everyone and everything exactly as they are. I want to share what I have learned to help others. Without a doubt, I feel that everything that happened or didn't happen has served me and others in my life.

There are two sides to my mom's rape. My biological father is the dark side, but he also gave me life and is part of the reason I have this life-giving mission: I help people shift perceptions so they can also realize there are two sides to their experiences. They say over and over again, "I never thought of it that way." That's why I am thankful my mom was raped – out of all the ugliness and terror, beauty and compassion unfolded. If things were not exactly as they were, I would not have been born or become the person I am today, serving others.

I was not conceived in love. I encourage children of rape to not take on shame or guilt, because it does not matter how you got here. An astrologer once said to me, "You came into this life – it is important to work on your issues in this lifetime." I think I have and I am helping others do the same.

I've studied a lot personal growth courses, such as Logosynthesis, synergistic play therapy and The Demartini Method. Each one has helped me understand and come to realize my mission is to help and assist others while remaining balanced, self-supporting and authentic. Believing in myself, developing new skills and appreciating things around me is very important.

Afterthought:

I don't really think of being the product of rape that much, but when I met you (Deb) I had a sense of relief, awareness and connection. Naming it to tame it.

I have recently fallen in love and with a man named Danny, who is the father of two boys. He is passionate, caring and affectionate. We both feel we have been preparing for this relationship our whole lives. It is wonderful to be in a relationship filled with mutual love and acceptance.

(Open To Love, Facebook).

A Victim's statement is presented to the court, by the victim or representative or in some cases, in the form of a video tape. The statement is restricted by guidelines dictating what may be included. Generally, the individual is permitted to discuss specifically the direct harm or trauma he or she suffered and problems that have resulted from the crime, for example, loss of income. Some jurisdictions allow individuals to include medical and psychiatric reports that demonstrate harm to themselves. They can also discuss the impact the crime has had on their ambitions or plans for the future, and how this has also impacted their extended family. The statement must only include the specific person before the board. In this case, the father.

A Victim's Statement
Hope

When I was five years old, my father began molesting me and he started fully raping me at the age of seven. He continued to rape me until I was seventeen years old. Now I am twenty four years old. Putting into words the impact of a crime is hard enough on its own, but putting into words the impact of a childhood full of suffering that was caused by your own parents is virtually impossible. In this statement I will do my best to explain some of the many ways that the childhood abuse I lived through has affected me emotionally, physically and financially, and how it has forever left me on a journey where I have no choice and no freedom.

Growing up, my friends all had families who loved them, cared for them and kept them safe. I always felt different. I felt like I didn't belong and wasn't good enough, and that I would never be able to connect with anyone. I felt ashamed, guilty and worthless. I lived in fear of what was coming next — every minute of every day. No one was ever allowed to set foot inside our house and this ostracized me all the more. When we went out we were the perfect family, with rehearsed lies, excuses and happy answers. No one was there when I needed someone and there was no safe place. I never had the chance to be a kid.

To this day, there is still no freedom or relief from the abuse. While the physical, sexual and emotional abuse has ended, the memories, nightmares, flashbacks, fear, anxiety, pain and brokenness remain. Because of the abuse I suffered as a child, I hate myself. I feel ashamed, dirty, guilty and worthless. I have almost no confidence in myself or my abilities; if you were to ask me what I'm good at, I wouldn't be able to tell you. I feel like a waste of time and space in everyone's lives and it's a struggle to keep going every day. I was made to feel like less than nothing and I have carried that with me into adulthood.

I live every day in fear. Nighttime is especially hard for me because most nights of the week my father would come to my bed and rape or molest me. As soon as the sun begins to set, I become anxious and fearful. I jump at every sound. I feel absolutely alone, vulnerable and helpless — as if someone is going to hurt me at any moment. I haven't slept properly since I was eleven or twelve years old. In the past five years, I have developed PTSD and I have violent, vivid nightmares and flashbacks replay incidences of the abuse I suffered as a child. I no longer sleep because of fear of these nightmares. I'm also terrified to be off guard during the night, so I stay awake and listen to every sound and replay the abuse all, the while feeling completely and utterly alone.

Along with my inability to sleep and feel safe, I also struggle with eating. Food was controlled and used as punishment when I was a child and so I have developed a fear of eating or preparing food. I can go several days without eating and I feel ashamed and scared to eat in front of others or to go out for a meal. The lack of food and sleep combined make day-to-day tasks incredibly difficult.

My fear and anxiety control my life. I make decisions and plans based around my fears and anxieties. I rarely go to social gatherings because the large crowds and face-to-face conversations are too stressful. At work, I am often too anxious to leave my classroom to go to the staffroom, the office, or even the bathroom for fear that I might run into someone and have to speak to or interact with them. I am always worried about making someone angry or upset with me because I'm afraid of what they might do or that they might reject me. I don't know how to say no or stand up for myself, as those opportunities were never presented to me as a child. It was always, comply or pay for it.

My father taped himself molesting and raping me from the age of six. This has caused enormous amounts of distrust and fearfulness. I always feel as though someone is watching me and that I am never safe. I don't trust anyone or anything and this has caused a lot of problems with my relationships and in my life. I can't let anyone get close to me. Some days even holding hands or a simple pat on the back causes panic and flashbacks. Because I am unable to trust anyone, the healing process has not come easily. I am so afraid of losing the few people I have left in my life that I don't express any of my own feelings, memories, emotions or stories in fear of their leaving me out of disgust or hatred.

I lost my entire family because of this abuse. My mother was arrested in March of 2007 and my father shortly afterwards. My brother and I were kept apart for the duration of the trial and we have never reconnected. It has now been almost six years since I have seen my brother. When I last saw him, he was sixteen years old and he is now twenty-two. I don't know where he is, how he is doing, or what his life has become. I love him with my whole heart and I miss him every day. He was the one person who knew what was going on and, when there was no one else around, he was there. I blame myself for not being able to save him and I hope that someday we are able to see each other again.

Because of the abuse, I also lost my extended family. My Oma died during the trial and I was unable to attend her funeral. It has been almost six years since I have seen, spoken to, or heard from any of my aunts, uncles, cousins or my grandmother. I also lost all of my friends and contacts from my childhood. Everyone left when they found out about what my parents had done to me. No one stayed around to help or support me. I have been truly alone in the world from the age of eighteen.

Friendships are few and far between. Because of my inability to trust — and all of the secrets and shame and pain that I carry — I am unable to easily connect with others. I withdraw into myself and hide all of the pain I carry within me. I always feel it necessary to buy people's friendships and time because I don't feel worthy of it on my own. I am the teacher at school that no one really knows or hangs out with. I am so extremely shy and fearful that many days at work I only speak to the children or other adults out of necessity.

I have had to seek counselling and therapy because of the fourteen years of abuse that I suffered at the hands of my mother and father. I have been diagnosed with extreme PTSD, anxiety disorder, depression, and suicidal tendencies. I am currently in group therapy and individual therapy three times a week to get me through each day. These therapists are true lifesavers. They are the first people in my life who have shown me care, compassion and love. I am also taking many medications to help control my symptoms, emotions and anxieties so that l can lead as close to a normal life as is possible.

I sustained many physical injuries as a child that continue to affect me in my adulthood. For instance, due to the fistula, I have constant infections, I cannot control when I need to urinate, and have a lot of pain and embarrassment. Because I was raped at such a young age and over such a long period of time, it is highly unlikely that I will ever be able to have a child naturally. The damage that was done to my genitals and internal organs was immense. The scarring left from tearing and burns will never go away. I will always have to deal with these injuries. These injuries make having an intimate relationship very difficult both emotionally and physically.

Along with losing my family, my safety and my friends, I also lost all of my belongings. After my parents were arrested, they sold the house and everything in it was taken away. I have no belongings from before the age of eighteen. When everyone else shows their children photos and mementos of themselves as a child, I have nothing to share — no yearbooks, graduation certificates, photographs, or childhood toys or comforts. It feels as though my house caught fire and not only did everything burn but my family and friends were all killed in the blaze as well. I was left completely alone with absolutely nothing and no one.

The expenses that I have incurred because of this abuse are also immense. I had to take out loans of upwards of $50,000 in order to get through school. I also owe lawyer fees of $20,000 for representation, documentation, emancipation and safety. Medical expenses have also piled up for continuous treatments. When my parents were first arrested and sentenced, I had no health insurance and so I spent thousands of dollars on my medications, treatments, and therapy. Today my individual therapy is still not covered by my benefits and costs $240 a week.

There are many times when I just think that ending my life would be a better solution than continuing to live. I could end the pain and suffering and the world would be a better place without me. I don't know how to hope for the future or how to dream. It's a struggle to get from minute to minute and day to day.

My father once told me that no matter what the outcome of the trial, he would always be there right behind me and two steps ahead — that I would never get away and I would never be free. He said he would be there every moment of my life including my wedding and graduation. That fear and constantly looking over my shoulder has been my experience for years. At every holiday, birthday or special event, I'm reminded of what I lived through and what I lost. But I'm here to tell you, dad, that I'm still fighting and, while life may be hard for me and I may have to struggle until the day I die, I won't give up. I will make it and I will never be like you.

I worry all the time about the day my father is let out. I'm terrified that he will come after me or send others to make me pay as he's done in the past. I've just barely begun this life without daily abuse.

The fear of my father remains constant. I hope you understand.

The victim's statement, though powerful, does not emphasize the enormity of how horrific Hope's abuse was. As you read these next pages, ask yourself what a sexual predator has to do to receive a life sentence.

Where's the Justice?
A Victim's Statement
Author's note

When I asked Hope (not her real name) how many times she had been raped by her father, she nervously laughed, then replied, "He didn't rape me when I was at camp." I met Hope when I joined a sexual abuse therapy group to ensure self-care through the process of writing *Unlock the Door*. The best description I can give of her, when I first saw her, is of a frightened fragile little bird. She sat rocking, with her arms pulling her knees tightly into her chest. She smiled nervously. I knew nothing about her life, but felt I wanted to protect her from the nightmare I instinctively knew she lived. I felt compelled to sit beside her every week.

As I began to learn about the violence and terror her parents inflicted upon her and her younger brother, I was repulsed by their actions, yet grew to respect Hope more and more. I was continually impressed by her strength and courage. She is haunted by demons daily as she experiments with every imaginable treatment to help her cope and assist her recovery. The night we sat listening to her victim's statement, I became angry at how the legal system re-victimizes innocent people. Hope struggled through sobs and tears to reveal her heartache. I will never forget the support our group provided as we rallied around her. She agonized whether or not to attend her father's hearing to read her rendition of reasons justifying her request to keep him incarcerated. She is terrified of him.

Is it logical for Hope to be asked to enter a room where he awaits her – a man who videotaped himself raping his daughter, a man who has threatened her life, a man who watched, allowed, and even encouraged his depraved wife as she broke and dislocated bones and burned their children, a man who sent thugs to rape and kill his daughter? Only a miracle kept Hope alive. It is completely unfathomable and unimaginable to expose her to the living nightmare of having to face him, particularly when there are volumes of evidence to incarcerate him indefinitely.

How is it possible to sentence someone to twelve years, then have it reduced to nine, then probably to allow him to serve only two thirds of that – approximately six years? Six years for thirteen years of sexual attacks? How is it that he has not been labelled a dangerous offender? She believes, beyond a shadow of doubt, that he will torture her and have her killed when he gets out of prison. The thought, understandably, weighs heavily on her mind. She has considered suicide more than once, as a means of avoiding his wrath – something I strongly do not want her to do, but would not blame her for. She waits in fear, always in fear. He will be released in approximately two years.

In this country, punishment for this type of sexual crime defies logical thinking. Raping anyone, particularly a child, is inhuman behaviour and not tolerable. Sentences must match offences. Forget basing sentence lengths on past sentences. The whole rational isn't reasonable because the sentences were extremely short – probably a result of little value being placed on women (who were typically the ones who reported sexual assaults).

Hope's father is not even receiving one day in jail for every time he molested her. The physical and emotional damage he caused is not lessened because it was his child – or is it? If an individual committed these acts against multiple people, there would be charges for each offence. He would not see the light of day when the convictions were added up. How is it any less of a crime when the perpetrator attacks one person that many times? There is no justice and certainly no peace of mind, even if the full twelve years were being served. None.

In the United States, Jerry Sandusky received a sentence of thirty to sixty years for forty-five counts of abuse. Hope was assaulted almost every day, by both parents, over a fifteen-year period. Is Hope's father's abuse not as bad as Sandusky's? Imagine a man who takes his daughter down from a coat rack, where she is hanging in the basement with her brother, rapes her and then hangs her back up. How do you release that man? Correction, *monster*.

For Hope, the witness protection program was and is an option, or was it? Take every household item as evidence of the crimes, every personal possession such as memorabilia and photographs, separate her from her brother, re-victimize her in court, leave her with incredible medical and legal fees, then advise her to go into hiding where she undoubtedly loses the friendships she has developed post sentencing. Who has received the greatest punishment, the guilty or the innocent?

The verdict is out. What can we do about this lack of justice? I have never thought of myself as a political person, but this utter disregard for the safety of Hope has awakened an activist. How do we, as a group, ensure the safety of people like Hope? She is doing everything possible to create a life that is tolerable and productive, yet she lives in constant fear. I was inspired by our justice system when Guy Paul Morin was released, when David Milgaard was declared innocent and when Steven Truscott was exonerated. However, today I sit here praying that a guilty man will never be released and that somehow there is political and societal pressure to correct this injustice.

Oh, did I forget to mention Hope's mother? She was charged before her husband, in 2007. Due to mental illness, she was placed in a psychiatric facility, rather than a prison. It was during her trial while searching for evidence against her that investigators found evidence that led to the arrest of Hope's father. As much as her father was a sexual predator, her mother was a physical predator. In Hope's statement she was not permitted to include anything about her mother, such as how her father witnessed continual physical abuse and not only tolerated it, but often encouraged it by irritating his wife. He knew the outcome of his actions or statements would be her violence toward their children.

Hit once? No. Multiply each attack by seven because in addition to her mental illness Hope's mother was also experiencing symptoms of obsessive–compulsive disorder. Dislocate seven joints or break seven bones, fingers, shoulder, jaw, or drown and revive Hope seven times – not to mention *regular* striking and burning. Add poisoning your daughter also. When Hope's mother discovered Hope has a severe allergy to tomatoes, she would occasionally contaminate Hope's food. Hope did not eat the lunches sent to school by her mother and remains frightened to eat. She is currently attending therapy to manage her anxieties around eating.

There is an endless stream of reasons to incarcerate Hope's parents indefinitely. Yet, as their sentencing reads, they will be free to harm Hope, or possibly other innocent people, to fulfill their need to watch human suffering at the breaking limit of physical tolerance. Torture.

I cannot help but question who is responsible for Hope's safety, and who will be accountable, if and when her parents either singly or jointly hurt her again. There is little doubt her father will seek retribution when he is released. Why would any government, institution or individual seek to integrate such malfunctioning people into society? In cases like this, there is a significant failure to protect the innocent.

Where is the support? *We* must be her family. *We* must ensure her safety. *How* do we do that? *Who* will do that?

Yes, this is a call to action. Hopefully this will inspire an experienced and well connected activist to take up the cause to ensure that criminals such as these two are never released, never given the opportunity to reoffend and never forgotten for the horrific monsters they are.

Unforgive You Now
Kristin

Whatever I forgave you for
Somewhere, sometime, somehow
Whatever I forgave you for
I unforgive you now

Allegiance I had pledged to you
To whatever I swore
Though once you were my family
You're not my kin no more

Whatever things I said to you
Promises, oaths, or vows
Whoever I once said you were
You're nothing to me now

Half my life wasted at your side
Blind loving spilt like blood
Whatever I once thought of you
Now I know you're no good

Whatever I forgave you for
Somewhere, sometime, somehow
Whatever I forgave you for
I unforgive you now

Good luck with all your sorrows now
Your vices, pain, and doubt
I'd wish for you what you deserve
But you're living it out

Trusted

Others

Love You Like a Brother
Paulie

First of all, thanks for taking the time to share your story. I think you are a very courageous young man. I am sure your fans on Facebook appreciate having a place to share with others who have gone through similar experiences. We are all part of this movement to get sexual abuse out of the closet and I want you to know I appreciate your work.
Thank you very much.

You're very welcome. I know you've shared your story several times. It has been over six years, right?
Yeah, six years since the assault. It gets easier every time. In the beginning it was tough to tell my story without breaking down and getting emotional. I'm not afraid to talk about the sexual abuse anymore.

What happened after you reported the assault?
I went to the police the night it happened, but I didn't realize the press would get involved. The man who molested me was a high-profile member of his community. I was ridiculed quite a bit. I almost regretted reporting it because I felt a lot of shame afterwards and received a lot of criticism. I wasn't taught, at any point in my life, how to respond to that appropriately. I mostly took it out on myself. When I did share what happened, I took it out on the people in my life. I'm glad I've finally gained the courage to talk about it openly. It took me about a year and a half to walk into a sexual assault centre for help. Then I was asked to leave because I was a male and they only worked with females. That was pretty discouraging.

I guess they don't have many men dropping by?
No. After that I didn't talk about it again for a while.

First of all, good for you for going to the police right away. You are
probably aware most people do not report sexual abuse?
Yeah, but after the assault the last thing the guy said to me was that
he'd be back next week to do the same thing again. I couldn't let
that happen.

What happened after charges were pressed?
It came out in the newspapers and television the following day.
They said, "Minor hockey president was charged with sex assault
on a twenty-one-year-old man." Then, I was accused of lying.
They questioned why I didn't fight back. They said he would never
do something like that. "He's an outstanding citizen, the president
of legions club and also a fire fighter." They had him up on a
pedestal; therefore, a sexual assault allegation must be wrong.
Afterwards, when he admitted assaulting me, no one from the press
apologized. It was discouraging.

I can see how you would be discouraged and very frustrated. In preparing
for this interview, I read Theo Fleury's book, *Playing with Fire*. (Theo was
sexually assaulted as a teenager by his coach). It's the same thing over and
over. Victims, who come forward not only have to deal with being violated,
assaulted, and molested, they also get blamed or accused of something. Re-
victimization. The other person is charged, you go to court, and they're
taking you down as much or more than the offender. Then, in your case,
when he admits it there is no apology from anyone.
It was pretty depressing to read, in the paper, how great he was.
There were pages of comments in the newspapers and websites
stating that I was a bad guy and I wanted to take him down. I
would say about 100 per cent of the people who wrote a comment
had no idea what was going on. I only knew him for three days. He
wasn't an acquaintance or a friend. He was giving me a job. It was
tough to go on the Internet and read everything. It was devastating.
I didn't know how to deal with it. I immediately turned to drugs
and alcohol. I had to numb the pain. I was always taking more,
regardless of whether I was drunk or high. I numbed the pain to a
manageable point – to what I thought was manageable. However, I
was hurting everyone else around me and I was hurting myself
more than anything.

Many people turn to *something* to reduce the pain after experiencing sexual abuse. Emotionally, what were you going through? What changed because of that one-hour incident?

My whole life changed: my morals, my positive attitude about life and my life goals. I thought I would spend the rest of my life in the hockey industry. In a matter of forty-five minutes, I wanted nothing to do with the sport of hockey. That really affected my psychological well-being because I had dreamed of being involved with hockey since I was a little boy. I was going to have a place there regardless and no one was going to stop me. Afterwards, it was tough for me to get back on the ice. Last winter I finally went back out. It was the most powerful experience of my life. I was able to strap on my skates and teach kids about the greatest sport.

Have you shared your experience with the kids or their parents?

Not at first. Most people didn't know who I was. Coaching was for my well-being; it was a personal goal to get back on the ice. This year I helped out with a training camp, and I told a lot of people what I had and am still going through. I've been sober and clean from alcohol and drugs now for 500+ days and I wouldn't have been able to conquer, or even address, my sexual abuse, if I was still using. I think that was a big thing for me – to get sober and clean before I tackled the subject. I started speaking in August 2011.

What prompted your desire to talk?

It was a combination of things. Theo Fleury has worked with me quite a bit. He promised he'd never give up on me and that I was going to be okay. For the first time in my life I really understood. I took what he said to heart. I will be okay. The biggest thing I can do is help others by sharing my experience. If I help one person then it's worth it. Theo has been a great supporter and a mentor to me through all of this.

How did you meet him?

I met him through Facebook. A friend of mine knew him. He knew I'd been struggling quite a bit with alcohol and drugs and was heading toward homelessness. He figured out the root cause and contacted Theo. The very first time I looked at the phone and it said "Theo Fleury" on the call display, I was thrown off that he wanted to talk to me. Right from the start we talked like we were brothers. That was huge for me. I grew up watching him in the NHL and I had no idea he was sexually abused until his book came out. He wanted to help me through the process of revealing what I'd been through. He taught me a lot about life and educated me about sexual abuse – that it happens to guys. Prior to meeting Theo, and reading his book, I thought I was one of only a few men to ever be sexually abused. I thought I was alone. I learned I'm one of about eight million people in Canada who have gone through sexual abuse.

Staggering isn't it? I want to mention that you can be found on Facebook under the name I'm 1 in 5. Your page is a place where many other people are sharing their stories. It's true; we're very aware of child abuse, we're very aware of women being assaulted, but to hear about a young man of twenty-one, you just don't think of that happening.

I started I'm 1 in 5 in August 2011. We've had quite a few people come on the site and share their experience of sexual abuse. Two guys spoke up for the very first time. That's what the page is designed to do. They have a lot of courage. A guy from Pennsylvania had enough trust in me to share his story. It feels absolutely amazing to help someone I've never met.

That's the power of sharing and being open. What was the reaction of your peers when your story came out?

I got mixed reactions from my friends. I convinced a bunch of guys I had hung out with in high school and after college into thinking the abuse didn't happen to me. I pushed them away because I was so mad at myself. It took almost two years for me to tell them what had happened.

They didn't hear about it in the papers?

They heard about the story but didn't realize I was the victim. My name wasn't in the press. When I did tell them, it shocked them and they didn't really say anything. Also, I was engaged at the time and my fiancée didn't believe me. She was the person I thought I was going to marry and she didn't believe me. She was vocal about not believing me and that was super tough. I trusted her; you know what I mean? She knew what happened. She came to the police station that night and saw me. It was awful knowing that she didn't believe me. Many people didn't believe it happened.

Why would you make up a story like that for your fiancée?
Right. The person I loved with all my heart didn't believe me – that affected everything about me. We haven't been together for a number of years. I couldn't respect her like she deserved because she didn't believe me. She finally believed me after the court case because he admitted he'd done it and pled guilty, but it was a little too late. I felt alone, even though there were two other complaints against my offender.

Feeling alone and isolated is common for people who are sexually abused. We feel alone because we don't talk about the abuse to each other. If we did, everyone would know how many of us share similar stories. What punishment did he receive?
He was charged with one count of sexual assault. It was a plea bargain. His sentence was three months' house arrest, eighteen months' probation, and ten years on the National Sex Offender Registry (NSOR). I wasn't too happy on the day of sentencing. He got into his truck and drove back to work or home and resumed is *normal* life. I had to live with the fact that he had *ruined* my life. That afternoon I went and put a rifle in my mouth and was ready to kill myself. I was devastated that he was free. He should have gone to jail.

How long would you have put him in jail for what he did to you?
It's took me almost six years to start the healing process. So, six years in jail would probably be sufficient punishment. He never lost a day of work and I've been basically unemployed or unemployable since the abuse. I completely changed. He had a wife and three boys and I believe his wife is still with him, though I don't know for sure. I do know his wife became the president of the same hockey association. I'm not sure what happened with his firefighting or with his work at the legion. He was relieved of his role in minor hockey, which he should have been because he shouldn't be around children.

Looking back, were there any signs he might harm you?

I had no idea he would sexually assault me. We'd gone to an arena and there was no one there. I guess that was a warning sign, but I didn't know at the time. Same when he took me to the bar and tried to get me drunk. He came into my house and locked the door. He said he wanted to help me out with my knee injury – he had training and could help. He basically brainwashed me into doing what he wanted. There were signs, looking back.

What advice would you give a guy in your situation? The difficulty with this one, Paulie, is a twenty-one-year-old guy would probably never guess what the offender was building up to.

Yeah. Well, the advice I can give is to do a bit of research on a person in a position of authority and to trust your instincts. If your instincts say something's wrong, regardless of what you think it may be, trust your instincts. I would also say don't let someone else tell you when to take your clothes off. If you feel uncomfortable, you need to speak up right away. Also, a big thing for me afterwards was to talk. Find someone you trust, like Theo, because you need to talk. The best way to start the healing process is to tell someone and to get it off your chest. It feels absolutely amazing when you finally tell someone and they don't judge you. They become an ear to listen and a shoulder to cry on. It's an emotional journey. Recovery takes time but it can be deadly if you don't get help. It nearly took my life.

Very good advice. It is an emotional journey filled with confusion, sadness, blame, shame, guilt, embarrassment, and more. Do you feel we should talk more about abuse before it happens, or do you feel we should talk less about it after it happens?

Pre-intervention is probably the best way to go: speak about it before it happens. Especially with male sexual abuse, a lot of people shove it under the rug and don't want to talk about it: it's taboo. If I had known about sexual abuse, I probably would have been able to handle it better than I did. I had no education about sexual abuse with regard to males. I didn't think I could be sexually abused, especially at twenty-one. I think the sooner we start a conversation about sexual abuse, and feel comfortable talking about it, the better. I go out and talk to clubs and teens in schools. It's a way to share the message that sexual abuse can happen to anyone. The subject should be discussed in boardrooms and around water coolers.

I'm smiling as you talk because I have been saying the same thing: let's talk about sexual abuse at the water cooler. "Well, I'm having a rough day because I'm reliving some of the sexual abuse that happened to me when I was child." No shame, just talking.
Right, yeah. We should be free to speak about it. The ultimate goal is to be able to talk about it and not feel uncomfortable.

Exactly. We agree on that one. Paulie, where are you with respect to your healing? There are a series of things people go through: shock, denial, confusion, and even blame and guilt and anger and fear and then, maybe, forgiveness. Where are you along the healing path?
I still have a lot of anger toward my offender. I realize it wasn't my fault and there's really nothing I could have done to stop it. I think he is a pathetic man. He is a sick individual and he needs serious psychiatric help. I'm trying to move along in my life, remembering what happened to me, but not reliving it every day. I went through quite a bit of time where I had nightmares, but they have gone away now. I don't rely on antidepressants anymore and I'm no longer dependent on prescription pills to sleep. I try to inspire people by telling my story – if I can help someone else, that really helps me out. I may forgive him one day, but right now I haven't.

Should someone like your offender have to enter a rehabilitation program?
Yeah. I think he should have to take a psychological test to find the root of his issues. There are things he needs to deal with. With sex offenders, the urge to offend is greater than common sense. I don't know if sexual offenders can be rehabilitated or if we need to lock them up for the rest of their lives. My offender molested at least three people, and there are probably more. I was the only one who charged him. I pray for those people every night. May they have the strength to come forward and say something. This man was forty-seven years old. I can't imagine sexual abuse is a hobby you pick up or stop at that age. I know that if I hadn't charged him he would have done it again.

You said he has kids.

Yeah. I feel bad for his kids. They were in high school when he was charged and I can't imagine what they thought.

There's a passage in Theo's book when his perpetrator (Graham James) has just been charged. Graham said that Sheldon Kennedy and he were in love. He wished that he had been born in Roman times because back then it was acceptable to have boys as partners – it was the manly thing to do.
He's just rationalizing his own decision to sexually abuse Sheldon. (Sheldon Kennedy was sexually molested by his hockey coach. His book is called, *Why Didn't I Say Anything?*). I don't think Sheldon felt Graham was his boyfriend or that they were partners. I've read a little bit of Sheldon's story – Graham did a great job manipulating both Sheldon and Theo. That's what most offenders do. They have the control and power. I think Graham has serious psychological problems.

What's the hardest thing you've had to deal with because of your abuse?
Trusting anyone is difficult. Being sexually abused took away my trust. The abuse has affected my relationships with partners and friends. I can't really trust an employer because my employer raped me, and I can't really trust a partner because my partner didn't believe me. Another tough thing I've had to deal with probably more than anything are my addictions. I really couldn't have started this healing journey if I was still using. I tried to talk, but I would get so filled with fear; then I would get drunk or high and wouldn't talk about it. Once I got sober, it was a big goal to start talking about it. I'm glad I've done this sober. I can tell survivors of sexual abuse, in order to heal, if you're using drugs and alcohol you need to get sober first. If we don't have a sound mind or people in our lives who support us, then it's going to make it a hell of a lot worse to talk about it if we're still using.

What's next for you? What are you working on right now?
I started "I'm 1 in 5" to raise awareness and provide education and knowledge about sexual abuse. Every single person knows someone who has been affected by sexual abuse. I'm training to stickhandle a hockey ball across Canada in 2013. I'm doing it to raise money and awareness for male sexual abuse. It's inspiring to be able to inspire other people.

Through 1 in 5 I hope to get the word out that abuse happens to guys. I hope we can raise some money to build healing centres and a network of people throughout Canada so guys won't have to search so far to find a male sexual assault centre. My goal is to have one in every major city in Canada. So, right now, most of my life is wrapped up in trying to educate people. I never planned to be here, but I am and I embrace it.

You have had quite a journey. I do support the idea that there should be more resources for men, women, children and families too. It's so important for people to have a place to go and talk, share, connect and heal. When my offender said to me, "unlock the door," he wanted me to open the door so he could hurt me. Little did he know that I would write a book called "Unlock the Door" and mean that it's time we all opened up and talked. We need to share our stories so everyone understands that they are not alone.
Yes.

Paulie, please go ahead and share what happened to you.
On September 19, 2006, I was in a small town in Ontario. My fiancée and I had moved there a few months earlier and we were starting fresh. She was pregnant. I saw a sign advertising a coaching position for minor hockey so I went into the store and filled out an application. I received a call within a week. I was told to go to a community barbeque and talk to the president at the minor hockey booth.

I went down and met the president, who seemed like a great, genuine guy, and he asked me about my experience in hockey. He told me there was a practice that afternoon with a major team and he'd like me to go out and see if I would be a fit with the other coach. I remember thinking things were moving really quickly. I went home and grabbed my skates, gloves, helmet and stick and went to the rink. The practice went really well.

Afterwards, I remember coming out of the dressing room and thinking that two coaches had to be in the dressing room at all times, and the door had to be open if the coaches were inside. I knew those regulations from hearing about Sheldon's case. I thought the bylaw was meant to protect players and not to protect me from another adult.

I remember the president hiring me. He said, "You're the guy for the team, welcome to the minor hockey association." He said he'd be by my house that week to pick up my coaching certificate. Three days later, when my fiancée was out of town, he called and told me he would be there that evening to pick it up. Once again, I remember thinking things were moving pretty quickly, but I went and got the certificate. He called me on his cellphone just before he arrived, so I went down to meet him. He asked if I wanted to go to a hockey practice in the next town over to see how the organization worked. Interested, I hopped into his truck.

We were maybe ten minutes out of town when he starting drinking while driving. When we arrived at the arena, there wasn't a hockey practice and I didn't know what to think other than it was odd. He also seemed kind of dumbfounded. He suggested that we go back to our community. I agreed. When we got back he pulled into a bar, which, again, I thought was odd. Our conversation was all about where I'd been in hockey and where I would like to go. He was the guy that was going to get me to the next level. He was the highest member of the minor hockey association in the community and he was making me one of the youngest coaches ever to coach there. He kept telling me that it would be the right fit and I would be right for the job. I wanted to believe him.

We sat at the bar for maybe an hour and a half. I had four beers and he had double that amount. I know now that he was trying to get me drunk, but I certainly wasn't drunk. Even when I went to give my statement to the police, the police acknowledged that I was clearly not drunk.

I asked him to leave an hour after we arrived, but he didn't want to. I now see it as a warning sign. I didn't drink any more after that first hour. I sat waiting for another half hour while he continued to drink. Finally, we left and drove back to my apartment. When we got there he got out of the truck with me and followed me into my apartment. Once inside he immediately turned around and locked the door; that's when shock set in. I knew something bad was going to happen, but I didn't know he would sexually assault me. I was basically following orders at that time.

The abuse lasted about forty-five minutes. He molested me in my own house, on my own couch. He took off my clothes and did really disgusting things to me. When it was all over, I was in shock lying on the couch. I was naked when he put his jacket on. He said he'd be back the next week to do the same thing again. I couldn't really comprehend anything that was going on, but I did comprehend that. He'd be back next week.

I sat there contemplating what to do. I knew what he had just done was wrong and I didn't know how to approach it. I was overwhelmed with feeling dirty and violated. I sat there another forty-five minutes without moving.

Finally, I put my clothes back on and started texting Bryan, a friend of mine, but he wasn't answering. Around midnight I decided to go to his house. I knocked on the door pretty loudly and his parents answered. I said, "I'm pretty sure I was just molested." Instantly they got on the phone and called the police, who arrived within fifteen minutes. The police took me to the police station and questioned me. I was severely, severely emotional. The police and my neighbours could see that something traumatic had just happened. Afterwards, the police said they would be in touch with me the following day. My fiancée came and picked me up at the police station. We didn't talk the whole way home. I didn't sleep that night. The next day I called into work and told them a lie, that somebody had broken into my house and there was a police investigation. I didn't want to tell them that I had been sexually abused. (I've since made amends to those people for not being truthful.)

The following day the inspectors and detectives called me and asked me to come to the police station. They told me they were going to make the arrest that afternoon and afterwards they'd be in touch with me. I said okay. I was still pretty emotional and still in shock. That evening they said they had arrested him. He admitted doing it. That really sent me into a big psychological circus in my brain. I remember thinking, "I can't believe this, I really can't believe this." I was hoping it was just a nightmare and it wasn't true. So, when they called and said he'd admitted it, I instantly felt dirty and filthy and sick to my stomach. For days and days after that I scalded myself in the shower to clean myself off, which never seemed to work. I figured out that drugs and alcohol were the way to go.

The whole court process lasted quite a long time and was frustrating. My case kept getting remanded every time we went to court. He would change his lawyer every three months. It was really frustrating. During that process, two other men came forward with complaints about him doing the same thing to them. During that time my drug use escalated rapidly. In September 2007, he pleaded guilty to sexual assault and his sentencing was set for the next month. As I said, he received three months' house arrest, ten years on the NSOR, and eighteen months' probation. I wasn't happy about the result. I wanted him to go to jail.

My son was born that September and I wasn't a very good father. I was addicted to cocaine and crystal meth and I was scared to even change his diaper. I felt like I was hurting him when I bathed him and that still hurts me to this day. I couldn't be the father I was meant to be. I felt very shameful seeing my son naked. Not that I wanted to hurt him by any means, I just felt very uncomfortable seeing anyone naked. He was my son and those feelings caused conflicts between me and his mom. I struggled and continued to surround myself with crime. Eventually I moved to Guelph with some friends and I got myself into more trouble. I really couldn't have a job because I was so angry at any employer that I wouldn't even apply for work.

In April 2008, I had a wakeup call and decided to go to a drug treatment centre in Hamilton. I haven't touched crystal meth since. I was there for ten weeks and afterwards got a job working on a tugboat for the summer. It was frustrating because there was quite a bit of drug and alcohol use on the boat. I tried hard to be sober and it didn't work very well.

I moved from place to place. I've lived in twenty-five places since I was twenty-one. I called it the *geographical cure* and I can tell you it doesn't work. Actually, I should go back a little bit and say I also tried to jump off the balcony of an apartment building. I was taken to the psychiatric ward, which didn't work out. I just told the doctors what they wanted to hear so I could get out of there. I didn't tell them how I was really feeling. I would spend the night and I'd be out the next day because I couldn't live without alcohol.

I've been to four treatment centres and four detox centres. The last time I went into one was in October of 2010. I was there for two weeks. I lived with eight other male addicts and I was really uncomfortable with them. I knew that something was going to break because I really needed to talk about the sexual abuse.

Theo Fleury was helping me out quite a bit through this time. I went to a twelve-step meeting one night, October 23, 2010, and I left that meeting halfway through and went to a bar and drank 200 dollars worth of booze in two hours. One of my roommates from the treatment centre had to come and get me out of the bar. The next day I was ready to start my life over. I haven't touched a substance since that day and don't plan to ever again.

My life has changed drastically since being sober. I was living in my car and drinking whiskey before I went to that treatment centre. Now I have a second chance to make something of my life. I've made some people proud because I've been able to stay sober for so long. More than anything I've made myself proud. In August, 2011 I was invited to Theo Fleury's golf tournament where they were raising money for male sexual assault. It was the most defining day of my life so far. I heard a guy say five words to me that changed my life: "Love you like a brother." I believed it and I actually felt he loved me like a brother. He also said, "You know what, you're going to be okay." I believed him. For the first time in my life, I trusted someone.

Since then there have been positive changes. I started speaking to groups and making YouTube videos about my sexual abuse. I'm embarking on the journey in 2013 across Canada to raise awareness, funds, and education for male sexual abuse, assault and victimization. I want to let people know this happens absolutely everywhere. The way I'm going to heal is to help somebody else who has been through the same thing.

I still struggle every single day waking up and knowing another person had power over me for a long time. I'm slowly getting my power back and it hasn't been easy. I live one day at a time and I try to stand up and trust this process of healing, trust I'm going to be okay. I really am going to be okay. I didn't choose this battle, but I need to embrace it with all my heart and soul.

I will still be involved in hockey, but I have to raise some awareness about sexual abuse first. I have to make sure that the kid who's raped by his hockey coach and the altar boy who's molested by his preacher have somewhere to go.

It's inevitable that this stuff is going to happen because there are sex offenders out there. We really need to educate ourselves and protect our kids. When it happens to our kids we have to make sure they have a safe and trusting place to go to. It happens to two-year-old kids; it happens to twenty-one-year-old men; it happens to ninety-year-olds in retirement homes. It happens everywhere and we must raise some awareness.

Paulie, when we spoke last week you mentioned *paralyzed shock*. Can you comment on that? If I may play devil's advocate, I'm saying, "Pal, why didn't you just do something? Why didn't you run away or fight back?" You've had that question, I'm sure.

Yes, I have. All I can say is "If I could have, I would have." I tried with all the physical, emotional and psychological power I had, but it was overwhelming. I could barely breathe let alone fight him off. I couldn't move a muscle. My psychological power was overpowered by this man and I couldn't do anything. I really wish I could have, but I couldn't.

Thank you for sharing. I personally don't feel it necessary to ask that question, but I want people to know that he had the power. One last question: I'm wondering where you see yourself in five years?

That's a pretty big question. Five years from now, I plan to still be talking to people about sexual abuse. I plan to be involved in hockey at a pretty high level of coaching. At the same time, that's a tough question because I live my life one day at a time – I just try to live on God's will and not my will. Theo tells me all the time: "When I drive the bus we go into the ditch. When God drives the bus we stay on the highway." In five years, if I'm with a hockey team, I'll be happy. If I'm helping kids out with sexual abuse, I'll be happy. I don't plan on going down the path I was on with my addiction, that's for sure. I'm trying to be clean and sober and, hopefully, I'm inspiring other people.

Thank you again, Paulie, for sharing your story and being a part of this book. I look forward to hearing about your trip stickhandling across Canada. You are building a great support network by coming out and talking about your sexual abuse. People are drawn to your story of survival and you're giving them the strength to share their stories and also, most importantly, to seek support and healing for themselves. It's all about finding strength in each other and also from within ourselves – having the courage to tell our stories. If, in doing so, we can help just a few people along the way every time we speak somewhere, every time we share a story, then it's all worth it. It's tough enough to be abused, more difficult to live with the feeling that you're alone. We are not alone; you are not alone. Yeah. Thank you so much for giving me the opportunity to do this and to get the word out.

You're more than welcome.

Author's note (April 4, 2013):

Today I received a message from Paulie. He relapsed and is heavy-hearted and guilt-ridden about it. He's had a very difficult time adjusting to his new surroundings in Calgary, without the presence of his Ontario support system. He is burdened by the knowledge that his perpetrator has a regular life when he, Paulie, suffers with haunting memories of sexual abuse.

In the face of a pending civil case against his perpetrator, a cross-Canada event postponed and ongoing trust issues sabotaging relationships and healing, Paulie remains determined to make a difference. He told me how important it is to be a part of this book: "It's part of my journey, and we are always connected now." Yes, Paulie, we are, and I want you to know that it's people like you who have given me the strength to finish this book. Recovery is a process. It takes time and effort and support. Believe.

I've heard that people stay in bad situations because a relationship like that gets turned up by degrees. It is said a frog will jump out of a pot of boiling water. Place him in a pot and turn it up a little at a time, he will stay until he is boiled to death. Us frogs understand this.
Deb Caletti

Author's note: Tim wrote his story prior to our interview. When I read it, it seemed as though his inner child was narrating. We agreed that I would do minimal editing to ensure his childhood voice rings true.

A Child's Perspective
Tim C.

I was born in Digby, Nova Scotia. I was a happy child, normal in every way. When I was two me and my brother decided to use a bag of flour to make roads for our dinky cars. I thought it was a logical thing to do, but our grandfather had other ideas. He wanted to tan our asses. My mom thought it was funny and told him it was her own fault for leaving us alone. Everything changed when I was about three years old. I was at the babysitter's and I remember her saying, "Don't tell anyone." My next batch of memories are of her playing with me, as in our sex games. This all happened between the age of three and eight. She was twenty-seven yrs old. In the beginning it was just touch, then it proceeded to her having me perform for her, playing with her big boobs. She would have me do sexual things I didn't like at first, but as time went by I didn't mind. She would experiment on me with belts, as in bondage, and we'd kiss.

When I was about seven, I was visiting my brother's school and had to pee. I went into a stall and was peeing when all of a sudden the door burst open and four kids came into my stall. Three boys and a girl and they were making fun of how small my penis was. That affected me to where I couldn't go to the bathroom if someone else is in the room or beside me. All of a sudden I realized I had a small penis. I just thought it was my play toy. I was always running around with no clothes on. My mother was always after me to put my pants on. When I was five, I got circumcised. My mom told me it's because I was always playing with it and it got infected, and the only way to treat it was to cut it off. When they did it, they pissed me off, cause everyone else got to watch but me, I fought with the doctor to see but he kept covering my eyes. I asked why can the nurse look and I can't, it's mine.

It was around that time I was cutting through the woods following my brother when I tripped and fell and landed on some glass, and had to get six stitches in my leg. And they found out about my temper. It took six people to hold me down to put in the needles in the open cut. The cut was six inches long. They had to dig glass out of it. And I'd cut my wrist three times before I was eight. We had a glass door and I was too short to reach the handle so I'd push the door open with my hand and the glass would break. After the second time my dad said if I do it one more time I'd have to pay for it. I did and I did have to pay for it. When you only get fifty cents allowance it takes a long time to pay and I never did it again. I was lucky the cut was always in the same spot. When I was three, I had my stomach pumped out from an overdose of children aspirin. They tasted like candy.

We moved around a lot, five times in Digby before we left to go over the mountain in Annapolis Co. Hillsburn a very small community. It was where my dad grew up. Not sure why we moved so much. I don't know where we lived when I was born. We moved to Hillsburn when I was in grade two. I didn't want to go. I liked our babysitter and didn't want it to stop. But we moved and it all stopped, until the next time we went back to visit. But it was different then, because I wanted it and couldn't wait to go back and play our games. We visited a few times. Then it all stopped.

When I was in grade three, I was in music class and we had a student who always forgot his book at home. I brought my desk up to his so he could share my book. When the teacher saw that, he got mad at me for sharing my book and came and knocked my book onto the floor. I went and picked it up. Then he did it again and as he told me to pick it up I bent over to pick it up and the teacher grabbed me and threw me over his shoulder and flung me against the wall and onto the floor, then mocked me for crying. He told me to stop sulking. I went to the principal's office and told him what happen. The principal asked him if he did it. He said, "No he didn't" and I went home and told mom what happened, and she didn't believe me. Nothing was ever done. I never shared my book again. About a month or so later my aunt, who was always telling my mother what I was doing, asked her what happened to the teacher that hurt me in music class. It was only then that she believed me. I learned that the only way she will believe me is if my aunt tells her, so I stopped telling her anything and just waited for my aunt to say something. I lived in my head a lot. I was always grounded for one thing or another, mostly for lying.

I started masturbating when I was about nine. I would play kissing cousins with two of my girl cousins and play house the same way I was taught by the babysitter. Only touch with one, and the other a little further. I applied all I learned from the babysitter, except intercourse, but I wanted to.

When I was young my brother showed me how to masturbate, but I already knew how but I couldn't tell him how I knew cause I didn't want it to stop. Around that time I didn't think they'd believe me. By the time I was ten my brother showed me where dad had kept his skin books. I thought I'd died and went to heaven. I remember being ten years old going to visit the babysitter and couldn't wait to get there so we could play our games. I started to crave the attention.

Something happened to my brother. He was my friend when we lived in Digby but when we moved to Hillsburn he changed. He didn't like me anymore. His new best friend was the bully who was paying all the attention to me. I'd get a beating from him once a week. By then I had a big mouth and I couldn't read. I kept that a secret as well. I had all the books on the book shelf but never read any. I went by the pictures. If my brother was reading I wanted to be like him so I'd get his comic books and try and figure out what the story was about. I learned to read to myself by reading Penthouse, but not out loud.

Whenever kids would laugh at me, I'd shut down and eventually the teacher wouldn't ask me or I'd pass. I was in grade four before someone noticed I couldn't read. They failed me. I was devastated that they sent me to see the school shrink to see what was wrong with me. I found out I had a learning disability and they put me in a learning disability school. My bully got a break until I got home from school. He lived down the road from our house about a mile but every time I'd walk to my grandmother's I'd have to walk by his house and he'd be waiting for me and I'd get hit. I rode my bike there one day and he stuck a broom stick in my front wheel causing me to go flying through the air and into the ditch. By the time I'd got back up to the road they were gone.

I'd fight back when I could but always got the worst of it. I always wanted my brother to stick up for me, but he never did. He always took sides with the bully. He'd tell mom it was my fault and she'd believed him. I'd get in trouble at school and by the time I got home, mom already knew about it. And every time she'd ask what happened, I told my version of the truth. But every time I'd come home with a fat lip it was my fault.

I didn't trust my parents to tell them what was going on. I was the middle child. My brother could do no wrong. My sister was the baby and she could do no wrong either. And everything I did was wrong. Almost every time I did something wrong I got a spanking. I know my sister never got one and I don't think my brother got one either. I think they named it mine. No matter how many times they'd spank me it didn't teach me to stop lying. In my head was better than living in the real world.

When I was eleven years old I got a bunch of cigarettes and some matches and we were in the old make-out barn smoking with a bunch of other kids. And I was playing with the matches and flung one onto the floor and the hay caught fire. I tried to put it out but it started to spread, so I told the other kids to leave and I stayed inside to try and put it out. But when I realized I couldn't. I stopped and watched the fire. And for a minute I thought about staying inside, cause I knew my ass was going to get sore for this. But at the last moment something told me to get out, and when I did only a couple of kids were still there and I said go home and play dumb. But that's not what happened. They went home and said it was all my fault. Which it was. But I thought if I denied it, they'd believe me. I had my mom believing it until the phone rang. My uncle saw me and the other kids go in, but only saw the other kids come out, so he called the fire department. By the time they got there the barn had burnt to the ground. I thought I was invisible.

That was the longest night of my life. My mom scared me by how angry she got at me. She wouldn't talk to me, just kept saying "Wait until your father gets home, you're going to get a spanking you'll never forget." Every time someone came through the door she'd tell them what I did and what I was in for. It was late when dad got home and he was furious with me. I was so scared and he lived up to what mom was scaring me with and it was the worst I'd ever got. It really hurt me. But that's what it was supposed to do, beat me into submission. That was the last time I remember being beaten.

I got grounded for one year. I was only allowed to go to school and church and if I left the property it had to be with supervision. But my brother didn't like me and never wanted to take me anywhere so I played by myself a lot that year. My brother took me once to a party and it was like having a parent there. I couldn't breathe without him bossing me around. I chose not to go anywhere with him. I went to church only as an escape from being grounded and I heard them say I was going to go to hell for what I was doing. When I went to school I was the talk of the town. All I heard was how embarrassing it must be for the parents to have such a rotten child. I got into a few more fights but never said anything about it. I felt I deserved them for burning the barn down and I didn't have anyone to help me.

Until a family from Ontario came to stay with us and their son was my brother's age and I'd come home from school with a fat lip and torn shirt and my dad gave me shit for ruining a new shirt. I talked back to him that if his precious son would just stick up for me once I wouldn't have to come home with a fat lip all the time. My dad was about to belt me for talking back when Curt asked me if that kid walking past the house was Blaine the bully. I said yes it was and Curt ran outside and started asking him why he's always picking on me. He didn't get a chance to answer when Curt started whaling on him. He beat the living crap out of him. I wanted to see blood. All the anguish he'd caused me. I was grateful to see someone finally stand up for me and I picked up a few pointers.

Curt's dad had to pull him off of Blaine. But I wanted him to beat him longer. But Curt broke his nose and jaw. When he unleashed that beating that was the rage I felt inside and about two weeks later Blaine came to my door. I figured it was for payback. But he shocked me and apologized for all the beatings. I said OK. But how do you forgive for all the beatings with a simple sorry. If he didn't say sorry he'd get another. That was the last time he ever bothered me.

I got into a few more fights at the special-ed school, but that was to show the bullies there I wasn't going to be their bitch. I walked up to the biggest one and belted him in the mouth. I used all the rage I had from all the beatings and I knocked him out. I wanted to give him some more but the teacher jumped in and took me to the office and gave me the strap, one on each hand. The secretary was the witness and I shed a tear. I swore I'd never let a woman see me cry 'cause that meant I was weak.

I went to high school the next year and my name was a regular over the PA to go to the office for the strap for fighting. The most I got was twenty-five on each hand and no more beatings when I got home. My father said he couldn't do anything anymore to me. But one day I backtalked to him and he slapped me on the face. It was the last time he ever hit me. My mom stepped in said, "Don't you ever hit him in the face again."

In 1978 there was a bad storm in the winter and my dad got hurt and dislocated a bone in his neck that left him a vegetable. Our whole life changed. After they operated they told him he could never fish again. My dad was a fisherman. Someone told him about an acupuncturist who could help him restore sixty per cent mobility. So we moved to Ontario.

I had my first drink after being up here one week and I liked it right away. I wanted another but my brother thought I'd had enough. I found my magic elixir. I felt six feet tall and I didn't give a shit what my brother said. He lost all the control he thought he had over me. I had no use for him or whatever he said. It was the freedom I'd been waiting for.

For the next four and a half years I drank as much as I could put into my body. It calmed the voices in my head, of all the things I did as a kid to cope with being molested. If anyone found out what I was doing I would have been sent to jail. I was already going to burn in hell. But that started to not work and I'd smoke as much drugs as I could afford. My thought was, what brain cells alcohol doesn't kill, the drugs would. I started selling drugs so I could afford more, until I ripped off my supplier. I'd dipped into his stash and a quarter pound went missing. I smoked most of it. I didn't know it but I was trying to kill myself. Then the day came when it wasn't working anymore. Every time I looked into the mirror I could see myself and I hated myself and what I saw. I didn't believe I deserved any help. Some people tried, but I knew it all. I had to fall hard before I was able to learn. During my last drunk I was arrested for sexual assault. I supposedly grabbed a woman's boob. I really didn't know if I did. I was in a blackout at the time. But I do recall what happened after that and I did try to assault a woman. When the cops threw me in jail, I thought that's what they caught me for. I was so drunk I really didn't know what I got arrested for until the next morning when I signed myself out. I went back to work, then home to tell my parents what I thought happened. The look of disgust on their faces said I'd shamed them again. Why bother. I hope I never forget that look. On April 28, 1985, I had my last drink. I have never had another drop since that day.

When I went for pre-trial I finally told a lady I was sexually molested. I was twenty years old. I accepted my guilt and I didn't fight the charge. I pleaded not guilty and was prepared to accept whatever they gave me. I started going to Alcoholics Anonymous and was so afraid of going to jail that I wrote a suicide note the day before my court case. I wasn't going to become Bubba bitch. I would rather take my own life. When I went to court I was nine months sober so the judge gave me a break and gave me my freedom. As I worked through the twelve steps and did my inventory I wrote about the sexual abuse and shared it and all my faults. In twenty-five years I'd scratched the surface, but my life wasn't improving.

My marriage fell apart because I wouldn't change into what my wife wanted me to be. I was getting flashbacks every time we'd have sex. I didn't know what was wrong with me. I just kept saying it was me, but I didn't know what it was. We tried counseling. I even went to the Clarke, in Toronto. Both me and my wife were trying to find an answer for why I didn't want to have sex with her. I told them how often I masturbate and they labelled me as having a deviant personality. They told me unless I lust after children there was nothing they could do for me, but to come back if I start to.

I found out I couldn't father a child because I was born with Klinefelter Syndrome and have a low hormone count. Because I was deviant, my doctor wasn't able to prescribe the hormones I needed. I was more fucked up then, I tried a few more times with different shrinks, and then gave up.

When I was twenty-five years sober my dad came and stayed

with me and helped me around the building. During that time my memories started to come back of what my childhood was really like – growing up in a dysfunctional house and not feeling like I lived in a nurturing home. I always felt like an outcast. By the end of his stay I told him to go home. I had snapped and beat up a fan that I was working with. I took out all my frustration on the poor fan and beat it to a pulp. The whole time he stayed with me he treated me like I was eight years old. I felt the same as I did when I was a kid. I couldn't do anything right. When I blew up, that's what I said to him. Deep down inside my mind it was him I was beating. I did this in front of my sister and nephew and I was ashamed of my actions and showing them that side of me.

Only I knew what caused the anger. After he left I was talking to a friend who went to Adult Children of Alcoholics, so I found out where there was a meeting and started going. That lead me to group counselling one and a half years later. It started me on the journey of journalling about my dysfunctional upbringing. Deep down inside I knew that was just a stopover until I found the right place to be. I learned how to be a responsible person while being sober and giving back to whoever asked for my help. I had to help myself first. I had to get so lonely that I could hear my own thoughts. I was just as confused as I was the day I sobered up – how and what I was feeling. I started going to other sexual survivor meetings, started one-on-one therapy and group therapy. They gave me a lot of support, which was what I needed.

When I was ten or so years sober I forgave my babysitter for molesting me. Not for what she did, but I couldn't hold onto that resentment anymore. I gained some freedom from the grip of her. I was able to forgive myself for what I thought I was responsible for. I was a child. I wasn't in any way responsible, no matter how my body responded. When I talked about my guilt and shame I'd been punishing myself all these years for my coping skills and behaviours. I was giving my perpetrator the power. I thank God for The Gatehouse. It gave me a safe place to work through these painful memories and get past them.

Tim, thank you for sending your story. I think the readers will benefit from hearing more about your journey of recovery. Please share what we have been discussing.

Thank you. I began to deal with my sexual abuse about a year ago. I joined Peel Family Services because they offered a program for male survivors. I attended meetings twice a month. I was also required to attend one-on-one counselling for extra support. The meetings gave me an opportunity to sit with other men and share what we had been through.

I also searched on the Internet and found Meetup.com, specifically a program called Soul Speak, which is a co-ed program for survivors of sexual abuse. I joined the monthly meetings and currently have stepped into the role of a co-facilitator. I'm excited to say that we now have two meetings each month, on the first and third Sundays. While attending those meetings, I was also able to get into a fifteen-week program for men at The Gatehouse, which saved my life. I felt comfortable in the room and that allowed me to open up with other survivors and get the garbage out: the shame of what happened to me and what I did to cope with it, for example drinking and taking drugs. It provided the fundamentals I was looking for, similar to AA steps of recovery, with an environment of peers. I have received more than I anticipated. Participating in these meetings has led to facilitating and has given me the opportunity to give back while further building on my own recovery. I'm definitely at a stage now where I want to give it back.

I find it remarkable that so many people I've met, through this process of writing, desire to give back. It seems at some point their healing shifts from *self* to *others*.

Yeah, it kind of goes hand in hand, similar to AA. In AA we have various slogans. One of them is to be responsible. When anyone, anywhere reaches out for help, we always want the hand of AA to be there. That's why I've reached out to others. When I'm helping somebody else I feel good inside; I learned that through recovery. Also, I discovered the more meetings I went to, the more I understood my own recovery. For example, for a long time I didn't understand my emotions. I'm still learning how to make the right associations between words and the correct emotions. Therefore, part of my motivation for becoming a co-facilitator was selfish. I did it with the goal of increasing the number of meetings from once a month to twice a month. Eventually I hope we meet every week. In AA we had meetings every day of the week, maybe we will have that too one day.

When we were talking earlier you mentioned *community*. Not only going to meetings with the people, but having the opportunity to incorporate these individuals into your life. I guess that's the idea of AA; you always have someone to call for support. We need more of that. Once you start on this journey, a lot of feelings are stirred up and having support is critical.

Yeah. That's why I sought more meetings. When somebody sent me an invite for Meetup.com, I had the idea to type in *sexual abuse*. I was hoping I would find another resource. I had searched on the Internet before, a lot of stabs in the dark because I couldn't find much information. Searching has taken me other places like meetings to deal with intimacy, inner child, and various other topics. I was grateful to find Soul Speak within Meetup.com. The lady that was hosting it is a survivor. I have found that one door seems to open up another door and another door. The more support the better.

A recent discovery was a program called Follow Your Bliss. They have a Tuesday meeting called Sacred Sexuality. I've always had issues surrounding touching because of being touched as a kid. By going to these meetings with other like-minded people, I've worked through boundary issues – specifically how to feel comfortable saying yes or no to being touched without feeling guilty. It has helped me to be with other people and not be afraid or uncomfortable.

That's a great resource. I am familiar with Meetup.com, but never would have thought to search for anything related to sexual abuse. You know, I was uncomfortable giving hugs for years when I was young and I've never attached that to my sexual abuse. Interesting. You said you didn't want to be touched because of what happened to you as a child. I'm sure there are a million people out there who feel the same way.

Yeah, on Tuesday I am going to what's called a Cuddling Party. I told my sister about it and she had a laugh.

I think it's fabulous. Learning safe touching is important.

It's non-sexual; a Soul Speak survivor member told me about it. It's a matter of just practising asking or being asked, "May I touch you?" with a response of no or yes. You give a person a hug and there are no expectations attached. You know, removing the *sex fear* that is sometimes attached to hugging – that's when you are hugging and wondering what the other person is thinking. The idea is to remove all the bullshit and just be you and give a simple hug and enjoy the warmth and feeling of unconditional love.

It sounds like you're really exploring a variety of areas.
Yes, because I don't know the answer. I don't know what it will take to heal. I know if I'm doing this in a safe environment then either I'll like it or I won't. It's a way to work on my boundaries. I never had a boundary, especially when it came to sexuality: yes, yes, yes was always the answer. I could never say no. I'm learning to be okay with either yes or no.

Good for you. It sounds like you're actually enjoying the discovery process.
It's nice having somebody point out options for me in a non-condemning way. My therapist has been able to show me that what I'm feeling is normal, rather than me thinking there is something wrong with me. It has taken constant courage for me to explore myself in a safe environment while more or less leaving my mind out of it. I've come a long way.

It is very confusing when we are abused at such a young age because we never learn normal, in terms of touching. We are manipulated to do what we were told to.
Yes, until the point, in my case, when I liked it. I learned to like it, or at least that's what my adult brain tells me today. I learned to like it and I didn't know it was wrong. The babysitter played with me when I was very young; then when she wasn't playing with me, I looked for other playmates to replicate the behaviour. Eventually, something happened and I thought, "Wait a second, this behaviour is wrong." I went from being an innocent child to being condemned for what I was doing. It formed so much shame in me that I was forty-six before I finally sought help.

At first I only told one person about being sexually molested as a child: the lawyer when I was arrested at twenty. When I was a child I didn't think my parents would believe me, so I never told them. They didn't believe me about other things, so I didn't trust them enough to believe me about the sexual abuse. I am still thinking and writing about this stuff like my child self. I assume that's why, even though I learn new information, when it comes out it's not all that I've learned – it's whatever is stored in my mind from my childhood.

Well, I think that will be the title of your chapter in this book then: "A Child's Perspective."
Sounds good.

When I read your story it was as though I heard your inner child speaking. That's why I didn't want to correct the grammar or spelling: it is as authentic as it can get. Talking to you now, I am speaking with a different person. Are you still okay with me doing minimal edits to the story portion?
Yes.

You said you were too young to know the sexual behaviour was wrong at first. When you realized it was wrong, you felt shame. That can be difficult to overcome: forty years' worth of confusion and shame.
Yes. I think it has a lot to do with society, especially in my case, being brought up in a religious environment. I was going to church and hearing that I was going to hell for what I was thinking – not to mention I was enjoying what I was doing. Between the combination of church and society, I was fighting a losing battle.

I can't imagine a god that is full of judgment and hate, or one that would not accept and love a child experiencing the aftermath of sexual abuse.
I didn't learn about that type of thinking until I joined AA. It wasn't until I was in my twenties that I learned my higher power is of my own choosing.

I feel that if we remove man's influence, we become spiritual in the sense that *God* is found in each and every one of us. Sadly, sometimes religious training leaves us nurturing shame and blame and tortures us for years.
Yes. Were you abused as a child as well?

Yes. I had a few unwelcomed encounters, the last of which was when I was about ten. I packaged and buried them for a number of years. I never really experienced things like guilt and self-blame. For me, it was suppressed hate and anger and I didn't fully understand why. We are all affected in various ways: that's why I am creating this book. I want people to know they are not alone, not the only one feeling what they are feeling. I want to encourage them to connect and create more healing communities.

It's interesting you mentioned that: connecting. I searched for a long time on the Internet looking for answers and I didn't find what I needed. I had to go to meetings and talk to a human to find that. It seemed to take forever to find information, but once I got going, one place led to another. By the way, that's how I learned that Ontario had opened up millions of dollars for male sexual abuse survivors.

That's a start. There are many people doing things at the grassroots level. We all need to share information and resources to make more people aware of what services are available. It's not like someone goes through an eight-week program and is miraculously healed.

Right.

Like you said, sexual abuse recovery resembles AA. You don't just go for fifteen weeks. It's a long-term commitment and that's why support is imperative. I see people wanting desperately to feel better and allowing themselves to be vulnerable in front of complete strangers – strangers with whom they often form strong bonds. Tim, I have really enjoyed our interview and I want to thank you for sharing some of what you have learned along the way. Is there anything else you'd like to mention before concluding?

For a while I've been considering creating a webpage to link us all together. So when someone sits at their computer and types in sexual abuse, there's a pop-up that links all the information together.

That's actually something I have been contemplating: how to best do that. How to organize the resources in such a way that anyone can easily find what they need, or so they can become aware of the various options. I think it's really important and I hope someone does it soon!

Yes, the information needs to be clearer. I've spoken to someone about my idea to generate a webpage; perhaps with their guidance it will become a reality. It's really more or less a matter of getting it started. I've been thinking and talking about it for a long time. Everything's slow. I want to do it right now, but things takes time.

I hear you. It's all good.

Yeah, it's all good, it's all good.

Thanks so much for everything, Tim.
Thank you. Bye.

Author and Thriver

Dana

I stand alone, so no one can see
The pain and fear I carry with me
Shut down, ignored, no longer free
They all pretended not to see
The lie was easier for them to believe
Left alone to understand
Their betrayal spilled over me
I will ignite the me I was meant to be

I'll start this story by saying I really don't have many memories of my childhood. I have blocked out many years of memories with friends and family...unless he was there. Those memories are forever engrained in my mind.

I was confident, outgoing, adventurous, and a ham who loved to be the centre of attention. I remember dressing up and performing for my family or anyone who would watch. I loved cross-country running and swimming. I spent many hours competing in the neighbourhood pool. I proudly held many titles, always trying to outdo myself and my competitors. The competitor is still present in my body and I love when she raises her hand to ask for another physical challenge. It creates a feeling of strength, energy and sheer happiness that overwhelms my body from head to toe – not to mention I smile like I really feel it. That's when I hear little Dana whispering to me.

I don't remember exactly how old I was, maybe eight or nine. It's hard to pinpoint the year. It was a typical weekend evening and we were visiting family friends. I had known this family since I was an infant. In fact, we had lived in their basement apartment before my parents purchased our first family home. We also attended the same church weekly, engaged in social and sporting events together, and travelled together annually. A perfect environment, or so it seemed.

I remember being in his room. We were playing Mouse Trap. I

loved that game, watching a marble travel through obstacles, rolling down slides and in and out of different traps. Ironically, I didn't know I was entering a trap myself.

He called me over to his bed and said, "Let's play a game." I loved games, so I was all for it. Looking back I see my innocence was clearly present but ready to be stolen. I trusted him; why not? My sister Elizabeth sat quietly on the floor continuing the game of Mouse Trap on her own, oblivious to the trap that was in front of me. He explained the game, and a rush of fear, confusion, and loss came over me at once. "Why was he asking me this?" "Why would he want to do this to me?" "My sister is here, does this mean it's okay?" My mind spiralled; my body froze. He tried his "game" and succeeded twice by fighting his hand down my pants and touching me inside my underwear. I squirmed and tried my best to fight him off. I cried silently. Fear stricken. There was no voice coming from me. Why was I so silent? I never had been. Our families were in the other room and yet I did not try to call for help. Why? I didn't ask Elizabeth for help either. Before the third round began, I sprung off the bed and headed straight to the bathroom across the hallway. I don't even think my feet touched the floor. I stood in a small bathroom: so still, so small, so shattered. I felt a rush of sadness, confusion and utter disgust. I cried silently for fear someone would hear. I don't remember opening the door again. I don't remember anything that evening after it happened. I don't remember how I acted once I left the bathroom. I do know little Dana was drowning in shame, guilt and fear and left the bathroom a different version of her original beautiful self.

That was the first time he molested me. I wish I could remember the days, weeks and months after the first time, but I can't. I can't remember how my life went on. I wish I could, but then again, maybe it's safer for me. My mind was in lockdown. I never shared my secret with anyone. Little Dana continued on as best as she knew how.

There was another time. One evening my mom casually mentioned to me that she and my father had plans and that he would be watching my younger sister and me since my oldest sister Leigh was busy with friends. A rush of anxiety came over me, a sense of losing control. Today I know this feeling all too well. I feel it on a daily basis. I told my mom I didn't want him watching us. She asked, "Why?" I had no answer, except, "I just don't want him to." No fault to my mom, but she didn't persist. He was going to watch us whether I liked it or not.

The next memory I have is sitting on the couch watching TV with him on one side of me and Elizabeth on the other. He wasted no time. He reached behind me and tried to shimmy his hand down the back of my pants. I squirmed. He tried again. I squirmed. I was dumbfounded. "Why was he doing this? Elizabeth is here. Doesn't he care?" I remember thinking, "Get up Dana, go to the bathroom, maybe he'll stop." I did. Again I stood there feeling sad, confused, and disgusted with myself. I cried and felt helpless. There was no one there to help me. When I returned to the couch, I sat beside Elizabeth. He sat beside her. Something was very clear to me: for some reason I knew he wouldn't touch Elizabeth. It was nothing he said, I just knew. Suddenly, I felt his hand down the back of my pants. I couldn't believe it. He bypassed Elizabeth to get to me. He was so brazen. I stood up immediately and said, "Elizabeth and I are going to bed." I thought we would be safe in our room, away from him and his hands.

Elizabeth and I fell asleep in our individual beds. I know this but don't remember it. Memories of events immediately before and after the actual abuse have disappeared or are so deeply buried I can't access them. The next memory I have is waking up feeling his hands between my legs and inside my underwear. As I slept he abused me. For how long I don't know. This pains me so deeply. Not knowing is frightening.

Suddenly a voice came out...of me! I said, "Stop doing this and leave my room now!" He didn't say a word, he left my room. It happened again. I can't believe I fell asleep again. I must find a way to forgive little Dana for being tired and for falling back asleep.

I thought of Elizabeth, who quietly and peacefully slept in her bed beside me. She was my protector, unaware to her. She was the one who could help me.

I slid into Elizabeth's bed and lay between the wall and her. I knew I'd be safe. She woke and asked me what I was doing. I told her something about what happened. I'm not sure exactly how I explained what had happened. She snuggled up and we both drifted off.

The next memory I have is standing in my parents' room. My dad was still in bed. He had summoned me to his room to ask me a question. When I entered, I remember walking up beside him and feeling scared. He said "Elizabeth mentioned something happened last night with Stephen. Did he do something to upset you?" I didn't know what to say. He asked me if I was okay. I said weakly, "Yes." No prodding. My dad mentioned briefly that he had spoken with Stephen as well, but never shared what words were exchanged. What did he say? What did Stephen say? I don't know the answers to these questions. I want to.

That was it. My dad didn't even get out of bed. I don't remember speaking with my mom about what happened. I do remember hearing a comment from her though, "He just lost his father and we can't burden his mom with this now." I felt helpless, confused and unimportant. I continued to see him every week for over eight years. My new life went on and my existence narrowed.

DANA'S REFLECTION

As I read my words above, I feel disconnected to the pain, fear and despair I experienced through the sexual abuse. I understand the abuse part, but what I can't understand is how my parents didn't protect me, their own child. Why did they pretend it didn't happen? Did they think it wasn't severe or damaging enough to me? Why didn't they get me help so I could understand it wasn't my fault?

The anger I carry around and the fuel I feed my anger is an outcome of what didn't happen instead of what did happen. I am still working on the anger that burns in my body daily. I know this is not how I want to live my life. Every day I step closer to a life that isn't led by negative energy. That's not who Dana is deep down. Through my path of healing today I know the fire that is burning inside is the desire to be free from the effects of my childhood abuse. I'm ready to channel this feeling of anger into something positive: healing and most of all acts of love and kindness toward others.

Daddy's Hands
© Colleen Laylon

Wish I could remember
gentle hands, that held me tight
and rocked me back to sleep
after a bad dream in the night

Wish they were warm and kind
like a fathers hands, should be
Instead of cold and scary
sneaking underneath my sheets

Laid there frozen like a statue
afraid to speak, or breathe
Pretending I was sleeping
praying he would let me be

But Daddy's hands were unforgiving
as he had his way with me
I can still feel the goosebumps
and fear rolling down my cheeks

Wish all Daddy's hands could feel
the pain that they can leave
Scars that run so damn deep
I still can't get no sleep

There are many who don't wish to sleep for fear of nightmares. Sadly, there are many who don't wish to wake for the same fear. *Richelle E. Goodrich*

I Want to Tell My Story
Lynne

Thank you for approaching me at the sexual abuse conference. When you said, "I've listened to so many people tell their stories and this time I want to tell mine," it really touched me. This is your time, Lynne, so please go ahead and share your story.

I've listened to a lot of people tell their story and there are often times when I thought I would like people to hear my story. One time, long ago, at a male survivors' weekend we decided we were all going to tell each other our stories — this was about ten years ago. I had only partly told my story when somebody broke down and I never finished or got any response. The incompleteness of it has bothered me for a long time.

Let me start at the beginning. I come from a French Canadian background and I am the eldest of two. I have a younger sister and I'm also the eldest of forty-one grandchildren. As such, I was expected to be the guide for all my cousins, who looked up to me. My parents separated after a lengthy, really horrible period of time. My mother was very promiscuous and wouldn't be home to cook supper so at the age of six, I would rush home from school and prepare dinner so she wouldn't get caught. When I was about nine years old my father had gathered enough evidence that my mother was being unfaithful and they separated.

We went to live with my paternal grandparents and my father wouldn't come home after work until he was drunk. He worked hard and he never missed work, but he never went to bed sober. He'd lost a leg in the war and many years later he confided in me, when I expressed concern about his drinking, that he couldn't sleep and that's why he had to drink. I work with many men who have PTSD (Post-Traumatic Stress Disorder), so I understand it now, but back then I didn't. I think my father had a strong sense of duty and responsibility, but he was not able to be a good parent. My mother was a full-blown alcoholic. As a result, there was a lack of parenting.

I was about eleven when we moved into my grandmother's house and I really felt like I had lost my place. I wasn't taking care of my sister anymore since she had my grandmother to take care of her and I wasn't covering for my mother anymore. I had a sense of loss – I felt like I didn't have a purpose so I decided I needed to get away. I decided I would enter the convent as an aspirant and become a nun. I lasted about three months there. It was just awful.

My father didn't want me to go because he had heard a rumour that if you didn't make it there, when you came out you would be *wild*. I came home and went back to high school. My dad would come home in a drunken blackout state and would somehow get mixed up and think I was my mother. He was always calling me names and accusing me of doing all kinds of ridiculous things. At the time I was a quiet, shy kid.

I started to dislike coming home and eventually I began running away because I was so unhappy. I left home for good when I was fifteen years old and by the time I was sixteen I was pregnant. My father told me I could come home, but only until I started to show because in those days it would be a shame and an embarrassment to the family. However, my grandfather was very supportive and wouldn't let me leave. I had my son and received further support from my aunt and uncle who let me live with them while I went to school and worked. Then, one day, I went out on a date with an old boyfriend and he raped me. That was the only time I'd had sex since my son was born and I got pregnant again. It was bad enough that I was an unwed mother but it was horrible that I was pregnant with my second child. I couldn't report the rape since I was an unwed mother and would be thought a *tramp*. No one would believe I was *not asking for it*. I asked my aunt and uncle to adopt my son, and when they agreed, I left for Toronto. I had my daughter and I immediately gave her up for adoption. I didn't think I could protect her or be a good mother. For the next ten years I was on a mission to self-destruct.

My first husband, who married two other women without bothering to get a divorce from me, wanted to be married to a prostitute. Little did I know what was going on. He'd set me up to have sex with somebody and then beat me so badly that my mother didn't recognize me. I was afraid to leave him and afraid to stay. It was a really bad scene. Following that I got involved with a man who was a professional criminal. He ended up in jail. I was on my own again making money, drinking and drugging until one night I had a vision. It was a wakeup call. I had a strong feeling I was going to live and die like my mother, who was an alcoholic and died from alcoholism at the age of forty-seven. I decided to make some changes in my life and went home to Windsor. At first I continued down the same path until I ended up in the hospital with hepatitis C. When I got out, I got help. I stopped drinking and drugging, and went to the University of Windsor and earned a degree. I was living a quiet life when an acquaintance from the past, Peter, came back into my life. He had been in trouble with the law all his life. I told him I couldn't live like that again so he had to either start a different life or go away. At the age of forty-seven he got his act together – he got his first job and shortly after that we got married.

My first experience working in a helping profession was on a committee to create a detox place for women. My mom had been picked up drunk, and there were no places for women to go in that condition so I decided to do something about it. When men got picked up drunk they would go to detox but there was no detox location for women. We created one and I worked there part-time. Then, after I was married, a friend asked me if I would help him at a new treatment centre and I said no. I didn't want to work in that kind of environment. He asked me to do him a favour and just help him out for a while because he thought if I could straighten out my husband I could straighten out anybody.

It was around that time I reconnected with my son, who was having a difficult time and had ended up in jail. He came to live with Peter and me for a while, but it was not a very happy time since he was to trying to get his life in order. He was a seventeen-year-old kid living with his biological mother whom he resented for abandoning him – it was a really tough time for all. By then I was working at a halfway house for men who were coming out of prison and I hated it. In the end, my son left us; we moved from London back to Windsor and I accepted the offer to work for my friend at the treatment centre. This was a six-month commitment that turned into five and half years. I really enjoyed the work.

I worked at a co-ed treatment facility. It seemed really difficult for the women because male alcoholics often express bravado whereas female alcoholics are socially more looked down on and also look down on themselves. I really didn't feel the program was very helpful for the women but my boss disagreed. In the end I decided to leave. My husband and I elected to come back to Toronto where I got a job working in a women's addiction treatment centre. During my twelve years there I started to recognize that the women had partners who were interfering with their recovery and often the partners had just as many problems. I started working with some men part-time in a private practice. While working with a variety of cases, I began to recognize that many people had trouble with recovery because there was an underlying sexual abuse issue.

There were places I could refer women to, but there weren't any places treating men who had experienced sexual abuse. I started to study and learned more and eventually began working specifically with men. My husband died at the age of fifty-seven and when I was forty-three years old I found myself alone again. Fortunately, my sister and I have always been close and we visited each other every weekend. Eventually, about twelve years ago, she moved to Toronto and we now share a home and a life together. I am very lucky – she is my best friend and my biggest supporter.

After my husband passed I threw myself into my work. I began discovering and understanding things that were really interesting to me, such as the different experiences of male and female survivors of sexual abuse, the symptoms of PTSD, and my parents' alcoholism. It all made sense. My mother was the daughter of a war vet who was quite brutal and my dad was a man who suffered from PTSD. I could see all the symptoms and what untreated trauma does to people and their families. I also realized how few services there are for men.

I created my small private practice and, interestingly enough, all the people who had known me for years continued to refer people to me. I thought I was going to be semi-retired but that plan did not last long; within no time at all, I was working full-time. I got involved with the organization malesurvivor.org and I still continue my work with them. All members volunteer their time to put on weekends of recovery for male survivors. In 2008, our team was given an award for the work we do with and for male survivors.

My childhood helped me to understand what happens to children when they're abused. On different occasions, when I was four and nine, two different uncles sexually abused me. Then, as a young woman, I was raped and beaten. I dismissed those things since I didn't think they were important. I didn't think I was important enough. I was damaged goods. Consequently, when the abuse happened to me, there was nobody I could tell and I didn't think anyone would believe me. When I was four years old, my great uncle tried to stick his tongue down my throat. I remember squirming to get off his lap and everyone thought it was funny. I don't think they understood what was really going on.

The abuse happened right in front of people. My uncle sexually abused me. It was fondling, not rape. The adults would be playing cards downstairs and he would come upstairs. How could he be upstairs for that long in a card game? It made no sense to me. I always thought it can't be too wrong – it can't be too serious.

When I first came to Toronto and I was pregnant with my daughter, a taxi driver helped me carry my bags upstairs into a hotel and he raped me. He said, "You can call whoever you want but they'll say you invited me in because you let me carry your bags upstairs." It was always that kind of thing. The first time my first husband beat me, I went home to my dad and he said, "Well, you know you made your bed, you got to lie in it." There was that kind of dismissal of abuse constantly going on.

On a professional level, I could understand very clearly why women and men didn't come forward about their trauma. When they are sexually abused or emotionally abused by their family, they don't think there's anyone to turn to. There is really nowhere for them to go. They don't think they have any value. For me, looking back, it was almost normal for women to get raped — not such a big deal for a woman, unlike a man.

That's a frightening statement, isn't it?
Yes, isn't it? I've seen many women who minimize the abuse and think it's no big deal unless it's a violent rape. If someone is date-raped or raped while drunk, many people assume they were complicit — that somehow they deserved this violence because they put themselves in a horrible situation. How can they possibly call it rape when they've been warned not to put themselves in

dangerous situations? That's kind of the normal thinking when they've been disrespected or not cared for as a child.

What do you say to a woman who's living with those thoughts?
I say, "Would someone's child deserve that? Would you say the same thing if this had happened to your best friend?" I try to reframe it by asking them, "What would you think if it were someone else? Is that what you want for your daughter?" When you put it like that women understand. They start realizing that if it isn't okay for other women to be abused, then it isn't okay for them either. They get that.

For men it's the same thing. They somehow think they deserved it and feel they were complicit or they were responsible. They were groomed, and often their parents are groomed, to recognize the perpetrator as a friend, so they trust him or her completely. I try to always help people look at the reality of the situation. If you've accepted a dinner invitation, that's what you were accepting. You weren't accepting rape. You weren't saying it is okay to have sex with me. I try to help them make those connections.

I really get the PTSD aspect of it all and I really, really, wish I'd understood at the time what was going on with my father. But it wasn't my job to understand him. It was his job to understand me. He wet the bed almost every night. There were a lot of mornings when the mattress was against the window drying out. My mom was obviously looking for love in all the wrong places – I don't know her history or why she was so sexually active. Usually the reason for promiscuous behaviour is because of a low sense of self-worth. I assume something happened to her to make her feel that way.

There is so much suffering that happens in silence. Did you ever make any contact with your daughter?
Oh, yes, after my husband passed. He didn't want me to contact her because my experience with my son was very painful. I had so much remorse and so much guilt and he didn't want me to experience that again. I found her when she was twenty-five. We have a good relationship. We have lunch together at least once a month. She has a close relationship with her adopted mother, which is wonderful, and found out she was adopted when she was

around thirteen years old. She experienced sexual abuse as a child, which was really gut-wrenching for me to find out about. She was able to tell me all about it and I connected her with a therapist so she could work through it. I'm very lucky. It hasn't been easy. It was awful with my son for many, many years and it was excruciating to find out that my daughter was abused. She's the one thing I tried to protect from my crazy lifestyle so she wouldn't have that kind of life but she had it anyway. That was really, really difficult to learn.

You mentioned the difference between men and women in terms of the effects of trauma. What would you say are the main differences?
There's one really important point. Shame seems to be worse for most men. Also, I think that men carefully guard the secret of the abuse because of the myth that if you were sexually abused, you become an abuser. Men have a really hard time coming forward because they are terrified that people will start looking at them out of the corner of their eye and watching them around their children. By and large, the men I have worked with, for over ten years now, have been over-protective of their children. For instance, one of the guys said, "I'm letting my son have a sleepover now. He's nineteen." That sounds funny but many men who have experienced abuse are very protective of their children and, in particular, their boys.

Sadly, men have a hard time admitting what happened – women don't struggle with this as much. I have rarely talked to a woman who hasn't been sexually abused or experienced some sexual impropriety in the form of gestures, touch or other behaviour. It happens way too often for women and we are just finding out that it happens a lot with men too.

It's being documented in the media more frequently now.
Every few months. Absolutely.

More people are coming forward and speaking out, which breaks the taboo that exists around people talking about sexual abuse. People are more knowledgeable now.
Absolutely.

How does a man get to the point of saying, "I've got to go to a therapist and talk about this?"

It could be something with his children, something in the newspaper, or that he's finally been such a horrible person to his partner that she tells him, "Get out or get help." I get calls when their children get to the age they were when they were abused. I began working closely with the Canadian Centre for Abuse Awareness. They have the Martin Kruze Memorial Fund, which is set up to support men who were abused at Maple Leaf Gardens. The folks at Suicide Studies at St. Mike's Hospital in Toronto have referred men to me and some called me after they saw the *Oprah* two-hundred-men show. They were shocked that there were so many men who have experienced abuse. After Theo Fleury declared he had been sexually abused, after Sandusky was arrested for abusing young men he coached at Penn State and after something like the Catholic priests being accused of sexual abuse, I received calls. Each situation triggered something.

Often men haven't told their wife or partner about the abuse and they have anger issues. For many men, the first time they talk about it is when they come to see me. One of the first things I may have them do is tell their partner and that's really hard. Imagine, if you can, being married for thirty years and now you're going home and have to say to your partner, "Oh, by the way, I forgot to tell you this." That's very, very hard but I encourage male survivors to tell the significant people in their life because that helps them to deal with the shame. Keeping a secret keeps the shame in.

I'm often told, "I'm not going to tell anyone about the abuse until after my parents are dead," or "I'm not going to say anything out loud until after my mom dies," but in the end most do tell and they're glad they did. I coach them how to do it because sometimes the parents will say something really stupid, like, "Oh, I wondered what was going on between you and that guy?" I coach them how to tell people in a way that they won't get re-traumatized by the response.

I'm sure there's potential for more trauma without this coaching. Most people are very afraid to speak about the abuse. Many have carried the secret and shame for decades. They haven't said anything and they don't want their children to know. What better way to build a closer relationship than by being honest and truthful with them.

Yes, absolutely. I've learned by listening to their responses. We role play and think about how the conversation may go. After one man told his teenage children, they understood and said, "That's why you wouldn't let us have sleepovers." They started to appreciate that their dad was trying to protect them because he knew far too well what possibly could happen. Often the partners want to come in and have a session with me with or without their significant other just because they want to understand and they want to know what to do and what not to do, as if there were a magic formula. But there isn't.

When you allow yourself to be vulnerable, then you really open the door in the relationship. It provides an opportunity to really grow as a couple.

Yes.

It's an opportunity to address the underlying issues: the shame, the guilt, the anger, the depression...

The lies. It's been my experience, all too often that a person who has been abused, especially in childhood, tells people what they think they want to hear. So, they're lying all the time and not because they're meaning to be evil or vindictive or dishonest; they're lying because they want to be safe. It's often about little things and when confronted they'll say, "I don't want you to know exactly what's going on with me, so I'll just tell you something else." It gives them a little bit of control.

What's the real issue that's stirring within these people?

A need to feel safe and in control. They often self-medicate for the pain. I think that's where the addiction treatment centres are starting to wake up, because they're starting to recognize that sometimes there is trauma underlying the addiction. There was a time when they would say, "You have to deal with the addiction first and then you can deal with the other issues." Sometimes that's true, but sometimes the person will never get clean and sober unless they deal with the trauma.

I guess part of a therapist's job is recognizing which one to address first?

Yes, but sometimes individuals need to deal with both at the same time. Fortunately, I have experience with both addiction and sexual abuse. We can talk about harm reduction by reducing substances and we can talk about quitting and how hard it will be. We look at all of it — the addiction and the abuse.

Sometimes people just aren't talkative or forthcoming about the abuse or related addictions.
Exactly. I'm really, really, fortunate in that by the time people get to me they want to do the work. The biggest challenge is the person who is addicted to something and they can access financial resources through their parents or a partner who keeps enabling them to continue spiralling down their dangerous and negative path. The people who are fairly well off financially have the hardest time. I think they're in a tough spot. It's very easy for them to avoid the issues. The ones who come independently are the easiest ones to work with. They know they have a problem and they'll do whatever it takes to get help. The people who have someone holding their hand and supporting them do well too. For the ones who are enabled to continue using, it's too easy and convenient to slip back. It's hard. If you love somebody and you see them suffering — crying, having nightmares and waking up screaming — it's hard to not give into them.

You come to a point where you just want the pain to go away.
Exactly and there's no easy answer. Support is important, but how to give the support is the tricky part.

And what is needed is different for different people.
Absolutely.

What does a healthy person look like after they've gone through sexual abuse therapy? What can they hope for?
That's an excellent question and I have a clear answer for you. First, they can reach a point where what happened to them is an event in their life and not who they are. Second, although they wouldn't want to go through it again, they start to recognize that the abuse made them who they are today and that they like who they are today.

What if they don't like who they are and they're only going to therapy because they don't want to devastate someone else?

Then they're not a healthy, recovered, sexually abused person. By the time they're healthy and have reached that point of healing, they do like who they are. They recognize what happened to them made them who they are — every bit of it, every piece of it.

If you had one piece of advice to share with someone who is sitting at home night after night very depressed and reliving their childhood sexual abuse, what type of advice would you give them?

I would tell them to reach out for help and don't give up on themselves. Don't let the abuser win. The abuser has moved on and is doing whatever the heck he or she is doing. People who stay home by themselves and relive the abuse day after day have taken over abusing themselves.

That's an interesting line and very true. I'm sort of resonating with that for a moment. Some stories I've heard about lately would imply that very thing: survivors often take over the abuse and they are not able to move forward toward healing.

Yes, they can't heal unless they reach out, tell their stories, and get help. There is help out there but it's often not easy to find.

It seems like there are a lot of different places on the Internet. I guess it's like looking for a doctor. Do you need the general practitioner, the chiropractor, the massage therapist or the acupuncturist?

Exactly.

Probably referrals are best. You must get a lot.

I do. I get referrals from my clients, witness support people, lawyers and the police. I've been around long enough now that my name's really out there.

You must be pretty busy.

Well I am and I'm not. I'm not covered by OHIP so some people can't afford me. I do have a sliding scale but I'm very cautious with that because I found people who come for very little money don't value it as much – which is really interesting.

You have gone through a lot, learned a lot, and have a huge base of knowledge to help people. You need and deserve to get paid fairly. You put in more than your share of volunteer time and, in fact, I heard you recently received an award.

I do a lot of volunteer work and thirty per cent of my practice is at a nominal rate. In October of 2012, along with many others, I was honoured to receive the Queen Elizabeth II Diamond Jubilee Medal for contributions to Canada and the Canadian community. I know my parents would have been very proud. My sister, my children, and the rest of my family certainly were.

Wonderful! Do you do individual or group counselling?

Oh, I love groups. I have two groups running currently and I need to start a third. I do individual work for men and women but mostly men. I do online therapy over Skype and I am starting an online group for men who are not able to get help in their community and for men who are isolated by their geographical location and/or their fears.

Group work is an amazing journey. It allows you to explore yourself and learn that you're not alone.

Yes, it helps the healing immensely.

Like you said, when you are a child, and you're going through all this, you don't feel you can talk to anybody about it. Later, it continues to eat at you in various ways, and yet you can't really stand in line at the grocery store and say, "Excuse me miss — I'd like to tell you my life's story. I was sexually abused..." We don't do this.

No, we don't. I was raised Catholic and went to Catholic schools. I was a really good student. I was always first or second in my class and then, all of a sudden, I stopped going to school and I was a runaway. I was angry because nobody asked me, "What's going on?"

They probably didn't want to get involved.

Yeah. All those records went with me to the next school and no one ever asked, "What is happening in your life?" No one seemed to care enough. I had to deal with that anger too.

What happened to your son?

After a long time, we reconnected and now have a wonderful relationship. He has four children and two grandchildren, so I'm a grandmother and a great grandmother.

Lynne, it has been fabulous listening to and learning from you today. I really appreciate your taking the time to share so many important points. After such a rough start, you've made a huge social contribution. I respect that way of life. Is there anything else you'd like to share?

Yes. Getting involved in your community is a really good way to help change society for the better. Thank you, Debbie. You're doing a great thing here.

Thank you.

Then
why don't I tell on him?

If they don't,
why don't I?

Because.

Because I am safe this way,
silent
unnoticed.

Thalia Chaltas

A Sign on My Head
Stewart

Stewart, I appreciate your taking the time to talk to me today. Thanks again for offering to participate. I know you have talked about your story; have you ever written it?

I've written little bits from time to time, mostly about my thoughts and feelings. I'm hoping to share the complete story today. I'm no longer shy about what happened.

I've been looking forward to speaking with you and hearing about your journey. If you're comfortable, start at the beginning.

Okay, sounds great. I want to be quite clear before I begin that my perpetrators were never family members; they were always a stranger or an acquaintance of the family. The abuse began when I was seven years old. My first predator was an adult male neighbour. I pretty much had to let it happen. The sexual abuse escalated and happened multiple times. It stopped when my father and stepmother split up and I moved away with my grandparents. Things were good there until I was sexually abused again by an acquaintance of the family. That time it also included physical abuse.

I became very confused and angry. I still refer to myself as somewhat of a bastard child. It's a harsh thing to say, but that was reality. In school, I behaved poorly, showing acts of aggression and anger. I didn't understand what was going on. Of course, now I say my behaviour was the result of the abuse.

As time went by I felt like I had a sign on my head that said, "Come and touch me." Just when I thought it had stopped for good, it happened again. The third time was a couple, the aunt and uncle of two of my schoolmates. It happened several times over a couple years when I went to my friend's place. I was getting more and more screwed up and more and more angry.

I'm surprised I never did anything really detrimental, although I once chased my stepsister around with a knife. I don't remember exactly what happened, but we got into an argument and I acted like I was going to stab her. Kids will be kids? I was extremely frustrated and I know I misdirected my rage at her that day. I couldn't talk about the abuse to anybody because in my era, more so than today, sexual abuse was never discussed. My sister probably still hates me for that attack. I'm surprised I didn't get sent to jail for the outburst, or at least get thrown into a home for delinquent children. Aside from that, I never did anything seriously bad. I was a very nice person to your face, but a bastard behind your back. Forgive me for using the harsh word, but that's who I was; that's what the abuse did to me. The pain was almost unbearable. Starting at about age eleven, I began using drugs and alcohol to try to forget my anguish.

What made the experience more confusing was that I never heard about sexual abuse in school, the media or anywhere. It was taboo to discuss it. I didn't understand why it was happening to me and I couldn't ask. I had to be secretive. I held everything inside and it turned into aggression.

I started getting into fights. I never backed down and anyone who tried to pick a fight with me got one. My attitude, combined with the drinking and drugs, landed me in jail for fighting. My grandparents became frustrated with my behaviour. At the same time, my younger brother and I had the opportunity to live with my biological mother on the East Coast, so we moved. I thought moving would separate me from the abuse. Unbelievably, it happened again. By then I was eleven and had begun slashing my wrists to get attention. My mother tried to help by sending me to a psychiatrist, but nothing came out of it. As far as I'm concerned, all the psychiatrist did was prescribe medication. I remember briefly mentioning the abuse to my mother, in a conversation about what was going on with me. She never pursued it or checked it out.

While we were living with my biological mother, I know my brother was also sexually abused. I know who did it too. That was very sad for me. I was devastated and frustrated to think it could happen without consequences. That caused continuous anxiety, self-doubt, and thoughts about why I should have to live through this crap! It was daunting and I continued to misbehave erratically. I questioned whether the abuse was right or wrong. It felt wrong, but it was so persistent, I just didn't know. It was very dodgy and confusing.

After two more individuals molested me, I had to separate myself from it, so I went back to Ontario. I was about thirteen and I started to fight back. I decided I wasn't going to let it happen to me again. When I left the East Coast, I left the sexual abuse behind. That was the end of it.

Yet, I could not leave the effects behind. I couldn't concentrate; I couldn't do much of anything. I had a hard time at school; I was into alcohol and drugs and struggled with major anger issues. I struggled in all my relationships, including those with my family, even my younger brother.

I had a hard time communicating or talking about anything. As my behaviour progressively worsened, I ended up in jail again for fighting more than once. Ultimately, I quit school and got a job. I wasn't achieving anything at school, so I figured I might as well make some money. I worked off and on. Work kept me occupied and paid for my habits. At that time I was about eighteen. I got fed up living in Ontario and decided to move to Saskatchewan to finish my high school education. I hadn't been able to shake the constant thoughts and feelings about the abuse. I felt that if I moved somewhere new, I could start fresh and put everything behind me. While taking university and college courses, I wasn't as distracted as I had been in Ontario. The relocation helped me, temporarily.

When I completed school, I took a step backwards. The feelings attached to what happened kept kicking me in the pants. I couldn't shut them out of my head. There wasn't a day I didn't think about it: no matter how busy I was, it would always creep up and catch me. Then, there were the nightmares. Oh gosh, the nightmares. What can I say? Whenever I tried to forget, I'd have a nightmare about one of my abusers. I never had peace.

Regardless of my education, I pursued drugs and alcohol again and again. Combined with the never-ending anger, it was a bad mix. I didn't take crap from anybody. I quit my job, and even ended up living on the street for a while. I didn't give a shit and didn't care about anything. I didn't know how to deal with the thoughts and feelings about the abuse – it knocked me back to the point where I thought maybe I should take my life. That's what it did to me. That's what it made me feel. I remember being in a hospital because I attempted suicide. All that got me were shock treatments and a lot of drugs I didn't particularly care for. They made me forget and not feel. That didn't help me. I was really discouraged with the treatment. You'd think I would have learned something from that experience, but I didn't; I tried to take my life again, failed and received the same treatment.

While I was living on the streets, my grandmother managed to locate me and told me my grandfather had passed away. So, at twenty-one, I reluctantly headed back to Ontario. I remember feeling like I didn't belong anywhere. I had a lot of doubts, no self-worth and felt like I shouldn't be alive. I felt dirty and disgusting. Even the shock treatment and medication couldn't release me. The nightmares haunted me.

After my grandfather's funeral, I continued to struggle. I came into a chunk of money and it escalated my problems. I got deeper into the booze and drugs and it caused me a whole lot of grief. The funny part was the street drugs seemed to work better at cancelling my thoughts than the medical treatments.

Eventually, I got a job and shook it off for a while. I met a woman, got married, and had a child. That experience lifted me out of my lost state. It created some emotional distance and helped me forget what had happened. Even when my wife and I divorced, I had my daughter part-time and managed okay. I was able to walk away from the drugs and alcohol while I was raising her. I did all the responsible things. That carried me until she was almost twenty.

I am fifty-one now and have managed to stay responsible, keep a job, and pretty much lay off the alcohol and drugs. Years ago a friend convinced me to study martial arts, and the training affected my behaviour significantly. I still have anger issues, but have learned to control myself through martial arts training. It was important for me to control my anger because I didn't want to be an angry person around my daughter. I wanted to learn to be calm, cool and collected. I knew if I didn't suppress my temper I wouldn't be a good father for her. I was uncontrollable before and now I have control of my deepest feelings. I can stay cool even in the weirdest situations when other people get angry. To this day I give much homage to my Sensei who helped me immensely. He taught me how to channel my anger into better thoughts and processes. I will always be grateful to him for pointing me in a new direction.

When I was no longer responsible for raising my daughter, I had free time for myself and it was easy to reflect on my past. I didn't have any distractions, which was really bad for me. I slipped backwards. Slowly that brought me to where I am now: memories, anger and struggles with intimate relationships.

I was abused by both men and women and as a result I have difficulty trusting either. I think about the things my female abuser had me do. The way she controlled me; it haunts me. I want to trust women because I do love a woman's company. I love the companionship and the magnitude of what happens between a man and a woman. I'm still trying to figure out why I think and feel the way I do. I am concerned I still have the same anger about what happened to me as a child. That's why I have misgivings and carry a lack of trust.

Whenever I'm in a relationship I always have mistrust. When a woman tells me something, I don't believe her. For as long as I can remember, when I start to trust somebody, deep down I know I do not trust them. I find it hard to believe a person when they talk about love. "How can you love me, I don't understand. I'm disgusting. Why would you want to have anything to do with me?" At the same time I'm thinking, "This person doesn't know what's happened to me or my thoughts doubting their love." I don't feel like I deserve love.

In a relationship I always fall, always crash. I shut down, keep to myself, and eventually want to escape. I'm afraid to get attached and I want to get past that. Without sounding weird, I have a lot to offer; it's not healthy to feel this way. I want to give myself completely and I want to share everything. I want to be honest. I want to have what others have. It just hasn't been possible. Why do I shut myself down? I'm fighting desperately and it's been a long frustrating battle to move toward healing.

I always considered myself a caring person. I was always giving to everybody else and putting myself last. Unfortunately, sometimes when I was in a relationship, my partner came last as well. While I was busy giving to everybody else and concerned about what others thought of me, I wasn't thinking about myself within my relationship or about my partner's needs. That has been detrimental to some of my past relationships.

Slowly my thought processes have changed and that's given me a new lease on life, or rather a new lease on my thoughts. I still struggle with self-worth, but it's improved with counselling. I'm willing to do just about anything to try to change my thoughts. I know the way I think and feel now is really different from before. I probably will struggle with this the rest of my life, but not as much as I did previously. The difference is that now I understand why I feel like I do.

I'm finally at a stage I never thought possible. I am feeling and seeing things I didn't see before. I still have issues, but I'm not running away like I did before. I'm striving to better myself so that I don't misbehave like in the past. Self-doubt and guilt are still a struggle, as are nightmares, although they haven't been as bad as in the past. I want the best for myself in the future, but at the same time I am very frightened. Living with the memories of sexual abuse is a daily struggle. As I move forward I want some kind of clarity or closure and I'm finding that really hard to uncover. I think I'm heading in the right direction with group counselling and look forward to seeing some light at the end of this scary tunnel I've been stuck in for over forty years.

I'm still a very angry person and it brings a tear to my eye when I think about what happened to me. However, I'm looking forward to helping others now. I actually can't believe I'm going to be helping someone with this same issue – I'm certainly going to try. I have a lot to share including what you should or shouldn't do to cope with sexual abuse. Hopefully I will be able to help. I feel there's enough hope for me and others to keep moving forward.

Thank you, Stewart. Just think of the tears as being the little angels coming out of your soul and helping you come alive again. They've given you a new awareness and there's absolutely nothing wrong with being emotional and being in touch with that. Are you okay to continue?
Yeah, I'm all right.

I'm wondering if you ever spoke to your stepsister about the knife incident – how old were you then?
Never. I never ever spoke to her about that. I was nine or ten years old. Something I didn't mention before is that she and her friend watched one time when I was being abused. She was young herself

and I don't know if she was scared or not, but she watched it happen.

You said you were aware that your brother was also abused – did you speak to him about it?
No, it was never spoken about. Around his eighteenth birthday, he committed suicide. I swear he did it because he didn't know how to deal with the sexual abuse.

That must have been very difficult.
It was a very, very difficult time. I felt abandoned, again.

Again?
First my parents split up, and then I was shipped here and there and all over the place. I always felt like I was abandoned – that's another one of my issues.

Understandably. What happened to make you realize you needed to seek help?
I was involved in a relationship and I couldn't deal with the memories anymore. I was having nightmares and couldn't shake them. I couldn't deal with my own life – I got fed up and said *screw it*. I walked away from everything, including a beautiful relationship. I knew if I didn't find help I would put a bullet into my head. That was my turning point. In the past, I had researched and tried to find help, but never saw anything that resembled what I thought help should look like. I did not want to go back to the hospital for more shock treatments or drugs, nor did I want to self-medicate with drugs and alcohol. I went online and ended up in group counselling thanks to a referral. That was two years ago.

You held an awful lot inside for a very long time.
Yes, over forty years.

Good for you for seeking resolution and not giving up.
It's very strange because I don't know where I got the strength that's driven me to do this work. Years ago I tried to commit suicide and didn't succeed for some crazy reason. There are powers greater than me. I guess I'm meant to be around a while

longer. There must be a reason.

Yes, I'm sure there is. It's unfortunate that people can't turn off the repetitive thoughts. You are starting to replace them by spending time helping other people. How do you feel about that?

I can't believe it – it's a positive thing. I think I've always given off a positive persona, but deep inside I've always been very negative. I am feeling positive about my role and this new direction. For me to even think this way is totally out of character.

Well maybe it's just that you have been trying to escape from the pain for so long: moving here and there, getting sidetracked focusing on your child, and then martial arts. All escapes and types of coping strategies, really... and now it's time to help others while still recovering. Helping others is helping you also.

Yes.

You mentioned lack of trust. When you've been sexually abused, that's a given. But let me ask you this: what does trust look like to you, in terms of a healthy relationship?

I'm still figuring that out; I'm not sure. I guess it's more of a gut feeling and maybe if I didn't have the self-doubt, then I would have the trust, right? I am struggling with that. Is that answering your question or not really?

If I said, *shoot from the hip* and pretend you know what a trusting relationship looks like, what would you say?

My perception of a trusting relationship is someone I can tolerate who won't judge me. I'm brutally honest. I care about people's feelings and I go out of my way to not hurt anybody, but at the same time I want to be able to communicate and not feel I've said or done something wrong. I don't want to feel like I have to run away. Running away does not help a relationship. You're supposed to work it out, right? I haven't been good at doing that because I've always thought I was trash. Why should I bother?

Right. Do you feel you've been judged in relationships because of the sexual abuse? Have you shared your experience with abuse with your intimate partners?

No, I've only shared it with one person and she was abused herself.

When I told her, it was like she cared but not really. It was like she believed me, but then again maybe not. Maybe she thought I was revealing it for attention or to take away her fears. I don't know.

I don't know why anybody would want to use that to get attention. I don't know.

When you talk about relationships and yourself in general, I am wondering if there's some self-sabotaging going on.
Oh, most definitely. It was self-sabotage.

In relationships, when you shut down or there is avoidance, is it actually a survival tool to not let anyone get too close to you?
That's right, definitely.

Well, it's good to be aware that you are doing it. That's one thing I get clearly from you: your awareness seems to expand with each lesson. Where are you currently with your feelings of anger?
Better, but I still struggle. I'm very good at keeping things to myself. I'm as solid as a rock in that area because I've had to carry so many secrets for so long. I don't display my anger in front of anybody. I may say a few words, but for the most part, I would never hurt anybody. I would hurt myself before that happened.

We share a history with martial arts; would you recommend martial arts as a means of healing?
Yes, I would definitely recommend it. It's a really good stepping stone, especially in dealing with anger. I would also recommend spiritual healing with First Nations people, which I'm starting to pursue.

You'll have to let me know how that is. If your abusers were in front of you, what type of things would you say to them? Did you ever meet up with any of them after the fact?
No, never. As far as what I would say, I really have no idea. Right now I'm trying to heal, so that might set me back. I'm focused on trying to repair myself, never mind facing them. I've never thought about taking that step.

I guess it's not part of your journey to write a letter to them, even to just

burn it?
No, nothing like that.

What does the ideal Stewart look like in the absence of anger, self-doubt and frustration? Where would you like to be with yourself?
I'd like to fully and completely like myself. I want to like and accept who I am.

What is it you don't like?
That I kept my mouth shut all these years. These perpetrators have probably abused others and if I had said something, maybe they would have been stopped.

That sounds like guilt?
Yes.

If you could go back is there some way you could have changed things? Do you think it would make you feel better now if you could change something?
I am not sure other than if I had said something maybe it would have stopped. I don't know; it's hard to say. I have a hard time, even to this day, reflecting on the past and thinking about whether I should have done something differently. Besides, it's too late for that. I can only try to learn something from what I've done and move forward.

If you came upon a child being sexually abused right now, would you have a voice?
I certainly would. I would not keep my mouth shut. I'm really not sure what I would do or how I would handle it, but I would not sit back and let it happen.

You said when you were twelve or thirteen years old you were prepared to fight back, you were empowered, and you were never going to let it happen again?

Yeah.

There was a shift that happened at that time and now you have a voice. I mean when you were younger than that, what could you do to fight back?

You can't really do anything. You really can't be much of anything.

You did what you needed to do. You survived and coped the best way possible at each stage of your life. It seems like you're actively doing something at each stage in order to get by.
Yes. That's how I dealt with it. I just kept very active, being very much a busybody.

Have you ever spoken to anybody about post-traumatic stress disorder, about your nightmares?
No, I have not spoken with anybody. I don't trust anybody enough to talk to them about my nightmares. I don't have a very high regard for doctors after my bad experiences in the past. I will not talk with a shrink. I'm sorry, I just won't. They're only reading out of a book and they don't understand.

Fair enough and this can go off the record.
No, you can write whatever I say. It doesn't matter. I really don't care from this point. I want to be heard. I cannot continue to be silent.

Okay. In another interview I was told that everybody who's been sexually abused in one way or another is experiencing post-traumatic stress disorder. The nightmares, they must be crippling?
Crippling is an understatement as far as I'm concerned, but yes, very much so.

Learning more about PTSD may help. Why is crippling an understatement?
Because the nightmares leave me sleep-deprived, and sometimes I think I'm thinking clearly, but I'm not. I've made poor decisions when I haven't had enough sleep. What I wouldn't do to have a good night's sleep. I'm lucky if I sleep four or five hours a night, sometimes not even that.

Wow, are you still having a lot of nightmares?
Not as often as I used to, but I still have them. I refuse to take sleeping pills. I refuse to take any pills. I don't want to take something to go to sleep or to get up or to change my thoughts. I want to feel; I don't want to be numb.

You're definitely going in the right direction and I am very interested to know what you find in terms of the spiritual healing. Western medicine is quick to provide a pill rather than exploring and looking deep into the spirit and soul of the person. I know some people think spiritual healing is way out there, but there is much to learn from other cultures. I hope you find some resolve.

Yes. I certainly hope so and I am looking forward to that now. I'm seeking to speak with a Shaman or a Medicine Man or Woman. I'm hoping they're going to help me on my journey.

I wish you much luck. Stewart, is there anything else you'd like to say in conclusion?

Well, this is me like it or not, I don't know what else to say. It happened and I can't change my past. The only thing I can do is reflect and change my future and try to better myself. I'll struggle with this for the rest of my life, but I've got nothing to hide now.

You're beginning to help other people and it's very courageous to switch your focus from yourself to others. Thank you so much for participating.

Well, thank you for taking the time to interview me. Thanks for hearing my story. I really, really appreciate it.

Coach or Predator?
Bonnie

The first thing I'd like to ask is why you want to remain anonymous?
The situation happened to my daughter so it's her private life and I think she still feels uncomfortable about it. I want her to be able to share her story with the people she feels comfortable sharing with. She already feels like her privacy and space was invaded by what happened and I don't want to contribute to that feeling.

I understand. Why are you participating in this book?
If there's anything I can share that will help anyone who's had a similar experience, I want to do that. Though my daughter was not sexually abused by her coach, she has struggled knowing he was arrested and charged, more than once, for having child pornography in his home. He is not the man we thought he was.

Thank you for making that clear. Why do you think there's so much silence surrounding sexual abuse?
I don't have a desire to remain silent, but for a teenager who's had a pedophile in her life, it's a different scenario. She's trying to figure out who she is, where she fits into the world and what her identity is, which is hard enough without talking about or having more people know about what happened. It was hard for her to go through this. Teenagers have enough problems trying to figure out life. No matter how many times you tell them that it had nothing to do with them and it wasn't their fault, kids internalize everything and they feel like they were bad or are somehow responsible. They think people will judge them if they hear that they were associated with a pedophile. It just makes them feel like they're not a good person, even though it shouldn't.

How can educators help children be prepared for something like this?
I understand we need to prepare kids but how many kids will come face to face with a pedophile? What's the percentage? It's not like

she didn't know what a pedophile was, but it's an entirely different world to read about it than to have one show up in your life.

Statistics state that one in three girls and one in five boys will be violated sexually in some way before their eighteenth birthday. Keep in mind this type of crime is also under-reported.
That is a very high percentage. In that case we probably don't talk about it enough.

Please share the story of what happened.
My daughter had taken gymnastics for many years and in the final three or so years she was in competitive gymnastics. That meant she was training three times a week, often for two hours or more at a time. She was between the ages of seven and nine and was being taught by the same coach most of the time. She's eighteen now. She was in a group coaching situation with four or five other girls and they practised on a gymnastics floor with a wide window where the parents sat and watched – that's why I don't think anything overt ever happened with her. The interaction she had with him was not behind closed doors. She decided to leave gymnastics and it was about a year later when I learned he had been arrested. The day I found out that he was arrested, she was away at a summer overnight camp. A neighbour called me around six o'clock and asked if I had seen the evening news. When I said no, she told me I needed to turn it on. When I did they were profiling my daughter's gymnastics coach, who was being charged with pedophilia activities. I remember feeling like every cell in my body changed and I thought, "Please tell me I'm not hearing this." I felt like it couldn't be happening. I wanted to get into my car right away and find out what was going on.

In hindsight, I am glad that my daughter was away at camp. It gave me time to calm down and learn about the whole situation before I had to sit face to face and talk to her about it. If you have to talk to your child when you're still reacting to the shock of something like this, you don't handle things nearly as well as if you have some time to think about it. I was grateful she was away.

I remember calling my husband, who was travelling at the time. He told me not to worry because he didn't think she'd been touched sexually. He didn't think there were any symptoms or behaviours evident with our daughter that would indicate that she had been harmed. He felt that until we had more information we shouldn't worry about it. He thought they may have caught the coach, and the allegations may be true, but he didn't think she'd ever been violated – other than being in his presence, which was a violation to some extent.

As soon as the news was over, the telephone rang and it was somebody from the police department saying they were contacting all the parents of the girls involved at gymnastics. I was asked to come to a meeting for all the parents of the children who had been taught by this coach. The police were going to talk about what they had learned and would tell us what they were going to be doing moving forward. The coach had instructed for a long time and there were quite a few parents at the meeting. I was also informed that each of our daughters would need to have an individual interview.

They had caught him by using an online detective, who works specifically on catching pedophiles by posing as a pedophile himself. He tries to get the pedophile to say things online so they can get a search warrant and search his home. I guess he started to get a lot more vocal online and talk about the fact that he was coaching girls. I don't know all the specifics, but they were able to get a search warrant and when they went into his place he had child pornography on his computer. That, in itself, is an offence. From there they were able to trace other things. For example, he'd been going into the girls' changing room. He took things that were left behind, like underwear. At that point they started to interview the girls who had been coached by him. They had conducted quite a few interviews and they had not found one girl who had been sexually violated. They thought all his illegal behaviours may have happened online. They stated that, to their knowledge, his behaviour with the girls never crossed the line. It was reassuring for us to hear that.

When he had his first court case, which seemed to go on forever, my husband went down and sat in the courtroom. He said he went because he wanted the coach to see him. He wanted the coach to see him because he wanted him to know, "Hey, you coached our daughter for all those years and I know what you did. I'm going to sit here and watch you and I want you to know that I know." It was really important for my husband to be face to face with him. I guess that was his way of saying, "Don't even think of going near her again."

When my daughter arrived back from camp, I sat her down and told her what had happened. Right away she told me she had not been sexually violated. She was definitely shocked and had a difficult time understanding how a coach she adored in so many ways could be a pedophile. During the time she was coached by him she was constantly making him cards that said "Best Coach." She really loved him as a coach.

My daughter was interviewed by the Children's Aid Society and a police officer. I was not allowed in the room during the interview. Afterwards, they asked to see me separately and told me they didn't think she'd been sexually violated by him. They said she had the choice of receiving therapy, if she wanted, but they didn't feel she was as upset as some of the other girls. They left it in our hands to decide. When I asked her if she wanted to see somebody to talk about it further, she said she didn't. Those are the main points of what happened.

Thanks for sharing. How is she doing now?

I would say she still doesn't trust people. Immediately following that experience she had a series of things happen to reinforce that she shouldn't trust others. She may have to deal with her feelings about her coach, in counselling at a later date. These experiences have reduced her ability to have intimate, trusting relationships. She doesn't let people get too close.

That's unfortunate. It would be pretty confusing for a young child. Who was aware that your daughter's coach had been charged with pedophilia-related crimes?"

Well, certainly our neighbours, the people at gymnastics and some of her close friends. Beyond that it wasn't something she wanted to talk about.

Does she ever mention it now?

I wish it would come up more often than it has. My feeling is that she still has some issues that haven't surfaced. My two daughters are very different. One wears her heart on her sleeve and the other one, the one who had the experience with the pedophile, tends to keep things inside. She doesn't share what she feels or thinks. Honestly, I do think there are still some unresolved feelings. After the incident some of the girls were very upset and they saw a therapist to talk about it. We were told our daughter seemed to have a fairly good understanding about everything so if she didn't want to see anyone, she didn't have to. I told her there were people she could talk to and I explained the whole process, but she said, "No, I'm good. I want to just leave it." Whether that was good or not, I'm not sure.

That's a tough one. I can understand a child trying to suppress or forget the feelings and thinking the whole thing will just go away.

Yes. Perhaps it wasn't the right call for the people working there to say she didn't necessarily need therapy. Maybe it would have been better to say, "We think it would be helpful for everybody who had contact with the pedophile to have therapy," but they didn't. I do believe to a certain extent, when children are ready to deal with their feelings, they will. Sometimes you can't push them until they're ready to talk.

Yes, for sure. I would have expected that there would have been professional help available for all the kids, as a group, to give them a chance to talk and share their feelings. Their unresolved feelings will stay within them and may show up later in their behaviour.

Yes, I agree. I don't know how much they talked among themselves. Based on the conversations I had with my daughter, she was confused because she wondered, "Was everything I saw about him false?" For example, he seemed to really love gymnastics, teaching and all of us and also wanted the kids to do well in gymnastics. She wanted to know if that was all a game. I said to her, "No, it wasn't a game. That was all real. He did have a passion for gymnastics, he did have passion for teaching and coaching and he was a great coach. Unfortunately, he was also a pedophile." It's so hard to put the two together and the main result of the experience for my daughter has been that she has a hard time trusting people – she definitely keeps her distance.

You can probably guess lack of trust is something I am hearing over and over again in these interviews.
Yes.

What guidelines are there in gymnastics? In most sports now, all coaches, trainers and managers have to have a police check completed when working with children. Is there anything like that in gymnastics?
Yes, but he didn't have a record at that time. He'd have a record now. It was his first offence.

Was he just coaching girls?
Yes, only girls. There were groups within the club that included boys but I think he made it quite clear he preferred to coach girls.

How old was he?
In his thirties.

How many kids actually ended up coming forward?
I'm not sure. There were a lot. The police focused on the girls who had spent considerable time with him. If they had to go through everyone he coached, there would have been hundreds. There were a lot of kids interviewed, but not one of them said he'd ever touched them sexually. In gymnastics there's a lot of spotting. Spotters make sure if the gymnasts fall, someone will be there to catch them. So, he often touched the kids, but it didn't look sexual. However, the specialist said for some pedophiles that type of touching is enough. The touching could possibly escalate as well. If there had been an opportunity, the outcome might have been different.

Fortunately that wasn't the case. Was he convicted?
It was a long court case. Yes, he was convicted. In fact, he has been convicted more than once at this point. He's no longer allowed to coach or work in any field related to kids.

Did you talk to the other parents at all? Had there been any red flags?
When he was charged, we were already out of gymnastics. I wasn't spending time with the other families then. But, looking back, I definitely think there were red flags. There were times when I had a gut feeling that there was something about him — something just

didn't sit well with me. When we went away for weekend competitions he would tell the parents he wanted us to relax and go have dinner together. He said he was going to entertain the girls in his room. They would watch a movie and have a pizza party. We just thought, he's a big friendly kid. He had a very kid-like quality about him and, because it was a group of girls, we thought it was safe. Now when I think back, I remember asking my daughter how their evening went and she said they had a huge pillow fight and were wrestling. Once again, he got his physical contact. There were also times at the club when some of the younger kids would sit on his lap and I felt uncomfortable with that.

It's so interesting that upon reflection, you see things more clearly. His behaviour was subtle and, in the absence of the online activity, he may not have been detected.
I never heard anything about him dating or having any interest in women. I believe he lived with his mother. He was at an age where there should have been some romantic interest.

I'm glad you're doing this interview because there's so much to learn from listening to other people's experiences. This is a good example of how subtle sexual abuse can be. It reminds me of the *grooming* or *building of trust* stage, in many stories.
My own personal feeling is that we know when abuse is happening, but we don't want to know. Many of us have learned to block our instincts but I think it's our natural ability to know.

Our intuition.
Yes.

If you watch animals, they know instinctively when there's danger lurking.
Exactly.

They're not only alerted, they respond. Sometimes we suppress knowing because our minds say, "Oh no, that couldn't happen to my child."
Yes. Exactly. I believe we all knew.

How do you feel about believing you knew?
I know I did the best I could at the time. If I could go back and do it better, I would. Do I wish I could have done better? Sure, but I

can't go back in time. The police officer who worked on the case is exposed to many pedophiles on a daily basis. He said he doesn't trust any male coach. Period. He doesn't give them the benefit of the doubt. He is more cautious, than anything. He said if I saw what he saw I would have probably picked up on it much earlier.

That makes sense since it's his occupation. Given what you went through, what's your advice to parents?
To be alert and aware, especially in coaching and teaching environments. They are a target area, providing lots of opportunities for predators who want to get close to kids. Be aware of anyone who works closely with kids. Be careful – that doesn't mean paranoid. You just need to watch closely.

The reason I didn't feel frightened of him is there were always a group of children training together and they were always in our view. We could see them going into the change room and that he wasn't going in there. What I would be particularly careful about is leaving your child alone or out of view. If a predator is alone with a child something could happen. Similarly, things can happen when your kids go to sleepovers. You never really know.

You can't watch them all the time and the person violating your child is typically a person who has established trust with them.
Yes.

I guess he didn't exhibit any strange behaviour.
No. He was friendly and happy. My younger daughter had him as a coach for a short time and he would do funny things. For instance, as he was walking, he would pretend to bump into a pole. The little children thought it was hilarious. He was always doing funny stuff and the kids loved him. When he'd say, "Oh, I'll watch them, we'll have a pizza party," it was no surprise because it was like "Of course that makes sense because he's a big kid." It was interesting because the police officer said, "I know you're all in shock. Don't beat yourself up that you didn't see this coming, because sometimes you just don't. Sometimes they hide it so well."

It must have been a real shock to your daughter as well. Did she have any idea that something was off with him?

No, no idea. Not until I told her. Like I said, the first thing out of her mouth, without even hesitating, was that he hadn't done anything inappropriate. I knew by the way she answered that she wasn't hiding anything. She said, "Mom, never, he never ever touched me."

Well, hopefully, he didn't touch any of them.
Yeah.

It's unfortunate that everyone was still violated, in terms of trust, and what you can only guess he was thinking while with the kids.
Yes, absolutely. Afterwards it was all about questioning who he really was. The worst part is that the kids looked up to him. They trusted him and he betrayed them. You feel like the whole relationship was a lie and then you think, "Can I trust anyone?" and "Who do I trust?" He seemed to love coaching and gymnastics. I thought he was a great coach, but then I heard this and I don't know how to put those two things together.

Who knows what he was thinking.
Absolutely. Although, based on what he said online, the police said he definitely had very sick thoughts.

It's fortunate he was caught, when he was, because maybe he was going to go to the next level.
Right.

How are mom and dad doing?
Well, we're good. I've been divorced for a while now, though that had nothing to do with what happened in this story. At the time, I feel we handled it really well. If I could go back and do anything over I would have encouraged my daughter to talk about it more at the time, either with a therapist or other people. I don't think I did that enough. At the time it happened, we weren't a family that talked about feelings enough. Today I'm a person who believes in embracing every feeling you have. A healthy home environment means that you discuss all your feelings. There's never an elephant in the room because you talk about everything openly and honestly. An open, honest environment is the safest environment

and that wasn't what our family had. I had grown up in a family where people didn't talk about their feelings. I've learned to talk and to be in touch with my emotions.

I think that's some of the best advice I've heard. Everybody can learn from what you just said. If people were open and shared with their child, starting at a young age, then when a child feels something's not quite right they would be more likely to talk about it. Likewise, if they haven't been taught how to share and express their emotions, they're going to be less likely to talk about something they feel ashamed or embarrassed about.

Oh, absolutely. I think it's best if we nurture our kids in that kind of environment.

Is there anything else you would like to share?

I think the most important thing is to get kids to talk about their experiences. The only other thing I would add is, talk about it not only when it happens, but also again at a later date. Ask them how they are feeling about it and if there is anything they want to talk about. A month later or six months later they may have had time to sit with it and be ready to talk. We have to give our kids the opportunity to talk about it when the time is right for them. We should take advantage of the times when we have a good dialogue with our kids and say, "Hey, that happened, how do you feel about it today?"

That's excellent advice, thank you.

The things we don't let out, we carry inside our bodies and they can do us a lot of harm.

I'm Not Gonna Hide
The Wisdom of a Ten-Year-Old
Fayth

I used to be insecure, shy, secretive,
I was scared they were going to judge me if I spoke,
Scared they weren't going to listen.
There were so many things going through my mind,
So many things I wanted to say but was always too shy.
So, I finally said something and when I did they all listened,
They all helped me get better…
Child abuse is a thing that can make you shut down
and hide from the world.
When I spoke about it
I felt like a weight was lifted off my shoulders.
I am no longer the insecure person I used to be,
I am no longer shy, secretive or wanting to be alone.
I'm in school clubs, school sports teams, I volunteer and
I'm not afraid to sign up for new things.
I have so many friends, I am not afraid to go out into
the world without the fear of being judged.
Talking about it helped me in so many ways that I am
no longer the quiet one in the group.
I speak my mind and stick up for people
and for the things I believe in.
I want to help others because it's not a bad thing
to talk about whatever happens at home.
Child abuse is a worldwide problem that needs to stop.
Though it can be a scary thing, it's a lot better living
happily than living in fear.

Stop masking your pain for it will bleed through somewhere else in your life.
Sherna Benjamin

Scout's Honour
Bob

It's nice to talk to you again. Thanks so much for participating in *Unlock the Door*.
You are welcome. Thank you.

Why don't we begin with you sharing the basic premise of what happened to you.
Sure. I am forty-five years old and when I was probably eleven, I was molested by a scout leader. It profoundly impacted my life in ways that I am only just beginning to understand. That's the very short version.

When did you start talking about your sexual abuse?
It's never been a secret with my wife – we've been married for eighteen years. She's the first person I told about it.

So, I'm guessing you would have been in your twenties the first time you spoke about the abuse?
Right. I had zero awareness of what sexual abuse does to a child's mind. I was completely unaware until recently. While I was open to talking about it, could speak about it, and it wasn't a secret, in a sense I didn't know what I was talking about. I just wasn't aware.

What have you learned and how did the process begin?
It started at my intake meeting for a sexual abuse group I wanted to attend. The questions I was asked were real and we had a very deep conversation. We covered a lot of bases: addiction, mental health, levels of vulnerability, history, suicide attempts and things of that nature. For me, the big one involved stress and anxiety. I have a high-stress career. I figured the symptoms of stress I have are normal for a person in my circumstance. The intake worker asked some deeper questions, after identifying stress and anxiety as

issues for me. She also identified physical symptoms of hyperventilation and flagged that as panic attacks. I was (a) completely unaware of what a panic attack is – I think it's actually a misnomer, and (b) I was completely unaware I was experiencing this and it's a symptom of child abuse. When I discovered that about myself, and I put together what I know about PTSD (post-traumatic stress disorder), I began to get very angry because I assumed those things were normal. I didn't realize they were caused by what other people had done to me. Once I realized this, I knew I had something to do. Not only was there work to do on myself, but I needed to do some things to bring dignity back into my life.

Can you elaborate? Tell me what you are referring to.
I grew up in a house where, because of the things I was subjected to, I was predisposed to being at risk. I was raised in an environment where the adults reigned with anger and maintained their will through physical harm or the threat of physical harm. I felt very unsafe. I didn't feel honoured or respected, and as a result, I felt alienated. My experience was what I would have to describe as *lonely*, but I think that's a misnomer also. I don't think that abused kids are lonely. I think abused kids are alienated. There's a key difference because *lonely* places the onus on the child, and that's not the case in my opinion.

Alienated and *lonely* are two common words a lot of people mention when they have been abused.
The two are used synonymously in everyday language. A child's experience of being alone becomes self-alienation after the fact. Abuse colours their perception of themselves and their perception of the world. The only rational way I was able to accept what was going on was to adopt the belief that it was right. It was correct. This was my reality and I had no choice. The people who were feeding me and putting a roof over my head, the people who I depended on for my existence, treated me very poorly. The only way I was able to cope was to think all of it was my fault, or I must deserve it. The human mind is always inventing reasons why things happen and justifying them.

It certainly does try, doesn't it?

Yeah. As a child your thought patterns are formed by these situations, circumstances and conditions. You learn to live a lie: *nothing happened.*

Children growing up in that environment don't know what a healthy family looks like do they?

Absolutely not. I remember seeing my friends being hugged and kissed by their parents. They were playful and I looked at them thinking, "Man you guys are fucked up." It's twisted but that was so alien to me that all I could do was perceive the weirdness of it – that's how alienated I was from the rest of humanity.

Clearly you were afraid in your home. You experienced more than one kind of abuse?

I need to make a key distinction here. The people in my immediate family did not sexually abuse me – I want to be explicit about that. I identify them as people who abused me, but not sexually. I'm doing my best to reconcile myself and to see if there is any possibility of reconciliation with them. It's a struggle. For so long I identified with them and that has recently shifted. I now recognize that what happened to me was wrong, was not my fault, and that I have been living a lie. My whole identity had been shaped around it. That realization was profound because it meant questioning my reality every moment until that point in my life.

That's pretty deep. Questioning your entire reality; it's pretty amazing what walking through one door can do.

Well, that's my truth.

So, it was the scout leader...

...who sexually abused me.

Were you afraid of him or were you drawn to him?

Yes to both. And here's the twist of the knife – it is significant to consider why and how I became predisposed to being at risk. I came from an environment where I was desperately seeking love and male attention. When I began to realize how sexual abuse within Canada is systemic, it caused another level of anger for me.

I realized I was let down, not only through my predispositions from my childhood environment, but also because of the system I was entering. My scout leader was warm, friendly and outgoing. He was the youngest and most macho of the scout leaders. I was drawn to him because I wanted attention – I'm sure he cultivated that.

You know what? I've never realized it until this moment, but in the back of my mind I can recall warning signals. There was a vacantness, hollowness, or falseness around the nicety he displayed. As an adult looking back, I can remember that feeling. His niceness was on the surface.

What does that look like? Part of what I'm doing with the book is trying to educate and help people recognize the warning signs. What should parents and children pay attention to?

I'll tell you, this is a long answer but I'm going to come around. There's another angle to the story. Last fall my sixteen-year-old son's eighth grade teacher was arrested on child pornography charges. Two years had passed since he taught my son. As a parent, alarm bells went off for me. My son indicated he had not been harmed and he had no idea that was part of his teacher's character. As a parent, I felt relieved, but you know what – even though my son is very aware, two years have passed and anything could have happened and who would know? If I had been asked about my situation when I was thirteen, two years after the fact, I may not have shared anything. I also may not have recognized anything was wrong – who knows, right?

Right. More than a few people have kept secrets for a very long time.

That was the trigger that sent me to the police to report that the scout leader had abused me. But back to the original question. When I think about that teacher there are similar patterns and feelings that I experienced before. The teacher has not been convicted and there is no indication that he actually ever abused any kids. What I do recall is a similar feeling when I was around him. He wasn't interested in me as a parent – he was more interested in the kids and kept more than a professional distance between himself and me. He made little eye contact and said as little as possible. He was one of the most popular teachers with the students. He was very active with video cameras and still cameras in the classroom and he was very, very close to the students, my son in particular.

Video cameras in the classroom?
Oh yes.

That's a little odd, scary?
Yes. But it's the field trips you want to be concerned with. So anyway, there's a similar distance. Even though in one instance I was a parent and in the other I was a child, it's the feeling that I had around him that is familiar.

You've had a lot of years to connect the dots.
It comes in bits and pieces. My mind reveals things to me as I'm ready to understand them. I don't have a complete memory of what happened when I was abused. I either blacked out or withdrew. I had to accept that I don't remember much though I tried for years. I'm at a place now where I believe what happened to me was so undignified that I really would rather not know.

What was it that makes you think something more happened?
I have a blank spot in my memory with a very vivid ending point and a very vivid starting point, but I don't know in what order they happened. The last sexual physical contact I recall is the act of being touched. The scout leader had his hands on my groin area inside my pants. It's like when you watch horror movies and the screen goes black and then it comes back. The next memory is running through the woods and hitting my head on a branch. But, I don't know why I'm running and can't remember whether it was before the touching or after it. I distinctly recall him giving me a pill in response to the bump on my head after hitting the branch.

You said you reported your sexual abuse years later, shortly after your son's teacher was arrested. Were there any other reports against the scout leader?
No. As far as I know I'm the first person to report it, but I know with a fair degree of certainty that he did this to other people because he normalized the behaviour and called it a massage. The

other scouts who were my age were all talking pleasantly about it and were urging me to ask for one. There was awareness from other kids who were in the same troop. I'm sure it happened to other kids.

At the age of eleven there were other kids saying go and get a massage?
Yeah. They said, "Ask him nicely and he'll give you a massage."

What do you think about that?
I wanted a massage and I'm pretty certain I asked him in front of adults and he sort of brushed me off. However, it wasn't long before he responded to my request because we went on an overnight weekend trip out of the city. Within twenty-four hours the guy had his hands down my pants. Now I look back and have to wonder how much of it was going on with other people.

As an adult overhearing that kind of thing, there were obvious red flags. Is he still a scout leader?
I don't know. The police are working with me to help find him, but we haven't located him yet.

Can you tell me why you are looking for him and what you hope to accomplish by finding him?
Well, the first thing is to do exactly what you're suggesting – to discover whether or not he's still active around children and interrupt that. The other thing is to locate other people who were also abused by him, if they exist, and make sure the best case is put forward to the authorities so he is brought to justice.

What do you think about everything in the media concerning child abuse?
I'm a member of the media so I have two opinions. I think it's great to be creating awareness for people who are being abused, or were abused as children, and to help them connect with each other and bring perpetrators to justice.

What is justice to you?
Justice is accountability, for starters.

And after that?

I don't know. I'm working things out with my parents and I am not necessarily a big believer in the penal system as a solution. From what I understand, the prison system is filled with people who were sexually abused as children.

How old was the scout leader and what would you want to happen to him all these years later? There's no statute of limitations, right?

That's correct. I'm guessing when he abused me he was in his late twenties or early thirties. I'm not sure how to answer your question because it's out of my control. That's the way the police handle it. I'm a witness and if they deem they have enough evidence to charge someone, then they do, and if they don't, they don't. So that's a question for the police. My focus is on healing myself. My focus is on doing what I need to do for me and that includes confronting him. I don't know if I would get that opportunity within the traditional justice system. I'm open to other things like healing circles or other approaches, but I don't know how effective they are. For me, my focus and my priority is looking at the upside of where my life goes from here and helping to create awareness around these issues.

This leads me to the second half of my response about the media. I believe the media is complicit in a certain way for keeping things the way they are around survivors of childhood sexual abuse particularly in the sense of creating awareness around what can happen to adult survivors when they recognize they've been living a lie. The focus in most of the media I've seen, I am talking about television, popular films and popular culture, is on the damage or problem and the suffering. Focusing on the negative is so typical. That's how an adult survivor of childhood sexual abuse is portrayed in the media, but my experience doesn't reflect that. My experience reflects something vastly different, because once that lie was discovered and once it was accepted, there was another truth for me – which was nothing less than emancipation.

What is your truth?

My truth is that I was innocent. When I was twelve or thirteen years old I started drinking. I was introduced to alcohol in my own home and I was completely unsupervised with unrestricted access.

I began binge drinking. By the time I was in grade eight, I was getting drunk before, after, and during school. I had severe challenges learning. My mind was not able to absorb information because it was scrambled by the PTSD and panic attacks.

Were you angry?
The truth is there are two kinds of anger. There's anger you turn outwards and there's anger you turn inwards. I was more of the type to keep it in. The things I did were turned inwards – I abused myself. Once I saw where the blame should be, for why I became the way I became, the guilt went away instantly. It was like the lid came off my life. It was like I was living inside of a toy box and that was my world. Then all of sudden, the lid was pushed open, and there was a whole cool version there. I thought, "Wow, it's not heavy and I don't feel cramped." It was a profound experience and the trigger was confronting my parents. Once I confronted them as an adult and stood eye-to-eye with them and said things like, "You punched me in the face when I was twelve years old and drew blood – that's called child abuse. Do you have any remorse?" The response was, "Well, let me tell you about how you provoked me": trying to reassert blame. I realized nothing had changed. They continued to believe it was my fault, as I had. So, I continued to hurt myself with drugs, alcohol, and unhealthy and risky behaviours. I became an extension of my parents, a tool of their thinking, and continued to hurt myself after they stopped.

Very powerful to confront your parents. Were they aware of the sexual abuse?
No they weren't aware. Here's the twist. Had they known about it they would have stood up, probably reported it, and probably would have made sure it went as far as possible in the courts. They would have done that because that's what's right in other people's eyes. But all the while, all the other abuse was going on in our house. This is why my mind was so screwed up – because on the outside everything appeared normal. They sent me to university, paying for half, and they supported me in things that I was interested in like sports and music programs. Outwardly I had all the support and they appeared to love me. That is why it's so terribly twisted to me: inside, abuse; outside, the appearance of

support.

That's very common. Everybody I've shared that stream of conversation with has said the same thing and that's what's sick about the whole thing – the outward appearance: "Oh, that's such a nice family" or "Wow, what a great person," and inside there's an abusive environment. All along it was a facade everybody was creating.

In my opinion, that's the worst part of it. You can heal from the physical harm; it's what the abuse does to your mind that's debilitating – your learning is interrupted and your voice is subverted. They say the first casualty of war is the truth. Well, the first casualty of childhood sexual abuse is your voice – and once your voice is gone, you're screwed.

Yes. It certainly reframes the way you approach life when you lose your voice. Regaining your voice is significant, life-changing in fact.

Add PTSD to that and your ability to learn becomes truncated because the symptoms are similar to ADD or ADHD. You can't properly orient to situations and your focus is constantly distracted. I once took a general math course, then took the advanced course, thinking, "All I need is a little bit of extra time to improve." It wasn't true. I didn't do well in either course and this is the burden of the survivor. We go through life with such tenacity because we realize and believe we can succeed. There's a deep part of us that knows we can get by and we become driven to succeed. Yet the harder you try, the harder it gets. It's like a receding goal. You're on a treadmill with a picture of the horizon and the harder you run, instead of getting closer to the horizon, you get farther and farther away from your destination. It's not about hard work; it's about healing.

What does healing look like to you?

It looks like what I'm going through right now: awareness, accepting the truth, and standing fast in my truth that I was sexually abused as a child. That is the truth: I was sexually abused by a scout leader, who was an authority figure in my life. Part of healing is an awareness of the symptoms of childhood sexual abuse. Understanding the universalities in the experience, which other survivors have shared with me in person and which I've read about, that resonate very strongly with me. For example, the harder you work the further behind you get, and the feeling that you can't be your true self with people because trust was broken. I went through life struggling to trust people, particularly around sharing my feelings.

We all agree with you on that one.
Yeah, trust of yourself, trust that everything is going to be okay, trust that everything is okay. The experience of feeling loved, allowing yourself to feel loved by other people.

Are you saying that you don't allow that?
I'm saying there were times I haven't.

What other symptoms did or do you have?
I've mentioned the big ones: PTSD, alcohol and substance abuse, addictions, and panic attacks. When I looked at the major symptoms I had nine out of ten. When I understood why I began drinking, that I was given alcohol and how inappropriate that was – and all the ways I misused it over my lifetime – I recognized, "That's not your fault, pal." It's perfectly understandable why I ended up the way I did. The irony is I grew up in the environment feeling proud of it. I wore it on my sleeve and became a tough guy. It's unreasonable to expect that on my eighteenth birthday I'd turn it all around and become a responsible adult. It wasn't going to happen. Though it was time to be responsible, I didn't know how. I hadn't been taught – rather, I was shaped into this other thing that was self-defeating.

Can you go back just a little bit to when you talked about losing your voice and combine that with when you mentioned confronting – what would you say to the scout leader now?
That's so far from my consciousness right now. I don't know where he is and I don't really have any hope of discovering where he is in the near future. I honestly can't tell you in this moment. I would need to get in touch with my anger around it and right now I'm not angry.

Do you think you would want to feel angry when you spoke to him?

Well, it would be appropriate to express anger, but the truth is I expressed anger to the people who first abused me. I don't know. Maybe there's nothing left in the tank; maybe I don't have anger to express to him anymore. I'm not quite sure what I would say. I may deal with that in a different way. I may have to deal with it in the way that is most appropriate for me in that moment, if and when that moment comes.

Are there questions you would like to ask him?
My style would be more of statements. Letting him know the damage he did. I think that's what the beginning of justice would look like for me. I would make sure he understands how profoundly he affected my life by what he did.

When you say, "How profoundly he affected you," what if someone said, "Come on man, you don't even remember what happened – just a little bit before and a little bit after, how could it be so profound?"
Part of preparing for that would be to ground myself. The effects – it's not only what happened to me. It sidelined me from making as big of a contribution to humanity as I might have done had I not been abused. There's a wider cost than meets the eye. But again, in this moment, I'm not in touch with the anger. I'm not in denial; it's so far away that it's not real for me and I can't go there.

The reason I asked was because I've heard sexual abuse, like your situation, be minimized. "Oh, that wasn't so bad, get over it." Those words seem to be as harmful as the act itself, often resulting in more anger.
My relationship with anger has shifted since I expressed my feelings to my parents. That experience was the first time I really confronted them with anger. Prior to that, I was carrying it around as resentment for myself and toward other people. There was weight behind and under my anger and once I expressed it in an appropriate way to the responsible people, I felt completely different.

I was able to (a) stand up for myself, and (b) express the anger back at the source. I was able to create a safer boundary for myself and to let them know what they did was not acceptable, by any standard. I told them it was wrong and that what happened was not normal. That was the demarcation point: the point at which, if they wanted to have a *real* relationship with me, they needed to get real and be sincere – find a way to make it work in a healthy manner. I continued to say if they wanted to reconcile, it might be possible, but they would have some work to do. I was returning the responsibility for what they had done to me at their feet and walking away.

Have you ever asked yourself why they are the way they are?
I identified with that for the longest time. I made excuses for them because they are children of war. They grew up with bombs being dropped in their neighbourhoods. I had more compassion for them than for myself.

They were somehow entitled to do what they did because they grew up in a war?
Not to make excuses, not to justify, not to say it's right – but I always had some level of understanding and compassion for why they might have done what they did. That was the other thing that broke when I confronted them. I stopped identifying with any excuse or any reason having to do with them. For the first time I began to identify with my own experience more strongly than theirs.

Good for you for having the courage to speak your truth. I can certainly see the connection between what you experienced in your home and how that could create a personality more susceptible and vulnerable to sexual abuse. It also makes me think about the cycle of abuse and why people are quiet for so long – they feel if people know what happened to them, they may presuppose they're involved in similar behaviour.
Right. Yes, that's a very, very significant point. There is the fear that if you identify as a person who was abused you're at risk for abusing other people – that's not necessarily the truth.

That's right – it's a myth that everyone who is sexually abused will abuse others. I held that fear for many, many years. In fact, that was a significant reason why I remained silent. The thought of someone thinking I'd touch a child in that manner turned my stomach.
Yes, that's a burden. I'm discovering that while there's a well-documented part about sexual abuse, like the negative effects on people who are abused (PTSD, panic attacks, alienation, learning

challenges, substance abuse and addictions) – there's more to it. There's less awareness about the flipside, which is equal in magnitude. When people recognize the lie and start telling the truth about their experience, they become empowered. I'm telling you it's emancipation and that is the phenomenon that people don't know about yet – it's the mirror.

I'm in total agreement with that. I resist speaking too much about it because I sometimes think people don't understand the other side: the positive. They remain in the negative aspects of the story. Depending on where people are in the healing process, they are sometimes more open to discuss these things. Often it is too difficult to even recognize what is positive because they are still dealing with the story itself and it's still a very tough time for them.

My experience is like training for a marathon in work boots. I train, train, train, train: it's hard, I sweat, I suffer, and I go through that for however long. Then the race day arrives and I put on a pair of sneakers and I've got the wind at my back. That's what it's been like.

It's been great talking with you. Would you like to add anything before my last question?

Yes. I can't emphasize in enough different ways the myth that you can't heal the overwhelming sense of dread and failure and lack of empowerment, all those things that are symptoms of childhood sexual abuse. That is an illusion. It's a spell and spells can be broken. It's experiential. Imagine the thinking of sailors, prior to discovering the world was round. Two things happened: exploring new worlds became a possibility that hadn't existed and the world got bigger and that was the new truth. Until that moment they all sailed along the coast and hugged the coast. No one went exploring too far out. But this is the kicker. The real shift was that the fear of falling off the edge of the world was removed. It wasn't just that they had a new place available to explore; it's that their experience of it shifted. That's what happened to me when I discovered I had been living a lie.

Thank you. One last question: there's an eleven-year-old boy who feels awful because something has happened to him similar to what happened to you; what would you tell him?

In the words of Marilyn Manson, I wouldn't say much, I'd be listening.

You must not lose faith in humanity. Humanity is an ocean; if a few drops of the ocean are dirty, the ocean does not become dirty.
Mahatma Gandhi

To Punish,

To Protect

Sergeant Shelley Tarnowski
Provincial Coordinator of Abuse Issues
Ontario Provincial Police, Crime Prevention Section

Sergeant Tarnowski, thanks for joining me today. Can you state your current position and job history?

I have been a police officer for twenty years. Currently I am a Sergeant with the Ontario Provincial Police (OPP), serving as the Provincial Abuse Issues Coordinator. I have been in this position for approximately five and a half years. Prior to that, I spent most of my career either investigating abuse or coordinating abuse investigations.

I spent approximately six years as the Regional Abuse Issues Coordinator for the Greater Toronto Region. I also spent time with our Criminal Investigations Bureau on homicide investigations. I spent some time in our Major Crime Unit, investigating other types of major crimes outside of abuse, and I spent two and half years in our Professional Standards Bureau investigating public and internal complaints against police officers. For most of my career, I've primarily been an investigator or supervisor for abuse investigations. I also assist with the development of training and policy on abuse-related topics.

You've pretty much seen it all then.

I'd like to think I haven't seen it all, but I've certainly seen enough throughout my career to no longer be surprised by much.

How did you get into the area of policing sexual abuse?

I fell into it by virtue of the type of investigations that came my way. I have to be honest – initially I really didn't understand these types of crimes. What causes people to do the things they do and what causes victims to react the way they do? The understanding I now have came from years of training and studying abuse and dealing with victims.

An officer's understanding can play a significant role in helping someone who has been violated.

That's right. I didn't really get that at first. The more time you spend with victims, the more opportunity you give them to explain and the less judgment you place on them. Also, with time, you gain more insight to empathize and really help the people who come forward.

I believe to my core that if you don't understand who it is that you are trying to help, you really can't help them in the way they need to be helped. It's not just about telling someone that they need help; it's about showing them what that help looks like. You need to take them by the hand and lead them to help because in many cases they can't find the way on their own.

What are your best recommendations of where to seek help?

It depends on the community. Unfortunately, not all communities are well resourced. For example, the OPP serve a number of communities that are very under-resourced and isolated. People have to travel a great distance to get to the resources. We always look for ways people can seek help from wherever they are – sometimes in unconventional ways such as webinars or online support groups. Ontario is fairly well-stocked with victim service agencies that provide emotional support and assistance. These agencies also provide referrals to resources in other communities.

What are the best online resources?

There are several: the Canadian Centre for Abuse Awareness (www.abusehurts.com) and the Sexual Assault Care and Treatment Centres (www.sacc.to). Various women's shelters. Online for men, there is www.malesurvivor.org. There's The Gatehouse in Toronto. Also, you can find information through provincial and federal support lines. You can also find blogs that may be helpful.

The most important thing is that people who come forward get the sense that they are not alone. Many victims feel isolated and alone in their abuse and don't realize the level or extent to which abuse is happening in every community. They're not alone. There are many people just like them and discovering that can be a tremendous support.

There are a number of resources on-and off-line and it's more about finding something that works well for you. You mentioned that when you first began working with sexual abuse, you didn't understand victims or the offenders. What do you understand about them now?

The things that impact their lives. For instance, I have found a strong link between domestic violence and sexual abuse. Children who are sexually abused are often more vulnerable because of dysfunction in the home – addictions, abuse and domestic violence. Oftentimes these children don't receive the attention they need for their emotional well-being, and that can lead them right into the arms of a predator.

Predators notice when children are alone. They see kids being dropped off at sporting events or practices and when parents don't stay. They see kids that seem to be introverted, sad and withdrawn. Often they'll target those kids and take full advantage of them.

One of the things I've found extremely prevalent, particularly with males who have been abused sexually as children, is that there is a lot of stigma. That stigma creates silence, which can be very detrimental to a man's ability to cope with those experiences. They experience a lot of the same things as females, but there are some unique things as well. One of the stigmas associated with males who have been sexually abused is that they will, in turn, abuse others sexually – when in fact, that couldn't be further from the truth. I think the statistic is that three per cent become sexual offenders. However, they do offend in other ways at a very high rate, just not necessarily sexually. We see anger, physical violence and addiction-related crimes. It doesn't have anything to do with sexual violence.

We see a lot of people who do dysfunctional things as a result of addictions – things that perhaps they wouldn't ordinarily do. The problem is that sometimes addicts try to seek help for the addiction, but they don't seek help for the root cause of the addiction. They don't disclose the sexual abuse. For instance, if you go to a twelve-step program, Alcoholics Anonymous for example, it helps people to deal with the alcohol issue and to stay clean and sober – if they follow the program. The problem is they only talk about alcohol. They don't talk about the abuse. If they don't deal with the root cause of the addiction, it's very hard to control the alcohol, because it's just one symptom. Alcohol is one way of self-medicating to cope with sexual abuse.

There are many symptoms of sexual abuse people perceive as being the root cause.

In my experience, the vast majority of people who have an addiction problem are self-medicating to cope with their experiences related to abuse. It might not be alcohol or drugs. It might be a sexual addiction, work-a-holism or a shopping addiction. People don't typically address these things, and in fact, some are praised: "Oh, he is such a hard worker." A man may spend day and night at work, but that is often an escape – so he can focus on something other than the abuse that's haunting him.

Gambling addictions, cutting. Look at people who are covered from head to toe in tattoos. Most people are very frightened of people that present with head to toe tattoos. I look at it in a different way. Yes, it can be somewhat frightening and intimidating at times, but to me, that person is hiding. They're covering themselves. Tattooing is a painful experience; it can be a form of cutting.

Some people would be upset with you for saying that. They would say, "Tattooing is a form of expression."

Not for everybody. Tattoos are a rage these days. Almost everybody is getting them, but for many people it is a form of cutting. It is a form of hiding – they don't want people to see who they are. They don't want to be perceived as weak and vulnerable. If they present as a person who looks very intimidating, that is a form of self-protection. While it's not always the case, behind all the shields that are put up, you will see that tattooing can be a coping mechanism for many things.

There certainly is a wide variety of coping mechanisms. Can you talk about the relationship dynamics between victim and offender?

You have to remember that when a home is riddled with domestic violence for instance, it is about power and control. Sexual violence is as well. When you're speaking about pornography and self-gratification, that is a different issue with other factors to consider. But when you're talking about people who are committing acts of domestic violence within a home, their primary focus is gaining power and control over the victim. This is particularly true when ongoing violence is part of everyday life.

Victims of violence are often consumed with trying to survive and cope and do a lot of dysfunctional things. They take antidepressants, sleep aids and nerve-related medication at a higher rate, from what I am told, than anybody else in the population.

A perpetrator's main focus is trying to control the victim. The victim is focused on coping day-to-day and surviving the abusive situation in whatever way they can. Who is focusing on the little people in the home? That is a huge problem time and time again. Children who are vulnerable in the home have found themselves vulnerable to other abusive situations outside of the home.

I know a man whose parents divorced and a stepfather came into the situation. The stepfather was very abusive to the mother and the children. The man, who was a young boy at the time, decided to go live with his father, who had remarried a very nice woman. That woman's brother came into the picture and the two became close. He absolutely loved the brother, who was considered a step-uncle, because he showed him love and attention that he should have been getting from his own parents. This gave him the attention he craved and they developed a loving and caring relationship. However, he did not know that this was all part of the grooming process. The person who he'd grown to love and respect in so many ways ultimately ended up sexually abusing him. That's the part that's hard for sexual assault victims to overcome. Sometimes they accept the sexual abuse as the price they have to pay to have a loving relationship. As a result, there's a lot of self-blame and shame later on.

This young fellow finally put a stop to the abuse when he was a few years older. It was the lesser of two evils to move back with his mom who had given up the first abusive husband and remarried someone twice as bad. The abuse continued and he finally said, "You have to pick him or me, because I can't stay in this situation." She ultimately chose the stepfather.

That happens too often.

It does, and at fifteen years of age this young boy was out on his own to fend for himself in the world. The shame and the pain he felt as a result of the abuse lasted for several years. It really wasn't the abuse, because he knows that wasn't his fault – it was the shame. The dysfunctional ways he acted out for many years have caused him the greatest pain. Luckily, he was quite young when he came forward and got help. If a child is abused at a young age, there is a lot of help available. The Children's Aid Societies have many resources, as do hospitals. However, most people who have a history of abuse don't say anything for years and when they try to find resources, they can't. This young man phoned a rape crisis centre and other similar places, but they couldn't help him. When he was attending university, he phoned the sexual assault crisis line and, while they were very sympathetic to him, they couldn't help him because their service is geared to women.

I've heard that a few times.

There's a huge shortfall in this country, and every other country, of services dealing with the abuse issues specific to men. The vast majority of our male population who are either incarcerated or committing violent crimes do so because of anger-related and addiction-related issues. These crimes are often acted out as a result of an inability to cope with the abuse they sustained as children – this is what statistics show us. I am speaking about all types of violence. The vast majority of offenders appear to be men. I believe to my core that this is a result of their inability to seek support and assistance. I believe if we could get a better handle on sexual abuse and provide more resources, particularly so males can get assistance at an earlier stage, we could probably close half the prisons in this country.

That's a serious statement. We need more resources for men and obviously the sooner they receive treatment, the better. If you have an infection and you don't deal with it, it can turn into something very serious. The same is true for abuse, where the side effects can develop into some significant problems. Yesterday when we were talking you mentioned conferences for men; can you share that information?

Back in 2008, I presented a one-day awareness session for police officers. It started out as a police training session, and we had some requests for other people to come. In the end, I had about a hundred and forty people attend: victim services agencies, Children's Aid, police services from all over southern Ontario, native friendship centres, crown attorneys and even clergy. Hearing the men speak had such an impact. They told their stories about what really helped them, what made a difference for them, and what *would* have made a difference. They also shared their struggles.

Afterwards, my phone didn't stop ringing. I had request after request to bring the awareness session to other areas of the province, and as far away as Germany and the United Kingdom, because it was so enlightening to people who were dealing with male abuse and had no resources. They wanted to help but didn't understand the best way to do that. I do a lot of presentations and training sessions about male sexual abuse for community groups, probation and parole boards, and youth workers – on top of the twenty-two conferences we've run across the province.

The great thing about the sessions is that survivors also attend. It validates them. It helps them understand that they're not alone and that there's hope. They realize they too can have a good life and become as happy as the male presenters that accompany me. It's not that these men don't have struggles from time to time, but they were clearly able to turn their lives around once they got the help they needed.

People now see the need to establish resources within their communities. They finally understand the magnitude of the problem and that services need to be in place to treat people who have been violated. All people.

Exactly, move the taboo out of the closet. We need more people coming out.

That's right. By broadening the awareness in the wider community, it helps. Three of my co-presenters went on *Oprah* two years ago when she ran a two-part series with Tyler Perry on sexual abuse involving males. They were identified as a result of their advocacy efforts and were asked to appear on the show. Millions of people worldwide watched the show and felt hope. People who have suffered from abuse and never spoken out saw these men on TV talking about the same things they experienced as children. They saw other men come forward and say, "I don't want to bear that shame anymore, I want to get help and I want to know what's available to me."

We continue to do awareness sessions so people in the broader community understand the widespread dysfunction as a result of sexual abuse. Sexual abuse is not your issue or my issue; it's everybody's issue. Any dysfunction that is happening in your community affects everyone. It's not just that person, their children, their spouses and their other family members; it impacts everything in their life: their ability to work and function as a normal, healthy, happy, contributing member of the community. If they're not well, we all see what happens.

When people come forward their focus is often on healing. From your experience, what are the key points to healing?
I see the most impact toward healing when men receive long-term care and support. Not eight-week programs, not ten-or sixteen-week programs, but ongoing support. People cannot be penalized if they miss two or three sessions – that doesn't cut it. They cannot be dropped if they miss and need to be able to come and go as needed. They need to feel like they can get the help they need when they are ready to ask for it. Asking for help is a process, not an event. Facilitators need to recognize that people will stumble along the way, but they need a place to go where they will always be among people who understand them. That is *key* in my view.

Like in AA?

Similar. Lynne McDonnell (www.lmtherapy.com) runs a group called A Time for Men. She's very well known. I think there are two groups going now and there is a need for many more. I've seen people go through programs two times and come back for a third because they need more assistance.

Through the process of writing this book, I learned that healing equals community. Since we flock to likeminded people, it only makes sense that in this situation, where nobody is judging anybody, we have the greatest opportunity to heal. Support needs to be ongoing for most.
That's the problem. They come out of the program after eight weeks and say, "I finished the program. I'm healed." And then a couple weeks later they're back to what they were doing because they aren't really healed. In eight to fifteen weeks you've only

scratched the surface. Lynne will tell you that she had someone come to see her every Wednesday morning at nine o'clock for two years. Then he came in one day and said, "Okay, now I'm going to start telling you the truth."

It's a long process before someone can fully disclose. There are many things they don't want to say they don't want to call it what it is. Whether it's rape, or other ways they were violated, they feel responsible for what happened to them. "I didn't say no, I could have stopped it, why didn't I stop it?" They think of these things as a forty-five-year-old man would, not as a seven-year-old child. It is hard for them to make that distinction.

That's a key point.

It is a key point because they fail to realize that they did not have the emotional maturity at that age. A child is unable to make adult decisions and take adult actions. As a forty-five-year-old man he has the knowledge and understanding to not be vulnerable to sexual abuse. He now understands what was happening – he now would likely see it ahead of time. Those types of things are hard to accept. When a person discloses, no matter how old they are when they disclose, the abuse comes back and at that moment they are seven, eight, or twelve years old again. We have to recognize that those people are very vulnerable when they disclose and they need a lot of support and validation. They need a lot of encouragement to carry on.

I have always said that in the end, it doesn't matter what happens to the perpetrator. If the victim can't get closure or find the help they need to move forward and lead a happy and productive life, what difference does it make what happens to the perpetrator? We have an obligation to keep the peace and bring safety to our communities. Yet, I always tell the victims, and this is what I train our officers to understand as well, the most important person in this equation is the person who was violated.

If you don't deal with the victim up front and provide the help and assistance they need, then you've got two problems: the perpetrator and the victim. If a pedophile or sexual predator is committing crimes, society expects the police to take care of the problem. However, we also need to take care of the victim. We didn't always focus on victims for many years – and you know what, we earned that stigma. We do a much better job now in responding to victims.

The criminal justice system was very cruel to victims. It is still very difficult, and it's important for the victim to understand that up front. Every victim who comes to a police officer must be told what to expect: the best-case scenarios and the worst-case scenarios. I never want a victim to say, "I would never have done this if you had told me this could happen."

That's a valid concern: the legal process re-traumatizing the victim. What does a victim need to know?
They need to know the whole process. They need to have information about services to assist them, emotionally and financially, and their rights through the criminal justice system. Knowing what they can expect in terms of procedures is also important. Something as simple as knowing the perpetrator will get disclosure of their statement may affect their decision or what they say.

Adults typically, unlike children, can choose whether or not they want to proceed with charges. Maybe they just want to make sure the information is known to the police, but they don't want to press charges. Sometimes they want to tell somebody and they don't know who else to tell. I had a female victim come to me one time and say, "I'm here because I had three choices: kill him, kill myself, or go to the police." How tragic is it that she was at the breaking point where those were the only three options? Thank goodness she chose the police. We see a lot of people who have not been able to cope, resulting in very tragic results.

We're limited by the options we perceive we have.
That's right. Perception is reality at that given time.

Do you get anonymous calls from people just wanting to know their options?
Absolutely. I've had many conversations with people who simply want information. I tell them exactly what to expect. What I stress first and foremost is that we can provide support and ensure they get what they need. They have options. They can come in and talk to me or one of our officers and not go forward with charges, or

they can tell their story and press charges, if reasonable grounds exist. We have an obligation under the Police Services Act of Ontario to provide assistance to victims of crime. It is a core requirement regardless of whether charges are pressed. If a criminal charge is laid, then the Victim Witness Assistance Program is engaged through the Ministry of the Attorney General. They can provide support, referrals and court accompaniment. They also keep victims updated on the progress of the case through the court system.

Are there enough officers to deal with this epidemic?
I believe so, although we could always use more specialized officers. Most police agencies and services do a very good job responding to this issue with qualified investigators in the area of sexual offences. I will say we need more funding and services. There is a terrible imbalance with respect to the number of services for men versus women. When we look at the statistics, one in three girls and one in five boys will be sexually abused in some way by the time they're eighteen years of age. It's a big number and a lot of people out there are hurting and in need of help.

I always say, too, that within those numbers many individuals have been abused more than once by more than one abuser.
You're absolutely right. People fall prey and unfortunately sometimes the victim has very low self-worth and feels they are only worthy through sex. Men have spoken to me about experiences where they've gone into prostitution. They say, "I'm good at this and someone wants to pay me for it." It is very sad and unfortunate, but all of these things impact the direction their lives take because of their diminished self-worth.

What are the rewards of being in your position?
There is a great deal of personal satisfaction. Nothing can compare to knowing you've helped someone who really needs your help. Sexual abuse victims really need help. Knowing I've had an impact that's allowed someone to move forward to a happier place in their life – there's nothing more rewarding than that.

What's the biggest challenge with your position?

The biggest challenge is getting victims to come forward. Then it's difficult, particularly in historical cases, to obtain evidence to support successful prosecutions in the court system. Also, getting victims the resources they need and seeing the results we want within the court system for people who are perpetrating these types of offences. Prosecutions are very, very difficult and we are often disappointed by the sentences offenders receive.

Are sentences for sexual abuse long enough generally?
In my view, no. They're structured. They're based on case law, meaning judges are guided by the previous sentences for similar cases. However, victims of sexual abuse are delivered a life sentence. There's absolutely no doubt for some, the abuse has cost them their life, their happiness for the rest of their days and their ability to function as a normal human being. Historical cases typically have lesser sentencing than what we see for a recent attack. Bear in mind that most offenders are familiar to the victims. Yes, we do have serial rapists and we have unknown attackers, but the vast majority of sexual offences are perpetrated by known, trusted individuals. That has an even bigger effect on the victims, their families and their communities. Many victims are silent for many years. By the time the abuser is sentenced, the court does not always recognize the toll on that person's life because of the lengthy silence. The shame, worry and self-blame they have carried all of this time never went away. If they could have forgotten about it, they would have. It's a life sentence for them and it deserves recognition, regardless of the passage of time.

How do we get the length of sentences increased?
Theo Fleury's Victor Walk (www.victorwalk.com) is happening in the spring. Efforts like that are needed and more people need to get on board. Talk to your political leaders and to anyone who has any influence whatsoever in getting the sentencing structure changed. The Canadian Centre for Abuse Awareness has been a driving force in that area. They were instrumental in getting the age of consent increased from fourteen to sixteen and they wrote "Martin's Hope," a document presented to government through the Office of the Victims of Crime. "Martin's Hope" is named after Martin Cruz, who was the first victim to come forward in the

Toronto Maple Leaf Gardens sexual abuse scandal. Martin couldn't bear his pain any longer and ultimately took his own life upon hearing the news that his perpetrator received two years less a day. Look at people like Theo Fleury, Sheldon Kennedy and R.A. Dickey from the Toronto Blue Jays, who have come forward. And other big names like Oprah Winfrey and Tyler Perry – they're famous. It gives hope to regular, everyday people when those respected people speak out about their own experiences with abuse.

It's really about recognizing abuse within the community and stopping it from happening altogether. I believe it takes a village to raise a child. If the villagers bury their heads in the sand and pretend it doesn't happen, as they have done for far too long, we'll never get ahead of this issue. That's why we need awareness sessions – the more we talk about it, the more people will come forward. Every time an event is brought to the attention of the media, it draws attention and broadens everyone's awareness. That is what it will take to have people outraged. People need to be outraged by what's happening right under their noses. You know somebody. It doesn't matter who you are or whether you are aware of it or not, you will know somebody who has been affected by sexual abuse. Awareness is what it will take to make changes.

How do people find out about your awareness conference and how do people get involved? Also, are you instructing people to teach what you're teaching, so it can reach more people?
At this point, people are in the developing stages and there are more conferences being requested everywhere – it's spreading throughout the province. It's not confirmed, but we're hoping to do some training for the RCMP in Manitoba later this year. What we do in the awareness sessions is the first of its kind in North America, or anywhere. We have not seen this type of awareness training with respect to the abuse of males anywhere.

If somebody approaches you and says, "we're going to put two hundred people in the room," will you come and talk?
Yes, we will go wherever we are requested. If they have training dollars and they're able to fund it, we'll go. I did six conferences back in 2011 that were funded through the proceeds of crime grant

funding. Unfortunately, funding is limited. All we try to do is cover the expenses for the speakers.

My last questions are about Internet safety. What are some safety issues that children and parents should be aware of?

It's important to understand how widespread the Internet is. Once you post something there, it's permanent. Understand that people hide behind the Internet and we never know who we're dealing with. Predators love this venue and it has fuelled them over the last several years. It gives them much more opportunity to prey on vulnerable people than ever before. It's important to educate children at a very early age how to use the Internet safely. I believe that it is a big mistake to deny them access as it's the way of the world. Teaching them how to use it safely is the answer. In order to do that, parents need to understand the Internet and how it works.

Can you give some specific tips for Internet use?

First of all, if younger children want to be on things like Facebook, parents need to set up the accounts. Parents have to know the password and log in on a regular basis to see what the children are doing. With my children, my first inclination was to say, no when they asked about Facebook – but it's the way of the world. Instead, I allowed them to get Facebook accounts at a fairly young age and taught them how to use Facebook safely.

I registered the accounts for them and I have the passwords. I read everything that is posted on their wall. They are never to accept or send a friend request without asking my permission. If I see a friend added and I didn't give permission, Facebook is gone. If they ever put anything inappropriate on the Internet, Facebook is gone. If anyone ever posts anything that's inappropriate that appears on their page, that friend is gone. They cannot tag photos. The privacy settings are structured. Make sure you go in and recheck your privacy settings often because they change from time to time.

If your children are on Facebook, you should be on Facebook. If they're on Twitter or if they are on any other sites, you should be there too. You need to be monitoring their activity. My children know if they dare try to unfriend me, their accounts are gone.

It's very, very important to understand what happens on the

Internet. Cyberbullying is a huge issue. Sexting is a huge issue among kids now. They take photos of themselves at fourteen because they're madly in love with someone and they think they're going to be with that person for the rest of their life. They are immature and they take a compromising photo and send it. They don't understand it's online forever. Sometimes after they break up, the other person is angry and spreads the picture around, in an attempt to embarrass or humiliate the person. At that point it may constitute distribution of child pornography.

One of the things I really recommend to parents is to stop trying to shield your children as much from things that you think are beyond their comprehension. Sexual content is everywhere these days: advertising, radio and television. We think it's inappropriate so every time it comes on we immediately turn it off. The kids see us doing that. What we're doing, without meaning to, is teaching our children that it's not okay to talk about sex. When we do that, guess what happens if something inappropriate happens to them and they need to talk about it? They think it's a taboo topic and they don't talk about it because they think they're not allowed to. We need to talk about these things with our children. Obviously not everything is age appropriate, but when these things happen inadvertently, don't overreact. Use every opportunity to generate conversation so you are the one they talk to about these things. Teach them that we need to talk about these things and explain and help to answer the questions they have.

One of the biggest pieces of advice I can give to parents is to always teach your children the correct terminology for their body parts. I've heard it all in my time, everything from hot dog, dinger-dinger, fish, muff, petunia, peter and birdie. You name it, I've heard it. The bottom line is a penis is a penis. A vagina is a vagina. When they say something like, "Old man Smith got my hot dog," we need to know what they are talking about. Did he get your hot dog or did he get your hot dog? There is no mistaking what the child is talking about if they use the correct terminology.

I understand. There's an example of that in this book in fact.

My children know my background and my oversensitivity. Given what I've seen, they've always known what's appropriate and what is not appropriate. Who's allowed to touch their body? No one. If your doctor has to for a medical reason or your mom or your dad needs to put cream on, that's one thing, but no one but you is allowed to touch your body. It's to the point where if I even broach the topic, my kids say, "I know mom, I know. Nobody's allowed to touch my body." You can't ever have too many of those conversations.

Back to the Internet, I've mentioned most of the critical points. Understand it's easy to hide behind a picture on the screen. It's easy to claim to be a fourteen-year-old highly athletic high school student when really you are a sixty-two-year-old three-hundred-pound man who preys on children.

Is there are lot of misrepresentation?
Yes. Watch where you and your children are going and what you are doing on those sites. Keep the computer in a central location where it's visible. My children don't have computers in their bedrooms because even the best kids with the best intention are curious. The computers need to be in a public spot in the house where my kids can't hide anything. They know if the screen gets minimized when I walk by, we have a problem. They have to understand, and I don't hesitate to explain to them, why these precautions have to be taken. Hiding the fact that abuse happens is not the answer. Protecting them and teaching them to protect themselves from being abused is the answer.

We need to move forward as a community, and it's not just about responding to this issue in a better way. We need to move forward to a point where we are raising a generation of children who will not have to recover from their childhood. That's the bottom line. We do that through education and knowledge. Knowledge is power.

Very good point. Is there anything else that you would like to add? We've talked about a lot and I really appreciate your time today.
I'd just like to mention the book *Rebuilding Your House of Self Respect*, by Tom Wilken. It's a good book for men who have experienced abuse to read.

Thank you so much for all the information and tips you have shared today. I enjoyed our conversation.

You're welcome, it's a big topic. Take care.

I learned that courage was not the absence of fear, but the triumph over it. The brave man is not he who does not feel afraid, but he who conquers that fear.
Nelson Mandela

Shame on You
Lorraine
Northampton, England

We live in a world where child sexual abuse is commonplace.

We live in a world where the victims of child sexual abuse are stigmatized along with the offenders.

We live in a world where most of the inhabitants prefer to ignore the ongoing abuse of its children rather than protect and safeguard them by properly dealing with the issue. We are obligated to get them the help they need to get over the ordeal with the least amount of damage to their mental health and future character.

We live in a world of willful ignorance!

If you're not part of the solution, you're part of the problem.
Shame on you!

Courage is not having the strength to go on; it is going on when you don't have the strength.
Theodore Roosevelt

It's Pretty Dismal
Ted

I really appreciate your offering to participate in the book and talking about offenders from the perspective of someone who has worked with them throughout his career. To start, can you describe the facility where you worked and a little about what you did. You have requested to be anonymous, correct?

Yes. I worked at a Provincial Psychiatric Facility that handled both the treatment and management of extremely high-risk people, primarily males. In addition, I worked in a Provincial Regional Psychiatric Facility with both males and females. It was at a lower level of risk to the public.

What is the typical kind of person in these facilities?

Primarily people suffering from some form of serious mental disorder. They would have committed the most serious of crimes – a capital case or typically murder, rape, or sexual or physical assault.

What percentage of people are typically there for some type of sexual crime?

That's hard to say, at least thirty per cent. However, even if the crime was not of a sexual nature, there was a usually a sexual component.

Can you explain that in more detail?

Well, once a person was in the facility, it became obvious that they were maladjusted or deviant in terms of their own sexuality. The people who tended to receive attention were the individuals who committed obvious sexual crimes such as rape or sexual assault. But somebody might have committed a murder, for example, and not been identified initially as potentially having deviant sexual problems. In other words this person was never charged or caught or labelled as such.

So, their sexual deviant behaviour was in the background somewhere?
Yes, for sure.

What's the difference between someone who gets sent to prison for a sex crime and someone who is sent to a psychiatric facility?
People who suffered from some sort of personality problem in the early seventies, especially if they were young and had committed a sexual crime, found themselves in facilities rather than jails because they themselves were vulnerable in the jail system. Imagine a young man having committed a sexual crime and then going to prison as an adult. At the time that was seen as extremely harsh. I think there was also some hope that treatment might be available and the person would have a positive outcome as a result of treatment and not reoffend. That was the ultimate goal, but that never happened.

And more recent than the seventies?
In the seventies and eighties they were protected from the prison experience. Today, if you commit the same sort of crime the likelihood of going to jail is pretty high.

Is there still a safety issue in prison or are these offenders kept in a separate area?
In prison they are probably kept in a more secure area for their own protection. It would be like solitary confinement management, as opposed to going into a hospital facility where they would be in a more open setting. In the hospital they wouldn't have to be managed with the same high level of personal security as in jail.

Some people would say, "Too bad for them, they'll get what they deserve."
Yes. Exactly.

Nothing is gained if that happens; don't we just end up with an angrier individual?
I don't think there's a positive outcome either way.

Would you say there's no hope in these types of cases?
I don't know of any research, at least while I was involved in the

centre, that would indicate that treatment of any kind had a positive outcome for these sorts of individuals – other than some sort of surveillance, and that's not really a treatment, that's management. They have to be monitored.

That's an interesting distinction. Are you suggesting a bracelet on the person's ankle?
I have no idea. That's one potential way of keeping track of the whereabouts of individuals, but even with that, there's a risk to the public, especially for people who would be identified by the perpetrator. I don't know how you would do that other than having somebody under an *eye hold* or a *mind hold.* Eye hold security is eye contact at all times. Mind hold security means I know where you're supposed to be from moment to moment. I don't have to have constant eye contact, but I'm always aware of where you should be, and if you're not where I expect you to be, then that level of surveillance isn't high enough for you and I need to go find you.

Does this type of security exist for these individuals when they are let out?
I'm not sure of the level of security when people actually leave a facility. If they leave the hospital and there was no legal way of tracking them, like probation or a parole hold, then they need some sort of caregiver surveillance – unless there's a specific court order related to the person. A community treatment program would be an example of that. It's mostly left up to the individuals in the community and depends on how comfortable they're feeling with the individual.

Probation and parole are a different matter completely, because the order specifies exactly how the person is going to report or be monitored. If it happens to be a sexual offender, they might have an ankle bracelet on. That tells you where they are, and where they should, be at certain times. In this situation, there's a need for someone to be monitoring him or her all the time. There are instances where known offenders have been hospitalized, released and subsequently reoffend, are jailed, parolled, and then end up working for the parole system, doing community service and reoffending as capital cases.

Now that is very frightening.
Isn't it?

I guess it can be done over time – they probably learn how to *work* the system.
Given the environment, and I don't mean to be totally negative, I really don't hold much hope that there's a cure for people who suffer from these conditions.

You talked about the seventies and eighties; are we more intelligent forty years later in dealing with these types of offenders? Can we anticipate what is going to happen?

Let's talk about Bernardo, for example. (Paul Bernardo is a serial rapist who, with his wife, abducted, tortured and murdered two teenage girls in the late eighties.) He would have been in the psychiatric system in the seventies and that's where he would have stayed because his case was high-profile. There are people like that in the psychiatric system now who committed crimes in the seventies. They're smart – kind of like him. When he committed his crime, the question would be, "Can you do anything for this guy? Was he crazy? Was he sick?" I would think, "Boy that guy is a sicko." Pardon me for using laymen's terms on this one. He's totally abnormal and sick. By the time his crimes were committed, it was pretty obvious the system couldn't do anything for him and he went to jail. There was no treatment for him; he's a psychopath. We need to keep him in jail indefinitely by labelling him a dangerous offender.

Do you think they'll ever release him?
I hope not. There's no treating that guy.

Exactly, but from time to time we hear about these violent offenders being released.
We have to consider the nature of the individual. I mean, if someone committed a nasty crime like murder and their illness was a classic psychiatric disorder like bipolar or a psychotic disorder like schizophrenia – it's almost explainable. When they get treatment for their disorders, a lot of those people wake up and realize what they've done. In many cases those people become

suicidal or attempt suicide because they realize what they did when they were ill. It's like they come alive again and figure out, "My God, I've done this," as opposed to somebody who is a psychopath. Psychopaths realize they've done it and they don't feel anything.

I understand what you're saying. There are so many scales to measure mental capacities and risk. But, one person is a psychopath and rapes women, another person is not a psychopath and rapes women – why would one get out and one not get out?

I don't have an answer for you. Is every person who commits a sexual crime a psychopath? I don't know that. Are they all a public risk or are there some who potentially would never offend again? If a sexual crime is really spectacular in that it involves something like dismemberment or post-mortem assault, then you have to wonder whether the person was responding to a level of anger and was just totally out of control.

Going back to your question, what is minor and major in all of this? Somebody who does something of a very minor nature, is that person potentially a high-risk individual for other kinds of behaviour? I don't know. Where does it lead? What do we do with someone when they have raped somebody? They get charged, they're found guilty, they go to jail, they spend six years or less in jail, they get parolled, and do they ever do it again? I don't know.

I guess a person could be drunk, commit rape, go to jail, come out and never do that again? The person isn't a psychopath. To be clear, I am not saying that is okay, just different.

Right, that's right.

That individual isn't the same as somebody who is going to be in a mental institution?

Or somebody who has been misidentified or somebody with Paul Bernardo's nature – those people are totally unusual and should never see the light of day. They need to be managed and in our society they need to be managed humanely, whatever that means, instead of sending them to the gallows.

Is it acceptable that Bernardo's wife was released, got married and has children?

I don't know much about his wife, just that she was part of it all and was also charged. Obviously, somebody felt that she wasn't a public risk and that's why she was let out. I can't think of anyone who would say Paul Bernardo himself would not be a future risk, regardless of how much treatment he has or how old he gets.

What I think the data shows now is that there's no successful treatment for this sort of problem. Any treatment that has been tried, in terms of either social therapy or psychotherapy, has only increased the risk of the individual offending. It makes the person a more effective psychopath, a better manipulator. Treatment actually makes them a higher risk. There was an extremely high recidivism rate for the psychopathic group, regardless of their crime. They reoffend in some way almost one hundred per cent of the time.

Isn't that interesting? Out of the people who you worked with who were violent sexual offenders, what percentage of them would you let out?
For that type of crime group, I wouldn't let them out. I would always have them under a level of security where they are monitored twenty-four hours a day.

Were you ever concerned for your safety when you worked there?
No.

Were there female employees?
Yes.

How were they with regards to their safety?
Okay. They were always supervised. The system has changed a lot since I was actually in the facility. It was almost an all-male caregiver facility for an all-male population. Now it's mixed and the potential for assault on anyone is still not that high. It doesn't happen often and if it does it's with very psychotic individuals, not the psychopathic groups who have committed the violent sexual crimes. Those people tend to be very compliant and get along with everybody – kind of the model citizen.

They control themselves in the institution.
I don't know of one sexual assault on anyone who has worked

there.

That suggests they are aware enough to control themselves.
It suggests that to me too. I don't know whether it is awareness or lack of opportunity. Would they force themselves on another client? I think the answer is probably yes.

Are there crimes among inmates?
I don't know if you would call it crime, it might be considered consensual. In an all-male population where the only opportunity to be sexual is with another male, there are people who are predisposed for that in the institutions and jails. You hear about more sexual assaults in jail than anywhere else. It doesn't happen much in health facilities because of the level of monitoring.

Are there signs in young people that they're likely to be or they're predisposed to be a psychopath or pedophile? Is there anything that distinguishes them?
A psychiatrist once said that by age three we can probably identify who could potentially develop a severe psychopathic personality because of a mal-nurturing connection to the mother. At a young age, this lack of connection can send a person on an extremely fast track toward destructive behaviours. That doesn't mean that people who didn't have that experience of trauma can't become very ill. There could be something else, like their genetic loading or an environmental patch that shapes their personality. You've heard the questions, "Did he abuse animals as a child?", "Was he antisocial or violent as a youth?", but these come into play after the fact rather than being used to figure out if these people are ill before they offend.

I guess there are many factors. Some people who have committed these crimes come from well-to-do families, others come from abusive environments. It's hard to pinpoint the one factor that made them cross the line. I don't have an answer to that one, Deb. I struggle with that, but in the end what do we do with extremely high-risk individuals, knowing that regardless of what we do for them to improve their situation or treat them, nothing works. Does that mean we should stop offering treatment? We offer treatment because there is nothing else, knowing full well that the treatment doesn't work.

Or it makes them worse – they learn how to manipulate the people running the system. That's particularly frightening.
Isn't that crazy?

Yes. It would be interesting to be able to backtrack and change some element of their lives, something traumatic that happened to them at a certain time, something that may have triggered a psychosis, to see if they would have taken another path.
And if you bury the trauma, if you bury the ability to respond effectively to a situation so you don't have any more feelings for something that's happening to you, you become like an observer. You're not feeling anything about it; once you reach that state you can do some pretty damaging things and not have to feel badly about them. Or maybe you never felt anything from the beginning.

I remember an experiment a long time ago in which they attempted to bring an individual back to a psychological condition that would get them to feel a normal emotional response such as remorse or guilt. In all cases it didn't work, and if any feelings of remorse were generated, they weren't authentic. If emotion was displayed it was as though there was a play going on and it was displayed for the audience. So, if the psychiatrist was expecting to see remorse, that's what he saw because that was the learned behaviour. Did the subject actually feel guilt or remorse? No, but he learned to display it.

And there is a huge difference between the two.
For sure. People who have this type of disorder have to be in total control of their environment. That's why institutions work really well for them – they're very predictable places. Their emotions are controlled well in those types of environments because they don't have to think; they can predict what's going to happen next. If you put them in a room, and then you walk into the room and remain silent for a while, they can't stand it. They have to do something in order to provide the control around what's supposed to be happening. If they know that remaining silent is a game, they can be silent forever. If you and your friends met me in a room and I said nothing, you'd all become pretty damn uncomfortable after a

while until I said something. With psychopaths, they'd quickly figure out the *game*: that I intended to remain silent and would not be uncomfortable. In a normal therapy group, they behave the way you want them to behave.

Incarcerated they perform for you; out in the world they don't?
The opportunity for them to do the negative things that got them placed in the institution is just not there. Whatever was driving them in the first place is not there because their environment has changed completely.

Though many of these people are lifers, do they have parole hearings and do victims come in and read victim statements?
Yes. Somebody who is hospitalized indefinitely has hearings at various stages. This rule might have changed over the years, but if they are found not criminally responsible they have a review; then they have another review within the first year and then subsequent reviews annually. They have legal representation to present their case to a review panel. The review panel has the authority to make recommendations to reduce the level of security or vacate the warrant.

At the hearings or panels, the victim's side is presented by the victim or by family members who present on behalf of the victim. The victim could also submit a statement or a lawyer could attend on the victim's behalf. A psychiatrist or lawyer from the offender's side could also come and present. It's more of a legal hearing to be fair to the person who has been incarcerated indefinitely.

What are your feelings on the course of action when somebody like this is released into the community? There are two options: either the public is informed and the offender's picture is released by the media, or the public isn't informed in order to protect the reformed offender.
That's a tough one because society values everyone's rights. I think the choice should be conditional upon the nature of the offence. I really don't know how to define the level of offence that should require public identification. It would have to be a clear-cut rape or a sexual assault. As far as identifying someone as a potential risk, I don't know how to do that either, but I think it would be more of a feeling that this person is likely to offend

again. I think you have to consider the conditions of the crime – for example, if the guy was drunk, if he was angry, if there were extenuating circumstances involved, or if it was totally unusual behaviour for him. Did he have an addiction problem that's been dealt with or is being dealt with? Maybe after additional treatment he's no longer a risk and will never be a risk again. If we're comfortable with that, then maybe he shouldn't be identified. But if it's an antisocial guy who did his time in jail or was one of the tough guys, and you think he's just another accident waiting to happen, then definitely identify him. But I still don't how they can assess some cases. However, for the obviously serious cases like Canadian Forces colonel Russell Williams in Trenton, we definitely want to identify him or somebody like him forever. He was at it for a long time before he got caught. This type of person is so smart and they're not going to stop.

That's a good example. He was in a high-profile position and wasn't discovered for years.
Smart, smart guy.

If this kind of guy is at a bar socializing, what are the warning signs?
You wouldn't know.

No signs? You could be living with that type of person and never know?
There's no way. It would be the biggest surprise in the world. You wouldn't have a clue. You'd be married to the kindest, most giving, loving, caring, friendly and decent person on one hand and on the other hand there's a completely different person there.

Is this why families protect these individuals, because they haven't seen any evidence?
They wouldn't know. If it's true – then what would they think of themselves? It would be awful. I just couldn't imagine what it would be like to find out you've been duped so badly when you have so much emotion invested in someone. How do you come to grips with the fact that they have a completely different abnormal and antisocial character that you've been totally unaware of? Sometimes people don't and they decide that life's not worth living.

I hear what you're saying; these people are master manipulators and for the family to have any guilt at all is really a waste of energy. You also won't know why they are the way they are?

There is no why. It's not something you did or your behaviour that caused the person to do whatever he did. You can't blame yourself from that perspective. You can blame yourself for not being able to identify, but how could you identify anything like that unless it became obvious to you and you were actually able to observe it? If you were actively involved in the person's deviant behaviour, well that's another matter.

So these people contribute to society somehow and go undetected until one day they get caught? They're productive people?

Yes. The guy we just talked about contributed and I don't think anybody had a clue.

Is a person who abuses his or her children for years a psychopath? This happens all the time. The more research I do, the more I hear about how much abuse goes undetected in families.

With abnormal sexual behaviour I don't think we're always talking about psychopaths. People who do that sort of thing often have very low self-esteem, poor impulse control and a victim mentality. They are secretive and who better to maintain the secrecy than a young family member?

I don't know if they do this knowingly, but I have encountered people over the years who have sexually assaulted their daughters and sons and I have also encountered the sons and daughters who have disclosed that they were sexually assaulted. In some cases the perpetrator has never been charged. The perpetrator has stopped the behaviour because it was specific to a family member and he or she hasn't gone beyond his or her own circle. Maybe the child gets big enough to stop it. Those people tend not to be psychopaths per se.

But is the outcome for the child any less severe because the parent isn't technically a psychopath? Shouldn't the perpetrator be in the same facility?

Or at least they should be receiving some form of counselling related to their behaviour, or treatment – is there a treatment for that?

I don't know. You tell me. Does this type of person respond to treatment?
Those people don't end up in mental institutions. We never see them.

Then how do we get a child, teenager or adult to report the abuse so those perpetrators receive treatment and stop the behaviour?
Can you get a child to tell someone else, a trusted individual like a teacher? I don't know. Teachers must report that kind of thing now. When I went to school there was never any education about that. Kids who were being sexually assaulted at home, or even at school for that matter, didn't want to say anything because they wouldn't have been believed. Today it's different. I think if a child came to school and said, "My father's sexually abusing me at home"; there would be an investigation in minutes.

Right.
That didn't happen in previous years, but it would happen now. Would a child report that? I bet the child would have feelings to keep them from reporting it, like they're "saying something bad about daddy." Although you would never say they're allowing it to happen, they don't do anything about it. They're still so young.

Exactly. What can a young child truly do?
Exactly. Unless the behavior gets identified, adults can't do anything about it either. Can anything be done about it?

I'm not thinking you're a psychologist or a prophet with the answer, but does this type of person respond to treatment? You mentioned low self-esteem and impulse control – could those be successfully rehabilitated?
Well, what if the person has an addiction problem that contributes to low impulse control? Probably the primary problem in that case is the addiction, and the secondary problem is the sexual abuse. In this type of person, stopping the addiction might result in stopping the abuse.

Right, but we hear about an uncle abusing a niece or nephew and it appears the abuse is isolated in the family circle, but then years later as people start to tell their stories we realize it was more widespread. Then there are the cases where a priest is discovered after thirty years because several altar boys come forward.

But is the priest a psychopath? Or are we just providing this person with an opportunity? And is sexual disorder the primary issue, or is there an addiction component? In terms of the Catholic Church, the tragedy is that the bishops just kept sending the priest to a new parish. They just kept giving him a new group of young boys, and I wonder who's going to hell for that? Put that one on paper.

It's a sad situation – same thing with the scouts. You involve your children in something you believe is good for them and really you've put them in a vulnerable situation.

Exactly. It could be a hockey coach also. We provide predators with a garden full of vegetables and they have their choice as parents innocently keep providing the produce. They have gone on unidentified and there's always a level of trust granted in the beginning. As a society we generally trust people in those positions. I think we trust our own ability to choose well and we make mistakes.

Well, you've talked about different labels we assign sexual offenders, but I still don't distinguish what the difference is in terms of the person who has been violated.

They're still a victim. If there was a serious assault how do they deal with that forever? I don't know.

It doesn't matter if the person is a psychopath or an uncle, there's still trauma.

Yes. I think the first step for people who have been assaulted is to acknowledge that they've been assaulted and they're not responsible. They were either too young at the time or they didn't know what was happening. They know now that it was wrong; they know what the person was doing to them was sick or maladjusted. If they have a relationship with that person, parental or family, identifying the person for what happened can help with healing. The people who identify their abusers tend to adjust better, partly because they now know the abuser isn't likely to violate them again. Then the victim doesn't necessarily attempt to disassociate mentally from the person, but just acknowledges that the person was sick and hopefully will never do it again. The victim may then feel that there's nothing to be done other than feel sorry for the abuser, rather than feeling angry, which just turns around and eats them up.

The priest who sexually assaulted altar boys, does that mean we should hate all priests or not trust all priests? Maybe. Does that mean that we're going to hate a perpetrator for the rest of our lives and just let that eat at us? Well, then you will have to deal with that resentment for the rest of your life. You really can't forget sexual abuse: it's going to sit in the back of your mind, but you don't have to think about it every day. There's got to be some point where you just forgive the people or person. Some people do forgive and they say they feel better because of it. I hope they do. It's a very tough thing to do, but it's a way to cope. Let me ask you, what are your thoughts? Could you forgive somebody for something like that, honestly?

I think it would be very difficult to forgive, especially if it was somebody in my family. Yet, if you don't resolve your feelings from the past and you see your offender at family gatherings – that must be brutal. I have a lot of different feelings about forgiveness actually. For years I thought I should forgive, yet the anger I suppressed kept me from getting a handle on forgiveness. I remember saying, "I forgive them," to myself, but I didn't. Feeling like I had to forgive made me feel like I was the bad one. Then I fought with the definition of the word itself.

Today I feel like I don't need to forgive because I would not change what happened, because if I changed it, I would not be me, nor would I know several people I treasure. I don't forgive; I accept what happened and the sexual abuse is a series of events in my past that shaped me, but is not me. Forgiving seems like a burden, a right or wrong moral or religious issue, and I don't feel a need or want to go there.

For a long time I hated the individuals who invaded my personal space. Now that's resolved and I am thankful for an alternative way of thinking. Forgiveness is different for everybody. Holding on to anger, blame and shame results in additional pain. On another note, I never felt I needed to forgive myself, whereas some people do.

Absolutely.

Anger breaks you down slowly over time and though I don't necessarily support forgiveness as it is defined, I do most definitely support conversing on a number of healing issues, one of which is forgiveness. Everybody has to figure out their way of moving forward and feeling good about themselves.

And feeling good about others as well. If we can't do that, then I think we lose sight of where we are and what we are achieving. However, I understand that if a family member has been abused by another family member and has resolved their issues, the person still has to look after themselves and avoid potential further abuse – either for themselves or other family members, like grandchildren. I would always wonder whether there's potential for the perpetrator to reoffend. When do you trust somebody who has done this?

For me I would simply never trust again. You just can't take a risk.
You make yourself safe and you make everybody else safe too. In that regard, I think you're potentially stopping future deviant behaviour.

Right. Thank you for sharing your perspective. Do you have any other final comments that you think somebody reading would be interested in?
It's pretty dismal you know. It's just like vomit. When you think about it, it's sad, its dismal – I'd hate to use the word *hopeless*. Many things have been tried: including chemical castration and castration, and even that hasn't worked. Obviously it takes away something, but the aggressive behaviour is essentially still there. I don't know of anything that works.

So would the last word in your chapter be *dismal*?
No, don't say that. Just say this guy was totally negative.

I think you're being pretty forthcoming after a career spent in an environment with these types of offenders. I appreciate your honesty – it's better to know what we're up against. In the past there have been so many cases where people have been aware of a dirty old uncle, a priest, or a scout leader who exhibited odd behaviours yet was overlooked. It has been going on too long; now finally there's a huge movement of people who are talking about sexual abuse. Many people are coming forward and reporting old and new crime. This generation is the one that can really shift our perceptions regarding sexual abuse: out with the taboos and the silence, in with awareness, support and healing. We need to share information and prevent so many people from being violated.
Yes.

I think this generation is starting to say things like, "No more, I want justice," "I don't want this to happen anymore," "What I've gone through, what I've had to deal with, I don't want the next generation to have to deal with," "I want them to get this resolved sooner than later." It does seem dismal in many ways, but it is not hopeless to prevent some offenders from offending and lead some victims to healing. Finally, you said one thing that really stood out for me: that sexual abuse is never anybody's fault except the perpetrators' and there's typically no way to detect them. It's absolutely never the victim's fault.

Yeah. That's for sure.

Thank you, I really appreciate your time and your contribution.

Well, good luck to you, Deb.

Sword and Wand

Alyssa Wright – www.katiefoundation.com

The unmade bed, the unwritten letter
The unspoken promise it would one day be better
The undying passion, the unchained melody
The uncaged canary not sure how to be free
    The war rages on between the sword and the wand
    For riches already gained
    Defend and defeat, peel away the conceit
    Until only the Truth remains
I have cleared the space, it's time to take my place
Open up my youth, stand up and be the proof

The unmentioned failures, the unavenged crimes
The uncaring marches of memory and time
The unfounded fears and the unexplored depths
The unvanquished hero on an unstarted quest
    The war carries on between the sword and the wand
    For riches already gained
    Advance and retreat, peel away the conceit
    Until only the Truth remains

Some say the devil's in the details
For some, it's the devil you know
Now that the devil can't stop me
Why am I unwilling to steal his show?
    Time to come down from the mountain
    Drown out the battle cries
    Be unabashed I'll always have the devil in my eye
I have cleared the space, it's time to take my place
Prepare to speak my truth, stand up and be the proof
Be the Proof

The war will linger on between the sword and the wand
And I'll keep the rewards I've gained
All advance, no retreat, peel away the conceit
Until only the Truth remains
Truth remains

A Time

to Heal

The Gatehouse
Arthur Lockhart
www.thegatehouse.org

Art, thank you for participating in Unlock the Door. *I'd like to begin with you sharing the story of how The Gatehouse came into being and a little bit about it. By the way, I have toured it and it is beautiful.*

Thank you. The Gatehouse has a unique beginning. I first noticed it when I was sitting with a criminology student of mine having coffee. It was boarded up and had holes in the roof. It had no wiring or plumbing. I had a vision of a place where people could meet and speak freely about sexual abuse. This house, to me, is a symbol — a living, breathing symbol of transformation. It was abandoned, neglected, abused and hurt. It was an eyesore and the city didn't know what to do with it for thirty years. They wanted to knock it down but couldn't because it's a heritage building. Nobody wanted to invest money in it because they didn't think it would be useful for anything.

I decided to try to get the house from the city and create a place for people to process their experiences with sexual abuse — a place where one human being could talk to another openly and without fear of judgment. When one person's words flow and another person listens, magic can happen. At The Gatehouse, people find ways to discover and reclaim their experiences through our central theme of storytelling. I have worked with people who have been sexually, physically and emotionally abused in every conceivable shape and form. Whether a person has been assessed with multiple personality disorders, clinical depression, schizophrenia, or a drug, alcohol, sex or violence addiction — the one thing that helps is storytelling. They may also undergo psychiatric intervention and medical intervention, which can be phenomenal and very helpful, but I think it's the storytelling that is vitally important. Oftentimes, by the end of a conversation between two people at The Gatehouse, the person who has experienced trauma feels stronger than when the conversation began. At The Gatehouse we don't say, "Why did it take you this many years to come here?" Rather, the message is, "Thanks for coming." The minute you walk through the door we're saying, "Great to meet you" and "I'm glad you're here." We don't ever treat a person as a client or a patient or anything like that.

A group of people worked together and repaired the house, which was a simple act that showed that there's a lot of beauty and strength in people who have experienced trauma. We want to let the beauty come out — that's what we try to accomplish here. We don't tell anyone what to do or think. When we let creativity, compassion and empathy come out, people grow. That's the atmosphere we have nurtured here at The Gatehouse since 1998. We have existed for fourteen years without funding from any ministry. We figure out ways to survive by ourselves. Many people have volunteered and created this house. In fact, with the exception of three people, it's run by volunteers. Everybody comes together; it's a real community initiative. Also, I want to emphasize, this house is open. People are always welcome to come in and see if we may be of service to them, and if we can't help with the services we provide, we can forward them onto someplace that can.

The facilitators are not clinicians or therapists. We're just guides who assist people in finding their own strength. We refer people to therapy and many people are referred here. What we want is a team of people going from a sense of isolation to inclusion. A man in his forties once explained that he had felt like an alien pretty much his entire life; then he said, "Now I am sitting in a room with a whole bunch of other aliens." It was just awesome, really fantastic.

Why do people wait to reveal their story and why do they come here?
We have discovered one reason people do not come forward is because other people tend to minimize what happened to them, which can be very upsetting. People may say things like, "You're a man. How could you have let that happen to you?" or "You should have done this and that." At The Gatehouse we do not *should* on people. People often say to survivors of sexual abuse, "Well, you should have told the teacher." The survivor may respond, "But it was the teacher who did this to me." At The Gatehouse, when people tell others what has happened to them, it is very likely that the person who is listening has also experienced sexual abuse.

Therefore, revealing here is really, really safe.

It's very difficult to come into The Gatehouse when you have been sexually abused or molested — I can't stress that enough. There is trauma from the abuse and the first thing that disappears is a person's voice because they don't know what to do with the trauma. It's so overwhelming that they don't know how to articulate or express what happened and how they feel. When a traumatic experience occurs we tend to tighten up and hold it in.

When a person who has experienced abuse finally starts to breathe and speak about what happened, they are expecting to hear "What! That happened to you? Oh, we're going to get that S.O.B." We've been conditioned to be enraged. That type of reaction takes the survivor's voice away again. The Gatehouse does not work that way. When people decide to talk, we say, "Okay let's hear more about it." That's why what we are doing at this house is so important — we are not judging, we are listening.

What other services do you provide?
One service we provide is to the police. In the past, in the event of childhood sexual abuse, a police officer, who was really well intentioned, would take a child to the police station. They put kids in the back of the police cruiser for their own safety. But who sits in the back of a police cruiser? Bad people do. Children may thus feel like they have done something wrong. When small children are taken to the police station and they are around police officers, their eyes are exactly at the height of zippers, belt buckles and guns. Is this supposed to feel safe for a child? And we wonder why kids are nervous when they get to the police station. The Gatehouse is very different for children and their families. We provide a comfortable home or office-like setting. The children sit upstairs and are interviewed in a gentle manner. The interview is recorded but the child can't see the recording devices. As a result, the recording reflects the state of the child at the time. In Canada, on average, it takes eighteen months for a case to go to court. It may take years after that to get a conviction. So, you end up with a fifteen or sixteen-year-old testifying about an event that happened when he or she was much younger. But when you put the video tape on in court, the child is seen as they were at the time of the abuse.

Share an example of something people learn at The Gatehouse.

They learn that they are not alone. The feeling of being alone is very common when you have experienced sexual abuse. People not only keep their stories to themselves but they feel like they are the only one who has experienced what they are going through. At The Gatehouse, they gain a new understanding. They have the opportunity to start to create their own sacred path. We ask, "What's the path you want for yourself? What are the steps you need to take on this path?"

We stress the importance of not dwelling on and staying stuck in the trauma. Horrible stuff happened to you but what are you going to do with this experience? We allow people to start to articulate their feelings and help them to get out of the state of being *stuck*. When we've been traumatized, we tend to replay the painful experiences continuously. At The Gatehouse, we have different methods of working through trauma. For example, we take the person's life story and stress that it can be rewritten and we can change the direction it's going. The person is now the author of the story and that is really exciting for them. They learn that they don't have to go around that same loop anymore. If something is not helpful then they can move to another path.

What are some signs that your child is being sexually abused?

A child may start to be withdrawn or place a lot of attention on different body parts. Also, you may see a child's behaviour change to the point of seeming more like an adult or someone in the late teens. The child may engage in sexual behaviour even though he or she is very young because he or she is basically imitating somebody's behaviour that's been imposed upon him or her. The parent should pay close attention to the child and watch for changes.

What are the implications if a teacher suspects sexual abuse?

There is protocol. If there's suspected child sexual abuse, teachers must contact the Children's Aid Society and call the police to begin the preliminary investigation. But we have to be incredibly mindful and gentle as we do this kind of thing since we don't want it to feel intimidating to the child. I think the adult who suspects abuse first needs to spend time with the child and gently and quietly see if there's anything to follow up on.

Even though the protocol is all nicely lined out in brochures, it's a very tricky area to navigate. If you suspect something, you must take action, but you have to do it gently and with patience. There's far too much attention and time and energy put into figuring out who the guilty party is instead of supporting the survivor. I think our culture, quite honestly, tends to ask questions about abuse from a retributive stance. We tend to say, "Let's get the offender." You hear that approach on the radio and see it on television and in newspapers. They use language like *moral outrage* and *moral indignation*. That language shifts the lens away from the people who have been victimized and focuses the energy on the offender. What people often don't realize is that's a second form of abuse.

In other words, the child has been traumatized already by the very specific act of abuse, but now there is another adult who is really angry and going to get the bad guy — as if that is going to make the child feel safe. That kind of behaviour makes a child feel even more insecure. Therefore, we have to move in a gentle way and sit with a child and listen to his or her story. As the story comes out and there's more and more information, then you can work with other people. It is important to continually think, "How can I be here to help and work with you now?" When you hear somebody talking, just pause, wait and listen before taking any other steps. We shouldn't get angry and, initially, we shouldn't worry about who the offender is. What needs to be focused on is the well-being of the person who has been harmed. What does he or she need to hear? We must give them space so they can talk.

There are a lot of emotions involved when the abuse hits the fan, so to speak. Old relationships may change and new ones may enter our life. When you think about it, relationships are everything. Relationships help give us our identity. You're somebody's daughter, somebody's son and somebody's teammate. The relationship is everything and I see abuse from a relational lens rather than a criminal justice perspective. I want to know what the person's tie to the other person is. How does that affect the sense of self-worth, self-esteem and identity? Not a single human being on the planet can grow in any shape or form without a relationship. It can't be done. When we look at abuse from the criminal justice perspective, we categorize people by breaking them up into victim and offender and we separate everybody and give a lot of energy to determining blame. We push the victims aside as if they have no strength.

Who typically do children turn to? Who do they want involved?
The tricky thing is that young adults often say, "All I want to do is talk. I don't want the police involved right now — maybe someday, but not right now." There's a tremendous fear of talking to anybody who might be connected to the police. It's a matter of trust. Children don't necessarily come and seek somebody out.

I find it very interesting that most people say they didn't tell anybody about the sexual abuse. Many spend their whole life silent. They bury it and experience self-torture deep inside. In my case, I don't know why I didn't tell anyone. I have no memory of consciously thinking I can't or shouldn't tell. I've asked myself several times, "Who could I have possibly told and why didn't I tell?"
Yeah, that's right. Our voice is part of our identity. It's like we were or are mute. We couldn't or can't speak. We are social beings and we don't want people to identify us as being abused. However, the abuse is part of our identity. Talking is letting the world know who we are. Now if we don't have the chance to vocalize that part of ourselves, it's going to wear on us and hold us back. We are trying to figure out who we are and within the context of abuse, we may start to second-guess ourselves, asking, "Did I deserve this?" or "Is it all my fault?" We become more and more isolated because we have no one to speak to. In some cases, the last person the survivor spoke to was the adult who was their abuser.

Overwhelmingly, abuse is enacted by a person in a position of power. The offender is usually somebody who's in a position of authority and this person abuses somebody who looks up to them because of their authority and for protection. When that happens the betrayal is absolutely massive. Try imagining what it would be like to go around thinking that you have nobody to speak to about something that affects you so profoundly. How would this impact your psychology, your psyche, your sense of self?
That's why everybody I interview mentions having a lack of trust.
Absolutely.

What happens to kids when sexual abuse is reported in their home?

These children may go to police stations, agencies and strange families. Though well intentioned, this can be confusing and disruptive. We take a kid away from the only home they know where we, as adults, determine that a horrible thing is happening to them. Home is the place a kid goes to for comfort. When that gets ripped away and they're put into another place that we deem "safe," that can make the child feel even more insecure. Then we start saying, "So tell us what happened" and we're surprised or even frustrated that the child won't tell us anything. That's where Zen Tao is needed — the ability to see and do nothing but do it really well. We need to just be with a child rather than do *for* them. To be with them so they feel safe and then, hopefully, later they will feel comfortable to speak.

When sexual abuse is suspected the police are typically called. Where else can people turn?

They can go to a hospital or a medical centre but all of these places use the approach of "We're going to fix you because you're broken." My view is the opposite. I don't think the person is broken. They have all kinds of capabilities if they are given an opportunity for them to come out. Hospitals and medical centres have their place but my focus is on the person's voice.

Please speak about the feelings of guilt people often experience when they've been abused.

Guilt is related to anger. When I feel guilty, I'm angry at myself. I think, "How could I have let this continue?" Guilt also has elements of fear. Anger and fear both feed into feelings of guilt. We always need to recognize that what we're really dealing with is someone who is frightened and feels that they have somehow let this happen. It is best to react to the sense of guilt with compassion, not accusations. Be gentle with them and start to build a relationship.

Can a minor come here to talk to someone without it being reported?

No, unfortunately we're bound by legislation. When they start to disclose we have to report it, in person or by phone. That's something I struggle with. I'd prefer if we didn't have to necessarily report. But right now we have to tell the minor that we have to report the abuse if they tell us.

That just doesn't seem logical to me. They are reaching out and get shut down.

I agree. You've hit on a really important issue. This is the difference between a culture of restorative justice and a culture of criminal justice. In the culture of restorative justice, a fourteen-year-old kid would be able to phone, walk in the door, or talk to us and tell their story without anybody having to report it — we could do what they want. In a criminal justice system, which is what dominates in Canada, the opposite occurs.

It is so incredibly frustrating because if they reach out to you and you cut them loose, they're likely not going to ask for help again anytime soon.

That's right. The system is, paradoxically, counterproductive. In this regard, I think we are doing the wrong thing. I know some people would be upset with me for saying it, but that's what I feel. I think the system, on occasion, can get in its own way. The minute we start putting obstacles in the way of talking about abuse — under the banner that we are doing this for the good of the children — we get in the way of children asking for help and finding their voice their own way. I hope we'll look at this more closely down the road. Is there a way people can tell their story without other interventions taking place automatically? Are there rules that we can have in place without, by default, having to go after the person in court? I honestly don't think putting somebody in jail automatically makes all the trouble go away for the person who has been harmed. I just don't see that.

No, it definitely does not.

But many people in our culture think, "Ah good, we got the bad guy." But that doesn't actually change much.

Well, I must say that I teach a lot of high school girls and they are very capable of expressing how they feel. I can imagine them shutting down if someone tried to force them to say something that they did not want to share.

Yeah. What they want to ask could very well help them. They may not want to report abuse but still want to talk and be helped that way. What if it happened to be their father or brother abusing them? In such a case, they know that if they report the abuse they will be pulled out of that home and then what?

Their whole life would change. They're already balancing the pros and cons of reporting the abuse. If they could just call and talk about it, somebody like you could advise them and really listen to them.

Yes, that's what we're doing right now for eighteen-year-olds.

I understand in one sense we need various interventions, but at some point we need to let young people decide what is best for them. Isn't a child who is old enough to make a call old enough to get an answer? It frightens me to think that we have to report everything and that a child who wants advice can be shut down. It makes me feel inclined to promote lying about your age when you call for support.

Yeah, that's right.

Who does The Gatehouse typically serve?

Anybody who has been sexually abused. We serve hundreds of people a year. We have people from every socio-economic background, including professionals and people who make their living on the street. In terms of children, we tend to focus on investigations dealing mostly with kids from three or four years old up to twelve or thirteen. In terms of adults, there are people who are currently working with therapists or psychiatrists, or who are in a program at a hospital and then they come to us. Also, there are people who have gone through drug or alcohol addiction counselling and then come to us. We've had people who've been self-harming or have attempted suicide.

What are the three biggest lessons you have learned since The Gatehouse opened?

First of all, to be invitational — that is, open to all who come for help. Secondly, to have a wide variety of organizations that work together. Thirdly, to focus on a person's capacity not their deficiencies. We don't look at people like they are broken or victims. I don't like the word *victim*. We focus on the person's strengths. What brought them here in the first place? Those are the three biggest things that I've learned.

Wonderful. I love that. I think that's why I appreciate so much what you're doing. It's my vision, with this book, to bring people together to share their knowledge and voices. What's your greatest hope in the area of sexual abuse?

That people feel more able to speak openly about it, to discuss and explore their feelings. In essence, that it is no longer a taboo to speak about sexual abuse and that somebody can feel free to talk about having been sexually abused as a child in the same way somebody might say, "My teeth are hurting." We've got to get to the place where it's okay to come forward and say, "I experienced this trauma."

We're on the same page on that one.

The biggest thing right now is that it's still a taboo — just like it is to have a mental illness. If somebody has a mental health problem, they don't want to disclose it either. People will walk around wearing a pink ribbon saying "I'm a survivor of cancer," but survivors of childhood sexual abuse aren't able to walk around with the same strength or bravado. Childhood sexual abuse survivor T-shirts aren't going to be in stores anytime soon.

Why not? We could make those T-shirts happen!

Yeah, that would be cool.

What would our society look like in the absence of sexual abuse?

It would be vibrant and flourishing — it would be a bright light. The darkness would start to disappear and we would hear voices and songs.

That's beautiful. That's an incredible way to put it. What does a success story look like to you?

A success story is first and foremost somebody having the courage to walk up the stairs, open the door, and come in and talk. To me, that is success. Another success story is to see people evolve — there's a young woman here who was huddled in a corner eight months ago. Today she's on our Board of Directors and is leading a committee on developing young adult programs. To me, that's an amazing story.

It must be difficult to keep this place open given how many people today are raising money for a cause.

Oh hell, yes. Here we are fourteen years later and we still don't have any core funding, though we try. Other programs in Canada started up and then died because they had core funding, then it was taken away. We're different since we don't want to be in the position where somebody who has no understanding of The Gatehouse can stop our services. I always came at it that way. Numbers matter because if they don't add up, we'll have obstacles to keeping the door open. But I feel we will find ways to build relationships and then money will come.

What message would you give to somebody who is sexually violating someone else or someone who is thinking about doing so and doesn't want to but can't get the thought out of his or her mind?

Imagine somebody walking up to you and putting a hand over your mouth and holding you down. Just imagine that person's going to do that now for the next thirty years. Imagine you can't move for thirty years because somebody is going to hold your mouth like that. That is what life is like for someone who has experienced childhood sexual abuse. Realize it's your hands harming the child, and then consider that you also have the option to extend your hand and hold the hand of a child and watch that child flourish in life. That's what I would say.

Where does someone who has been abusive or is contemplating being abusive go for help without being harmed themselves?

That's a great question. It's something we're exploring. Where do they go? Where can people go for help if they have a thought about abusing a child? There's something called the "circle of support." When offenders who get out of prison get the urge to offend again, they can call people who will meet with them and talk them through it. This is a very different approach than having people stand outside their house with placards saying "evil perpetrator" or "you're a monster." They are people who are ill — biochemically and physiologically something is unbalanced.

We have to figure out ways of not having a default response of retribution but, rather, a default response of trying to figure out how to work with these people so that they don't do it again. Throwing people in prison does not stop them from doing the offending behaviour — it doesn't help them resolve their issues. In fact, I think many people quietly smile when the offender goes to prison because they know he's likely to have the hardest time of anybody in prison. He will likely be abused and beaten up. But, if you think he won't abuse afterwards, that's absurd. That is why we have to figure out how to help all people – I am not referring to the small population of psychotic people. It might be helpful if we had people in custody and had the right programs for them while they're in there. The way we do it now just causes more pain for everybody.

Is there a correlation between being sexually abused as a child and becoming someone who abuses?
Being sexually abused as a child does not mean you are automatically going to be a sexual predator. That's just a myth. What we do know is that people who've been traumatized in a variety of ways, not just sexually, may have sexually deviant behavior, but this is not necessarily the case.

There must be some people who want to stop being abusive. Is there any place for them to go for help.
There doesn't seem to be. Even if there were, I don't know if abusers would go because the taboo surrounding childhood sexual abuse is massive. We live in a culture that sexualizes children by the time they're eleven or twelve years of age. They are used in ads to sell a variety of things like clothing and perfume. What I'm trying to say is, this is a cultural issue too. We can't just say, "Oh, it's that guy's fault only." We live in an environment where there's more and more sexualizing of children. Young kids even take suggestive pictures of themselves and put them on their cellphones. We have to look at what we are doing as a culture to make our kids vulnerable. We also put kids in places where we just assume they're going to be safe. For instance, Cub Scouts and Girl Guides of Canada. Do we educate our kids enough about healthy relationships? I don't think we do.
In order to reduce sexual abuse a lot of factors have to come together — education, support services, removing the taboo, and so on. We need to help the offenders and potential offenders. I understand the negative reaction our culture has to sexual abuse, and some abusers have to be put in prison indefinitely, but we need to consider how our reaction to the abuse

affects the child. I remember hearing if you get sexually abused you'll become an abuser. I was terrified that anyone would know I was abused because they would think I would do that to someone else. How can we expect offenders to seek help when they know, if discovered, they will have a target on their head?

Yeah. That's why I often say, "PAUSE and PAUSE," which stands for **P**aying **A**ttention **U**nveils **S**acred **E**xperiences. Let's just PAUSE. You had a horrific experience. Are you going to abuse anybody? We don't know. People who've never been sexually abused may abuse others. Let's just pause and then work to understand the trauma that's happened. It is important to not forecast that survivors will become abusers.

In probation and parole they have something called, a Risk Needs Inventory. It's a list of questions and based on your answer they assess which individuals are or are not likely to reoffend. But this assessment doesn't work all the time. No one can really forecast the future — we can have educated guesses but nothing is cast in stone and that is why we need to slow down and stop reacting the way we do.

Interesting, thank you, Art. I've written out some statements. I would like to read them to you and have you respond, okay?
Okay.

A woman: "Sexual abuse is something that should be hidden because it makes me feel dirty and like nobody would ever want me or love me."
If we believe that, we're never going to get any sense of resolve. When you use the word *should* you end up *shoulding* all over yourself. It holds you down like a heavy weight.

A child: "He told me not to tell my parents because it's our secret and he would be mad and punish me if I told."
It's totally understandable if you felt terrified when he said that to you. You're not wrong to have felt bad.

A man: "If I don't talk about my sexual abuse, I'll forget it — it will simply go away."
Talking is the first step toward the abuse truly going away. Not talking about it simply hides it. It's like putting something in the back of the drawer and you assume it's gone away but, guess what,

five years later you'll open the drawer, move a shirt and there it is.

A father: "I am supposed to take care of children. How can I live with myself knowing that a friend of mine sexually assaulted my daughter?"
Your insight is really fantastic. You should convey the feeling of love, caring and concern that you feel for her, to her right now.

A young girl: "If I tell my teacher about what happens at home, I'll be taken out of my home, put in a foster care program, and then I'll get assaulted there as well. I mean it could be worse there than here."
That could possibly happen. Unfortunately, it has happened. But your strength to come forward is what we want to focus on. We don't know what is going to happen but I want you to know that I'll be with you as we go through this process. You won't be going through this alone.

A wife: "I didn't realize that my husband was a pedophile. This has torn my family apart and I simply do not know what to do."
First, the wisest people I have ever known are the first ones who say, "I don't know what to do." That's a great starting point because it's going to lead you to meet people who can work with you and help you to figure out what to do.

A young girl: "I feel alone and don't know where to start or what to do. I'm getting abused at home."
Tell somebody that you feel alone – that's the first thing you want to do. Find one friend, one acquaintance, one human being who's going to listen to you, and tell them, "I feel alone" and let the conversation build from there.

A lady in her fifties who was abused as a child: 'What are the stages of recovery? I feel like I'm never going to get over this. I've gone through therapy and I've tried forgetting with alcohol. I feel like I might as well commit suicide since the pain never goes away."
What happened in the past will never go away but you are in the position right now to be the author of what happens next — that's the most powerful and beautiful thing you can have on this planet. Also, the fact that you said everything you just said is a demonstration of strength. Together we can build on that strength.

A girl at high school: "I was abused when I was really young by an uncle and I never told anybody. It's gross. I can't talk about it."

Well it's good that you're thinking about it again. You're not alone. It's important to actually talk about it. You have a wonderful opportunity in your life to let go of that *grossness* and the way you do that is by talking to somebody.

A young boy in high school: "My girlfriend revealed to me that her father is molesting her but made me swear that I won't tell anybody. How can kids help each other?"

Just by what you're doing right now — talking about it with her and bringing one other person into the mix to listen to you. We're not going to try to fix you — we're going to listen to you.

A nineteen-year-old male: "I was cornered and raped by my coach. I can't tell anybody. I never dreamed this could ever happen to me."

It has happened to you and it's happened to other people too. It's your voice that's going to help you and anybody else who's been in that same corner.

A mother and father: "We thought our four-year-old daughter was way too young to ever have had to deal with sexual abuse. A neighbour who was babysitting abused her and she had the courage to talk about it. Where do we go? There's no proof so it's his word against ours. Should we even tell anybody? Should we report this or what should we do?"

You've got an amazingly strong daughter who had the strength to talk with you and tell you the story. The next thing you want to do is to sit with the person who did this and the child, and have a conversation with them and see what they have to say about it. You begin there and then, based on what that conversation reveals, you may want to bring some other people into it.

Parents: "The guy across the street is always watching the children play. He sits on his porch and it's like he's reading but we know he's watching the kids. What if anything can we do?"

He may enjoy watching kids. He may be just enjoying the kids playing and we can't start imposing or projecting our fears onto other people. It may be one of the most innocent activities on the planet.

Thank you, that was informative. I have a few more questions. How should we go about teaching sexual awareness?

It begins as a conversation. Young children need a chance to hear from people who share their thoughts about what healthy sexual relationships look like. Our school systems tend to look at sexuality as a problem. I propose that in elementary school we talk with children about healthy relationships. What do they look like? Focus on healthy relationships and let the conversation spiral out from there instead of having somebody come in and talk about bad touch and secrets and so on.

That actually makes a lot of sense.

Good. It's always better for us to slow down and start from a position of strength. It's like martial arts. In my training we start in a position of *groundedness*. We need to consider how to stay grounded when dealing with sexual abuse.

I get it; most people are not grounded. Rather, they are ignited and react very quickly.

Yes, I'm glad what I said makes sense to you. It's like what you're saying with this book. What would be cool is to connect and have conversations that are not shrouded in mystery and darkness but, rather, conversations about how to live a healthy life. What does it look like to live a vibrant life? It would be really cool if we focused more on that. The reality is that our kids are rushed through the conveyer belt of education and rushed to get out and get a job and that's it. I like the idea of just slowing the whole damn thing down and enjoying the presence of each other. Celebrating relationships in the moment – that's where I would like to go so that we all just sit down and talk. That would be really healthy in my opinion.

That would require more family time and less television.

Absolutely, that's right. I was a probation officer for ten years. I wish I had a buck for every time a kid told me that his or her parents never talked to them. They grow up fast and along the way they need to gather around the family table and talk to their parents. Culturally, we need to slow the hell down. Slow it all down. What's the rush? We took away grade thirteen from kids so now I have kids in my class who say they want to be a cop at seventeen years old. I don't think so.

I have students telling me stories about siblings in grade six who are formally dating. What kind of pressures are we putting on kids at that age? What does it mean to date in grade six? What the hell is that? What are we doing to our kids? Just go on the Internet and pay attention to the language and demeanour. What does it mean to be a child today? Social anxiety disorder is growing among students. The number one issue now is mental health. We are dealing with more and more conflicts in schools. One of the reasons I've been called in to schools is because some of the kids have attempted suicide. This particular school is one of the richest schools in the country but kids are trying to kill themselves because they're not fitting in.

That's sad. Okay, we're almost out of time. Is there anything else that you would like to add?

I guess I would say thank you for writing this book. It's fantastic. I'd like to see the transcript from our conversation; that would be exciting. I think simply getting the word out is really, really vital.

Thank you.

When people hurt you over and over, think of them as sand paper. They may scratch and hurt you a bit, but in the end, you end up polished and they end up useless.
Chris Colfer

Harmony Integration Therapy
Satyen Raja
Founder and Master Facilitator of WarriorSage

Satyen, thanks for creating time in your busy schedule to talk with me today. I'm looking forward to learning more about your work. It's hard to believe that you are one of my last interviews for *Unlock the Door*. Please tell the readers about yourself as it relates to the topic of this book.

I'm the founder of WarriorSage training. WarriorSage is a personal development organization that leads events internationally. I have thirty years of experience helping people empower their lives physically, emotionally and spiritually. I'm trained and certified in many modalities of psychotherapy and the development of human potential.

Can you mention a couple of the methodologies that have influenced you?

Traditional psychotherapy, neuro-linguistic programming, forms of Shiatsu therapy, acupuncture, Harmony Integration Therapy – the list goes on and on.

Which is the one that you use to help people deal with trauma?

Harmony Integration Therapy. I'm a master coach.

How does it work?

First of all, it can be done in person, over Skype or on the phone.

The coach asks questions to determine what the major problems are that the individual is facing. All traumas are connected to a specific time in our life. An intense negative experience happened to you and you weren't able to take it all in. You weren't able to confront the intensity because you were young or the shock of it was overwhelming on your emotions, psychology and nervous system. Parts of your brain, body and cells got shocked and ended up traumatized in four areas.

The first area that is traumatized is the *pictures* that we see in our mind. Sometimes we relive these negative images and experiences in our mind visually over and over again. It can happen in our dreams or happen every day while we're awake. The negativity gets stuck in our internal pictures.

The second area is our *thoughts*. Our mind goes into shock, and the intense negative experience gets stuck. Sometimes we repeat the same type of thought or we create a generalized idea. For example, someone thinks, "All men are bad" or "All women are angry" or "All people who look like this are bad." We have these thoughts in our mind and they circulate over and over again. It's like we can't do anything about them and they haunt us.

Another place where the trauma affects us is our *emotions and feelings*. In the initial moment of shock and trauma, or repeated shock and trauma, our nervous system can't handle the intensity of the negative experience so it freezes. We get stuck in negative feelings: depression, anger, resentment, hopelessness, despair, and lack of self-worth or self-esteem. Emotions can be really shocked by these experiences.

The last place we have shock and trauma is in our *body sensations*. After trauma we can start to hold our body differently. We don't open up – we don't hold ourselves up with good posture and confidence because, although we don't know it, our body is trying to protect itself from having that negative experience again. We develop tension in our chest and breath, have digestive problems, aches and pains, poor posture and lack of energy. All of these things can become worse over time because the shock has not been cured or healed.

Those are the four areas where shock and trauma take root: our pictures, our thoughts, our feelings and emotions, and our body sensations. Unfortunately, this diverts us from living a full, positive and capable life – one full of self-esteem and possibility. The trauma sits in some part or parts of our pictures, thoughts, feelings, and body sensations and keeps us stuck and suspended in the past.

Without going into the whole course right now, how do you extract the trauma from the cells?

In Harmony Integration Therapy, we recognize that all of the problems you are having in your life are a result of a negative charge in the four areas I just mentioned. Through a simple process we guide clients through a very safe and, in a way, painless process. We take them back to the heart of the images, thoughts, feelings, and the body sensations they originally experienced. We get to the root of the trauma and help clients absorb it and move them back into flow.

Through Harmony Integration they become unstuck. It's like they are an ice cube that is frozen. In Harmony Integration Therapy we gently place warmth on the area that is frozen and then all of a sudden what was cold, tight and stiff with shock and trauma starts to become warm and breathes, expands and gains a fresh life. The negativity dissolves. What you're left with is all the energy that was trapped in the images, thoughts, feelings and body sensations. All of that energy is released and now floods into the present moment and you feel the sense of deep calm, tranquillity, and serenity and you also have a sense of strength and clarity. You realize your own inner power and wisdom is back and that it was already within you. It was just trapped.

Is the outcome from the session permanent?
Absolutely permanent.

With sexual abuse, the trauma may not lay in one incident that happened at one time. It could be over a period of ten years and involve more than one offender. Does a client have to sort through each event or person? How do you get rid of all the traumatic experiences?
You don't have to do a process for each traumatic experience. The Harmony Integration Practitioner finds the events that are filled with the most amount of negative charge. Sometimes we can't find it; sometimes it's just a vague feeling or clients can't remember parts of it because they were young at that time and things have gone fuzzy. Or they kept the memory stuffed way down because they didn't want to remember it. It doesn't matter what state the person is in; just knowing that something happened is enough.

When we dissolve some of the major incidents from the past, the positive energy flows and brings people into present time. It depends on the individual, but for most people with a chronic history of abuse, it takes a few sessions. The Harmony Integration Practitioner supports them through this process and also arms them with what they can do on their own to deal with things related to their trauma when feelings come up. So, rather than being a victim, you're now the one in power and you know what to do for yourself.

So, you wouldn't have to dissolve each individual experience?
No, not at all.

Who is your target audience and where do people find you?
Well, our audience is anyone who wishes to overcome past negative experiences and move forward in their life in a positive and empowered way with a sense of possibility. Also, it's very empowering to not only overcome this trauma, but to help guide others to overcome it.

Are you saying you train people to become practitioners in Harmony Integration Therapy?
Exactly.

Good to know. How do they do that?
Contact my office at WarriorSage and ask about the training.

What's the main thing you've learned about trauma?
The main thing I've learned about trauma is that rather than allowing the past negative experiences and perpetrators to have a hold on you in the present time, the trauma can actually catapult you to take your life further forward. You can make something good out of the trauma rather than getting stuck in it. The trauma does not have to trap you; you can use it to move forward.

Satyen, can you give an example? That's one of the things that's so hard to convince somebody of, someone who's been suffering replaying their story and is only able to see the negative. They want to heal, but they almost see healing as forgiving, not keeping the memory. They want to get rid of the memory.
Exactly. So, what's powerful about this is, it's not focused on forgiving the perpetrator. The focus of Harmony Integration Therapy is coming to peace and harmony within you. You may then be more empowered to take the perpetrator to justice; you may have more energy to support the cause of people being safe and treated well: in harmony and with integrity. I'll give you an

example.

One of my clients had been habitually molested from the time she was a young girl until she was about twelve. She was in a state of shock, looking emotionally stunned most of the time. I could relate to her; she could speak but it was always short and dry. No anger, no happiness – she was emotionless. She was very attractive but didn't do well in relationships. She had a long history of relationships that didn't go past a few dates. She didn't know how to be with someone without shutting down and becoming abrasive and pushing them away.

Part of her wanted a partner and someone to have a positive long-term relationship with, but she was never able to make it happen. As soon as intimacy came close, her body shut down, her images came back, her thoughts of "not me, I'm ugly" and "I don't deserve this" started ringing through her head. On an emotional level, she started having the feelings of deadness and not feeling sexy or attractive or that someone could find her attractive. At the same time on a body language level she had a constant rigidity that conveyed *keep away*.

She came into one of our sessions and we worked together for about an hour and a half. It was a very thorough session. I guided her through this very profound process in which she started thawing her experiences. She went through the whole process, and at the end, it was as if colour had returned to her face. She was breathing. She was experiencing herself as a feminine woman for the first time in years. She started honouring her femininity. Her trauma had caused her to associate femininity with being very weak, which makes sense given what happened to her.

Femininity can be strong. She has now become a world class dancer, dance instructor and also a martial artist. She's happily married to an amazing man who loves her deeply, honours her, values her, and treats her like a goddess. That's an example of a success story that's relatable.

Thanks for sharing that story. Just one more question – it has two parts. You talked about peace and you talked about harmony: what is peace and what is harmony?
Peace, harmony and tranquillity. They're all in the same vein. Peace is the sense of feeling deeply relaxed and deeply calm and

available to what life has to offer you. It's not pushing out life. Tranquillity and peace is a sense of calmness and a sense of inviting all the good things in life to come to you without feeling that you need to defend yourself from a big, bad, ugly world.

I'm glad I decided to interview you for this book after our conversation last week. Harmony Integration Therapy sounds valuable and cutting edge. You've made many good points and it certainly makes a lot of sense.
Yes.

So many of us, me included, don't realize we hold trauma in our body. For many years, I felt pretty strong, yet now with much more awareness of how sexual abuse affects people, I realize how the trauma is suppressed and stored in our bodies. Because of my experience, I believe body awareness information and exploration is important to people seeking alternatives to traditional therapy. Thank you for sharing this methodology. I think it could potentially make a big difference to many people.
Yes.
And that's how you connect with people – when they can relate to what you're talking about.
Exactly.

I know you are pressed for time; is there anything you want to add?
The best way to have justice over the negative things that have happened in your life is to integrate them. When you do, your words and actions will have so much more power. You will then be living from a place that opens you up to the good things in your future rather than having a ball and chain on your ankle from the past.

Author's note

Having spent countless hours studying martial arts, and realizing the mind-body-healing connection, I feel a responsibility to share a physical form of healing. Brad is now an owner where I trained for many years.

Shifting Paradigms about the Martial Arts

Brad Hutchinson

Beyond Kung Fu Inc.

Many people mistake martial arts primarily as fighting or self defense. Peering through the lens of the mainstream media, popular movies, and The Ultimate Fighting Championship it does look like that. But let's look to the discipline of Shaolin kung fu to shift our perspective and grasp the true purpose of the training.

Kung fu is a sharpening tool. It is the act of forever refining, honing, and becoming more competent in the art. At first you have to learn the basics, like in language you learn the alphabet before putting words and sentences together. In music you learn the notes and scales before being able to play. But this mental and physical learning is a medium that provides a channel to free your inherent creative spirit. For the writer it's finding the word or turn-of-phrase that is worth a thousand pictures; the silence between the notes brings music to life; for the martial artist it is efficient movements for greater dynamic physical power. In kung fu less is always more.

What many martial artists misunderstand is that the movements are the vehicle, not an end. Nobody mistakes the piano as the music or the pen as the story. When a martial artist sharpens his skills solely to become a better fighter he has missed the mark. When fear and ego are the driving force of the lessons physical skill grows but this channel of intuitive knowledge becomes clogged. As a result conflict, anger, resentment, and mistrust tend to grow.

The martial arts are not about acquiring anything. This is the shift. The practice is about letting go of the negative so the positive surfaces, naturally. There is creative wisdom in you waiting to materialize. It does not push, shout, or fight. It speaks softly so your mind and emotions must be tranquil and calm to hear.

Instead of contracting your heart in the face of conflict you must relax, open, expand. The healing creative spirit within you surfaces through a relaxed, peaceful heart. Negative emotions that are constricting it must be removed. Kung fu exercises balance energetic streams of Qi that flow inside and outside you and neutralize non-supporting emotions. Harmony is restored to the mind and body and a channel for spirit to surface naturally opens.

From childhood trauma all the way to yesterday's conflict with a spouse, co-worker, even traffic we all have become masters at burying minor and major tensions in our subconscious. Our bodies have become storehouses of hidden dark energy that tends to direct and control our life. Stress mounts, the body tightens, and disease manifests. Until recently there weren't many options for help for the plethora of stress related illnesses brought on by past traumas and further amplified by our hectic life-styles; save for the pharmaceutical approach. The martial arts have been around a long time but most of the history has been veiled in secrecy and mysticism.

Thankfully, over the past two decades a great deal of knowledge is surfacing from all over the world, stemming from Eastern wisdom of wholeness and connection. You are meeting some of those people in this book. Let their teachings and stories inspire and reawaken your spirit.

Find the vehicle right for you to help release the different shades of fear, anger, guilt and unresolved pain that may be guiding and controlling your behaviour. Peace, compassion, and joy are natural states of being alive. Breathe deeply, put attention on your heart, and you will intuit that this energy is ready to serve you. Now set a course to its realization.

Brad is the author of:
On the Fringes (Novel, 2002)
The Engaged Mind (Personal Development, 2004)
The Eye of the Storm (Chapter Book, 2007)

Emotional Freedom Technique
David Rourke
www.eftrecovery.com

Hi David, thanks for joining me today. Maybe you can start by saying a little about yourself and how you got involved in Emotional Freedom Techniques (EFT).

I was working as an addiction counsellor at the New Port Centre, Port Colborne, and I realized relapse was very high. Most people were suffering from trauma of some sort and using alcohol and drugs as a solution to their problems. They got clean and sober in a safe environment. But when they returned to their world, the unresolved traumas and other anxiety-provokers returned, and they didn't have the strategies to cope with them.

I started learning about trauma, and in the process became a trauma specialist. One of the alternative courses I took was energy psychology and it was about EFT (Emotional Freedom Techniques). I was blown away. I thought, "This is it," something simple that everybody can use.

I started learning more and I applied it in my practice, got scared of it, put it on the shelf for six months and went back to the methods I knew were going to make people cry. Then I returned again and studied once again. After about six years of using EFT, I was offered a Master's program. I applied and was accepted. I spent the next couple of years studying with Gary Craig, the founder of EFT, and I became an EFT Master. Of twenty-nine Masters on the planet, I am one.

That's pretty incredible. Congratulations.

Yeah, I'm kind of proud of that.

Why were you afraid of EFT?

The power of it, I imagine. It's a gentle technique. You can take people in incredible distress and bring the stress down in a matter of seconds or minutes. A person can touch specific spots on their upper body and reduce a lot of the trauma they are experiencing.

I've also been trained in Eye Movement Desensitization Reprocessing (EMDR) and Traumatic Incident Reduction (TIR), where you know people are going to cry when they have their discharge. When I witnessed that reaction in EFT, it scared me. I said, "Hey, wait a second, I thought this was supposed to be gentle." The fact is, I just didn't have enough experience at the time. I started learning more and learning the techniques and using it effectively, and it has made all the difference in the world. Now, it's the only technique I use.

When people aren't familiar with something they have a tendency to be afraid.
I'm kind of a skeptic, but I'm not a scaredy cat.

Can EFT be used for any trauma?
Yes. Any type of negative life experience.

Please describe what EFT is.
People are energy, just a bunch of vibrating molecules, as Einstein demonstrated back in the nineteen twenties. Throughout history in different cultures, there have been names for a life force that seems to go through us. In ancient China, they called it Chi, which means life force. The discovery statement for EFT is, "The cause of all negative emotions is the disruption in our energy system, and that is our life force, our Chi."

Trauma happens when an experience overwhelms us. It doesn't have to be something as violent as a rape or sexual abuse. It could be a three-year-old child who's drawing a Picasso on the kitchen wall and mom comes in. The child is expecting praise for his or her creativity, but mom slams the hamper down on the ground and yells and screams and sends the child to his or her room.

When your system gets overwhelmed, the energy system gets blocked and doesn't flow. We're supposed to flow, like a tap. If you put barriers in the way of the flow, it causes a backup. That, in turn, causes flooding and other problems. It seems to be the same with our energy system.

When we have an event we judge as negative, it overwhelms our senses, it overwhelms our energy force and it causes a disruption. It's much like taking a screwdriver and waving it around the back of an old style TV. It creates a disruption and you can't see the picture clearly. When I move the screwdriver away from the TV, the picture brightens up. The screwdriver interference is like a negative experience. Each time I wave the screwdriver around the TV, the picture is distorted. Likewise, when a negative event happens to us, our energy system gets distorted and creates negative emotions and our reactions to those emotions. We're using those emotions to try and make sense of our world. We're trying to heal, but we're getting a distorted perception of what's going on and that causes us, in a sense, to have blinders. We can't see the big picture and we don't have a lot of clarity.

Is it similar to acupuncture?
Acupuncture doesn't get specifically at emotions. In EFT, you stimulate the acupressure points while thinking about the event, and the trauma starts fading away. It opens up like a field of vision where you get a better perspective on what's going on. You get more opportunity for a different perception.

Tell the readers what you're physically doing to them or they're doing to themselves?
You stimulate acupressure points around the face and the upper part of the body. These points are close to the surface of your skin. You tap, with the first two fingers of your left or right hand. Basically, you are stimulating the major energy vessels.

Here comes the statement from the skeptic: "So, you're telling me that I poke my face and I'm going to get over my traumatic experience?"
I would say it's a good opportunity for you to get over the trauma, yes. If you're thinking about a specific part of the trauma while you're stimulating these acupressure points on your face, your anxiety will be reduced. What you have to keep in mind is that we all have these barometers within us. You cannot have an emotion of any type without some sort of physiological response, whether it's butterflies in the stomach, tightness in the chest, the sweats or a pain in your knee.

When you think of something that bothers you or creates stress for you, there's going to be a physiological response. All you have to do is monitor that response, because as you stimulate these acupressure points the physiological response starts to dissipate. It doesn't take away your memories, but it helps you find another perspective. You can't change what happened – it happened – but EFT does help you come to a better place of acceptance.

Frank Gerbode developed Traumatic Incident Reduction. He wrote a wonderful article on time and intention. He says that when something happens to us, we have a plan and we're moving in a particular direction. For example, I'm driving to the store and suddenly I get T-boned. In my mind, I'm still trying to get to the store, and just like an abuse survivor, trying to make sense of what happened. The survivors are struggling trying to heal. We have to consciously either complete the intention or consciously discontinue it. Most of this stuff is unconscious; we don't even realize we're acting out. When we're in distress, we have a set way of dealing with conflict, and when our senses become overwhelmed emotionally, we get stuck in that moment.

We're looking for some way to cope. If a behaviour or emotion helped us survive at the time of the trauma, that's something we're going to continue to use until we let go of that intention. As an adult you need to realize it was a long time ago. You don't need to have the child still be the authority in your life.

How does EFT actually work?
This is how the process works, step by step. First, you think about something that creates distress for you and you rate it on a scale of zero to ten. Not one to ten, because that means there's always going to be a piece of the problem there. Zero means it's a non-issue. Ten is almost a state of being overwhelmed – I'm ready to have a panic attack. Zero means there is no *charge*. No physiological response.

So you rate it, then you use what's called a setup statement which addresses the issue and adds an affirmation to it. For example, you say, "Even though I'm afraid of heights, I'm still a good person." At the same time, you're tapping the points to get your energy flowing in the right direction. You say the affirmations three times while tapping on the side of your hand (the fleshy part between your baby finger and your wrist.

Next we move into the sequence of tapping points. You need to have a *reminder phrase* to keep you focused. Let's stay with the fear of heights. I start tapping, directly on the top of my head. There's a meridian spot called *the meeting place of 100 meridians*, which is a powerful spot. It's going to pulse electricity all through your body. You tap on the top of your head and repeat the reminder statement, "Even though I'm afraid of heights...," because it keeps you focused.

The next spot is between your eyebrow and the bridge of your nose. You tap there and repeat your reminder statement. Then move to the side of the eye on the orbital bone, right in the corner of the eye. Stimulate that spot, seven to ten times, again saying your reminder statement.

Next, move directly underneath your eye. If you're looking straight ahead, it will be right below your pupil, again on the orbital bone. Tap there and repeat your fear-of-heights statement. Then you tap underneath your nose with the statement, then between your chin and your lower lip. The next place is the collarbone spot, on either side of your sternum, where the collarbones join. That's where the meridian end points are. The last spot is on the side of the body, about four inches down from your armpit. For a woman, it would be along the bra band.

That's a short-cut version for EFT, and you can do a lot of healing, just by tapping those places.

Where does somebody learn this technique, and how often do you have to repeat it for it to be effective?
You can learn EFT on YouTube. There are hundreds and hundreds of videos there; however, they don't guarantee quality. There are a lot of places where you can learn from a knowledgeable person and they can be found on the Internet. Every other week I'm instructing a training session somewhere. I teach at a lot of institutions and companies.

If you get all the aspects of the issue, you'll probably never have to tap on it again. An hour session with somebody who's a trained facilitator, somebody who knows what they're doing, is probably like having eight months of psychotherapy. A lot gets covered in one session. Psychotherapy and EFT are probably the best things that somebody could do to treat trauma.

Psychotherapy is about the *whys*. You're looking for insights. When your energy system is blocked, you can't get to the insights.

When you free your energy, it all just comes and it lands on you. It's incredible. I have a friend who is a psychotherapist. I am sure he doesn't mind me telling this story. He was my idol because of his leadership skills and his counselling abilities. I really admired the man. He came to my workshop and said, "I need you to work on me."

He told me he'd been in psychotherapy for twelve years trying to get over family issues and sexuality issues, as well as body image issues. He had been treated for all those years, yet, while he was telling me his history, he was crying. There was still a lot of emotional overwhelm. In an hour and a half we had everything cleared. It was gone completely.

If you've been in therapy for twelve years you'd better go find another therapist, no?
No. It's not so much the therapist. What I discovered was that as long as your energy system is disrupted, you can't get clarity. He had done the work but couldn't apply it because his energy system was so obstructed. He couldn't make all the connections. Once we did that, away he went.

How do you get through all the issues if somebody has eight years of incest, for example?
Each event or specific traumas are isolated incidents. With repetitive traumas, there's a sense of generalization. I think the psyche gets damaged more than anything. You can put everything in a bundle because generally there's going to be a lot of anger and shame. Those are the things you're going to want to work on. The process could take a little time. It's much like peeling an onion.

You could work on emotions, an event or a person or group?
You work on the event or you work on the emotions around it. There are different processes and everybody is different.

You alter the focus based on your conversation?
Yes. Whatever is coming up and creating chaos in the person's life or whatever is creating any distress. With repetitive traumas you get into complex traumas and there are layers that need to be peeled – that takes time. I've had some clients over a year because

they're so damaged because of their experiences. EFT is quite powerful, but it's still going to take some time.

So recovery depends on the severity of the trauma? If somebody's afraid of snakes you might be able to help them in a couple sessions.

Maybe in five minutes. When the fear of snakes or whatever goes away, we start unravelling all kinds of things, because the snake could be representing something else. Getting to that core is the trick. Stimulating the acupressure points, for whatever reason, helps pull in more information from your unconscious into the threshold between the unconscious and the conscious mind. This threshold can only handle one piece of information at a time; then it goes to the conscious mind for processing.

So in a complex trauma, the outcome can be related to the expertise of the Master or the therapist?

I'd hate to say something like that because the way I look at it, I'm just facilitating somebody's process. Maybe somebody else would have a different take on that, but I'm not the healer; they're healing themselves.

But isn't healing related, at least partly, to the questions?

I imagine it is. I'm trying to be humble here Deb.

Right, I'm simply thinking if the trauma is severe, go to the master.

Yes, absolutely.

As much as I'd like to say, go to YouTube and tap away on yourself, I'm wondering how effective that's going to be?

Yes, when I train my students, I show them a slide that says, "Don't go where you don't belong." But you see the interesting thing is, using EFT may bring up a repressed memory spontaneously. It may also bring up other issues, and people start to over-react, again just intense emotions. I think it's something they have been wanting to do for a long, long time. I have a hard time labelling it *over-reaction*, when it's a release of energy. There's a man named Peter Levine who's worth taking a look at. I thought I knew a lot about trauma until I went to one of his workshops. It turned my life upside down: my whole perspective on trauma changed. He was showing us a video clip of a polar bear running on the ice trying to get away from a helicopter that was chasing it.

As the bear was running, it was shot with the tranquilizer gun. It ran another 100 yards, then started to stumble, fell down and couldn't move. The plane landed, the people tagged the bear and the plane took off again. They circled the bear until it was coherent and moving about. The interesting thing is, the bear was lying on its side, and as soon as it started to come out of sedative, its front paws started going back and forth. It was like it was still trying to run. Then, all of a sudden, it looked as if it was having an epileptic fit. The whole bear was shaking like crazy, and then took a deep breath and relaxed. About a minute later, it wobbled to its feet and ambled off. When I saw that shaking, I said, "Oh my God, how cruel is this? Why are they doing things like that?" Levine pointed out that the most important part of what the bear was doing was shaking off the energy. You notice when it first came to, its intention was to keep running. What it did was, it discontinued its intention. It didn't need to run anymore. It shook off the intention and went from sympathetic nervous system into parasympathetic nervous system, deep relaxed breathing, and got up and ambled off.

Levine said, "All animals discharge, except for animals in captivity." Domestic pets get diabetes and all kinds of illnesses that they don't get in the wild. In captivity they don't get an opportunity to discharge. I think it's their masters that prevent that. Human beings are animals. We may think we live in a democratic society and we're free to do what we choose, but the thing is, we're culturally captive.

We get unhelpful messages such as *big boys don't cry* and *shut up or I'll give you something to cry about*. An eight-year-old who just lost her brother is told, "Okay Natalie, you need to be strong for mom and dad, okay? You need to take care of them." All Natalie wants to do is cry. She wants to discharge and she's been hampered or stopped. She can't complete her intention.

Most people would not think of things that way. That's pretty powerful and it makes a lot of sense. Could you share a case study of someone who used EFT specifically for sexual abuse recovery?

Yes. I think this one is on my website. A woman was diagnosed with multiple personality disorder and came to me, just after getting out of alcohol and drug treatment. A friend gave up her appointment so this lady could see me. I interviewed her to see if there was anything I could do. She was pretty remarkable. She had experienced childhood sexual abuse from her father. It had gone on for years and years – she experienced body betrayal and the whole nine yards. We worked together for about a year and now she's completely free. One of those personalities is gone. We have the right person in charge and there seems to be a complete integration. It has been over five years since her treatment.

Do people relapse?
The only time that happens is if you don't get all the aspects. Let's use an analogy of a tabletop and talk about a specific trauma. The tabletop is the core. It was a specific incident. A problem is not just a problem. If you look at it, a problem is a bunch of legs that each represent a piece of the table. With sexual abuse, you're going to have a leg of shame, a leg of anger, a leg of betrayal and a leg of more betrayal from another family member, "How come mom didn't rescue me?" You have all these different aspects, or legs.

In EFT, you pick one of those aspects and start working on it. That's where the tabletop would be the problem and the table legs are all the evidence supporting the problem. So, "Uncle Tom molested me" is the top of the table and "Mom didn't support me, Mom didn't even want to hear about it" and "Dad was drunk all the time so he never stood up for me," each of these are one leg supporting "Uncle Tom molested me."

When you start chopping off some of those table legs, a lot of times the table collapses on its own and you're free and clear. Sometimes, if you miss one of those aspects, the anxiety comes back. However, when you tap on it, it will go away. It worked once; it's going to work again and you'll probably never have another problem with the situation.

As triggers come up over time, do you work on that specific trigger?
Yes.

Is EFT always done one on one, or can it be used with a group?

I do group work. Absolutely. It's called *borrowing benefits*, which is really quite fascinating. I teach groups with ten people and they're a lot cheaper for everyone. With a group session, it's a third of the cost and you get more time. I have people write down a couple of issues they want to clear – I want them to feel it. I want them to get Subjective Unit of Distress or Discomfort: SUDS. I want them to imagine being there, feeling what it feels like, and write down a number between zero and ten. I bring someone up to the front and start tapping on their issue with everyone tapping along and listening to us. Then everyone checks into their issue. Participants find that most of the anxiety pertaining to their issue is significantly reduced. They start to get a better perspective, even though they were focused on us, not on themselves.

That sounds pretty interesting.
It's pretty spiritual.

You said there are only twenty-nine EFT Masters. The training must be difficult.
It was the most "brutiful" experience I've had in my life. We are called Founding Masters. We had to have at least five years using EFT professionally. We had to go to California regularly and study with the founder. He would fire all kinds of questions and ideas at us. We had to put everything together and see what worked and what didn't. The final exam was only fifteen questions, but the answers were all very lengthy.

Sorry for your pain, but it makes sense to me because you're working with people's lives.
You know, my idea of life is that every one of us is wounded. There's not a person on this planet who isn't walking around wounded. We're trying to heal; that's the bottom line. When I finally got that, it was the most freeing moment of my life. I realized I didn't have to be better than anyone or threatened by anyone because we're all wounded. Nobody wakes up in the morning with the intention of harming another person. Well, I can't say *nobody*: there are a few unfortunates who really, really struggle. They have obviously been wounded enough that they think harming others is the only way of living their life. But very

few people wake up in the morning with the intention of hurting another human being, yet it happens throughout the course of our day.

With that in mind, *everybody's wounded*, here's a question for you. I've never asked anybody this during these interviews. When someone has been sexually abused, they often feel that they're alone and isolated, right? They feel alienated.

Yes.

And then when a group of us come together and talk about what's happened to us, we discover we are not alone. Considering what you just said, everybody, regardless of sexual abuse, is wounded, just in different ways.

Yes, bottom line.

That's pretty profound. It's almost like it's us against them – our issues are a little different from their issues, but maybe everyone feels a little bit alone and alienated.

Absolutely. There's an expression I like to live by: "Hurt people, hurt people." It helps put things into perspective.

Have you worked with someone who is an abuser and tried to reduce that behaviour?

I've worked with several abusers, and there's hope. There really is hope. They're trying to complete intentions, just like the polar bear was trying to run away. I'll use a woman as an example. A girl with an alcoholic father ends up marrying an alcoholic. That's an attempt at completing an intention. She is just trying to heal. That girl, in making her pick, is trying to heal her relationship with her father, an unconscious relationship. Harville Hendrix wrote the book *Getting the Love You Want* and developed a therapy called Imago Therapy.

He says that in romantic love, you're attracted to somebody and you think, "Where have you been all my life, I've been waiting for you." Well, he says it's actually somebody who has wounded you that you're getting reconnected with. You either come to a place of acceptance of what happened in your life or you're going to have a power struggle. More often than not, we get into the power struggles, and that's what creates all the distress in our lives.

Both the victim and perpetrator are wounded.
Absolutely.

For most, it's hard to feel sympathy for the perpetrator.
I understand. It's hard to feel sympathy, but when you think about it, it's compassion in its truest form. That person wasn't born that way. Something happened to make him or her think it's okay to behave that way – power struggles. I'm sure that if you showed them a video of abuse, they would say, "Oh my god, that's horrible," even though they're committing the abuses themselves. You hear that all the time, the zealots, the hate mongers cleverly disguised as politicians and people in positions of power... the anti-gay, and so forth. These are the guys who get caught in the bathroom stalls in airports. All they are really trying to do is heal.

Any final things you would like to share?
Try EFT, it works. It's such a useful tool and it helps minimize the pain, torment and the always-trying-to-figure-things-out. It will open up perspectives that will put you in a place of forgiveness. My definition of forgiveness is abandoning all hope of a better past. When I talk about forgiveness, what I'm really saying is acceptance. Acceptance doesn't equal agreement; it's accepting the fact that something happened. If I forgive Uncle Jack, does that mean I've given him permission to do what he did? Not at all. You didn't have any power; you were eight years old. How could you figure this out? When we're kids, we're concrete thinkers: we think in terms of black and white. Abstract thinking doesn't develop until later on, when we actually see that there are more than fifty shades of grey. There's not a person on the planet who would agree that it's okay to be molested and have your power taken away from you like that. No one would agree that it's okay, but you have to accept the fact that it happened and it's done. EFT helps get to that place.

David, it has been a pleasure to talk to you I've learned many new insights. Thank you.
Oh, thank you so much. So did I; it's been fun.

The *Demartini Method*®

Dr. John Demartini
Founder of the Demartini Institute
Human behaviour specialist
www.drdemartini.com

Thank you for taking time out of your busy schedule to participate in my book. The first thing I'd like to ask is why a busy man such as you agreed to this interview?

Why did I agree? Well, you seem to be sincere in your objectives and appear to be dedicated to serving people with your expertise. I do a lot of interviews and whenever I receive the opportunity to share my inspired mission and desired message with another group of receptive people, where it may be of service to them, I attempt to make myself available. And your opportunity provides me with a new means of reaching a brand new audience and that's also my mission. I think we're both working toward accomplishing what we would love to fulfill and I think this will be mutually helping each other.

You have read over 29,300 books and written over 200. From that vast knowledge tell me why sexual abuse is more common in some cultures than others and why it is so prevalent?

Many factors are involved in what some individuals have *labelled* sexual abuse. Collective cultural values and socioeconomic structures are a couple of the factors. Sexual experiences considered to lie within a normal range in one culture's values may be considered taboo in yet another set of cultural values. The biological drive for sexual procreation and sexuality is normal and essential for our species' survival. We experience sex for pleasurable recreation as well as for procreation. And both of these drives are additional factors in what some have classified as sexual abuse. My studies have led me to see that nearly every imaginable action has been associated with sexuality, ranging from those involving pain to those involving pleasure. In biology the necessity for reproduction is wired into our neuroendocrine system. Since there are dopamine and oxytocin rewarding and bonding systems associated with sexuality, just about anything can become associated and attached with it. From my observation, sex has been associated with just about everything: food, pain, clothes, fetishes, spanking, total pleasure or ecstasy, and even nirvanic religious experiences – almost every imaginable noun and verb including even pain, violence, and ecstasy. Sexuality is genetically hardwired and epigenetically soft-wired into our systems from the point of our conception.

From our pre- and post-birth and youth to our most aged years, sexuality is present with all its various forms and associations. Each of us has different associations with our sexuality that can be compounded and lead us to have different sexual needs. There exists a dialectic involving complementary opposites within our global society on sexual preferences. And sexual repressions in society have their complementary opposite outlets or expressions. In other words, sexual repressions are counterbalanced globally by sexual expressions – things that are taboo are also expressed to compensate for the repressions. Chastity and promiscuity walk hand in hand. What collective society represses, selective society expresses. Hiding or suppressing one side only makes it flourish underground and initiates multi-billion dollar industries.

Some people have even made associations between their food and their sexuality. If some food items are put in front of them, they immediately translate their views into sensual or sexual experiences. If they look at a bowl of soup or a banana, it can become a sexual stimulus to them. Almost anything can be associated with sexuality and can stimulate the desire for sex – that's one of the challenges with socially governing it. Neither religious nor socio-political governance will ultimately disturb this balance.

Is that why rehabilitation for perpetrators is so rare?
Yes, partly, but I think the approaches that some correctional units and their psychologists are taking are also why rehabilitation is not usually a successful endeavour. I have my own theories and beliefs about the issue, but I do believe that there are ways of associating things with sexual behaviour in such a way that sex can be

moderated and so-called abuses dampened. I've seen it, I've worked with cases. I wouldn't say rehabilitation is low because it has to be low. It's low because of the approaches being implemented and because the paradigm being considered is imbalanced from the start. Trying to get rid of one side of a magnet is futile. Embracing the whole magnet is the key.

You teach around the world. The other day you mentioned a story that happened in the Bible Belt about repressing sexuality. Do you remember the story and could you share it here?

Yes I do, certainly. I was presenting my signature program the *Breakthrough Experience*® in Lubbock, Texas, commonly referred to as the Bible Belt region. Most major street corners had some sort of church. On average the percentage of incest in the women that attend my programs is about twenty-five per cent. It is more common than most people would imagine. If you have a hundred women present in attendance, about twenty-five per cent of them have had some sort of sexual interaction with a family member or an extended family member or close friend of the family. This usually happens at a very young age up until the teens.

At this particular program there were approximately seventy per cent of the women in the room who had experienced incest. Of that seventy per cent, the majority of them happened to be the daughters of religious leaders, which I thought was quite interesting and telling. I didn't anticipate that, but it was certainly obvious in the room and there was a very interesting discussion that came about as a result of the high percentage.

From my observation of working with over a thousand cases of incest, usually the repression of sexuality in family members is part of what's going on in the sexual dynamic. I definitely see patterns of repression in these family scenarios. There was a very high percentage, higher than I normally ever see, so I was quite intrigued. There was definitely a taboo hypocrisy associated with sexuality within the family.

I'm also fascinated by the correlations seen in the clergy of Catholicism. We see a high percentage of pedophilic expressions compensating for their attempts at celibacy. We have this sort of artificial environment where a man is isolated and celibate, yet we find sexual expression in alternative or pivotal forms. Sexuality is a natural urge and therefore it shows up in other forms – such as what we're hearing about in the news and television today. My personal feeling is that it would be wiser to allow marriage and moderate degrees of sexuality within the clergy. Ideally, I would think the allowance of husband and wife within Catholicism would probably help solve the concern they're facing. I think this is another one of the repression – expression dynamics.

One of the exercises given in my *Prophecy I Experience*™ seminar program is for my student attendees to go out and find somebody they feel they can learn wisdom and leadership principles from in their local society. They are instructed to interview a selected person and ask him or her to share ten things to do and not to do to master their life. Once in Sydney, Australia two of my students went into a coffee shop and as they were looking for a person to interview they were approached by a gentleman who happened to have been a priest. They entered into an unexpected discussion with him about his sexuality, which they found really fascinating, and as a result they invited him back to my seminar program. There were approximately a hundred participants at the program and we entered into an open discussion about the fact that the man had had periodic sexual interactions with his monsignor for well over a decade, which became public news. We talked about the experience and what led up to it. He went back and forth between showing his emotional satisfactions and being disgraced by their interactions. He had a very interesting combination of polar opposite perceptions about the whole sexual interaction. I then proceeded to take him through the *Demartini Method*®, which is a series of questions that when thoroughly answered, awakens new insights, perspectives, and feelings about previously emotionally charged events and liberates bound individuals from their sexual wounds or other wounds and baggage.

There are different values and morals for different people. What some individuals in society label as abnormal sexuality, or even evil, harmful, or criminal sexual habits, others may consider to be normal sexual actions that emerge out of deep affection and feelings of love between two people. In some cases, these extreme polarities are compensations for repressed or oppressed family dynamics. This family involvement has to be factored into these cases if true understanding is to be obtained. I have seen some really interesting family dynamics demonstrated. I advise counsellors, therapists, psychologists, and prison workers to remain objective and encourage a broader non-judgmental perspective and evaluation before jumping into immediate, socially sanctioned, and limited responses and labels. I probe to uncover the drives and motives of the involved parties and derive a fuller education out of it and strive to in turn educate the involved parties. If I go in with a predetermined set of moral assumptions, "this is morally bad or this is morally good," it biases my view and I don't have the opportunity to uncover a greater portion of the whole story. Working toward uncovering the whole story is a lot more educational, transformational, and meaningful and I can help people more when I get to the real core reasons for such sexual interactions. It also sets all parties free.

I first heard about you in 2008 when I was talking to a psychologist friend about sexual abuse. He said you teach people how to go beyond forgiveness and love the person who is believed to have "violated" them. Can you elaborate on that?

Well, I don't choose to use the words *violation* or *abuse* because they imply presuppositions of drawbacks without benefits, pains without pleasures, and losses without gains. They are presuppositions that are incomplete and biased once the cases are more fully scrutinized under investigation or analysis. I don't use that language because if I do, I'm perpetuating the very illusion that they're emotionally reacting to.

What I do is ask a series of precise questions. The *Demartini Method* is a series of specific questions that reveals to someone an underlying hidden order and a more comprehensive dynamic that allows them to start to see how their sexual experience, that they once thought to be *abusive*, could be useful and meaningful – and how it has actually also been a benefit in their life. I come from the perspective that it's not what happens to us, it's how we decide to perceive our events, what we decide to do with them, and how we respond to them that matters. I've seen too many people who have been through so-called *horrendous sexual experiences* and then gone on to do extraordinary things with their lives and use their experiences as great opportunities. I prefer to give them the wisdom of the ages without having to go through the aging process. Being a master of their destiny is wiser than remaining a victim of their history.

We have the capacity to take our sexual experiences that we have labelled terrible and turn them into incredible opportunities; therefore, it is not the event that is the determining factor – it is how we perceive and respond to the event. William James emphasized that the greatest discovery of his generation was that human beings can alter their lives by altering the perceptions and attitudes of their minds. I've been studying human perceptions extensively since I was twenty-three and it is truly fascinating to explore how we perceive and how we distort and bias our perceptions. We definitely have biased perceptions that are filtered and generalized, which can become even more distorted over time as we elaborate on our sexual histories.

I ask questions and initiate answers using the *Demartini Method* that allow people to see their sexual experiences in such a way that they turn them into opportunities that they actually feel love and appreciation for. You were in the program this weekend and you watched people end up with, "Thank you, I love you," when they had all kind of reasons to be upset with other people. What I've done is compiled a set of forty-eight questions that liberate people from any of their burdened perceptions. If a person asks these questions honestly and sticks to the facts and not the fictitious evaluations, distortions, generalizations, and assumptions, they will end up with a deep appreciation for what's happened and will actually get to a point where they feel appreciation and love for the person involved. It's hard to comprehend until you actually complete the method. People don't believe it's possible, or they think it has to be some form of brainwashing, but it's not. It is simply them honestly answering a series of questions. Of course that is sometimes because they may want to hold on to their misperceptions so they can remain a victim with secondary gains. The *Demartini Method* works every time if you work it as instructed and designed. It is the science of clearing emotional baggage and transforming incomplete perceptions.

I've been blessed to be able to work with tens of thousands of people around the world. I've worked with nine hundred cases of incest and almost the same number of rapes. There are also many more cases of beatings and abandonment and all the other classical actions people want to label themselves victims of. When I finish asking these same people the appropriate questions, these individuals become poised, present, empowered, and purposeful and simply state, "Thank you, I'm now grateful," and they show a lot of love and appreciation for their previously disturbing sexual events. I know that may sound shocking at first, but if you saw it every day like I do, you would think it's time that the broader psychology industry explored what's going on with the method. Psychologists or therapists who watch it live say, "I've got to see that again. Is it just one time or does it happen every time?" The answer is it happens every time – if people don't run out and avoid the method altogether and they just stay for the completion of the process. It works. It is a repeatable science.

In my two-day seminar program, the *Breakthrough Experience*, each attendee works through a series of questions that helps them discover the hidden order in some event or action they previously thought was meaningless chaos or emotionally burdensome. The questions help them have more gratitude and love for whatever is going on in their lives. They begin to understand that everything is "on the way, not in the way". It's not positive thinking – it's not blah, blah, cover-up, or hype, nor is it superficial affirmations and dissociations. It is simply a series of precise questions that balances their minds and allows them to see the hidden order and appreciate what's happened in their lives. To me, encouraging people to be imprisoned with the perpetrator – victim model tends to put them into a defensive mode for the rest of their lives. It puts them in their own prison and I think it's wiser to let them be free and no longer perceive themselves to be prey.

I've worked with people who have been raped, stabbed, beaten, or incested and who have, after completing the method, actually gone to the person (sometimes in prison) and thanked them for their experience. That assists the person in the prison to transform his or her life as well as transforming the visitor. I find the chain reaction of assisting both partners in this dynamic, in the long run, is the wiser transformation for society. If you understand the entire context of the individual who is involved you have a deeper appreciation of how the initial sexual situation came about.

If you had the opportunity to watch me or my facilitators work with an individual who has experienced rape: before, during, and after the process, you'd see a marked difference and you would better understand why I am making these statements. I once had the opportunity to work with a young girl who was thirteen years old. She was addicted to heroin and her dealer would only give it to her if she had sex with him – he was three hundred pounds and sixty years old. Some of the people in the room were just squirming and whispering, "Oh no, gross, I couldn't imagine that." The young lady described what she was required to do to get her heroin fix. It took just over two hours to work through her session and liberate her. Afterwards she gave us a video testimonial explaining how she saw things differently. She said she could look back on her life and not want it any other way. She saw the situations from a different perspective and was actually grateful for her events. She realized that because of them she had a deeper understanding of how to interact with and relate to people, the consequences of becoming cocky and manic and how to be present with people. She added that because of what happened she learned to listen really well and now had a focus on school that she wouldn't have had otherwise. She was starting to look at her life differently and she said she could see all the blessings that came out of the event and couldn't remain resentful. She said, "I'm actually grateful. My life changed because of that event."

I know that sounds shocking, but I'm not really concerned about people who have emotional reactions to such stories and remain fixed in their victim mode or model and remain stuck being hurt and right. I'm interested in the person who I'm working with and helping to be free of the burden he or she under with the perceptions they're living with – that's all I'm interested in at that moment – setting him or her free to appreciate and love again.

You saw this weekend that I'm interested in helping people reach a point where they can truly say, "Thank you, I love you" again. That's it. That's all I'm interested in because when you're down to the last twenty-four hours of your life, that's the most common, highest priority action step that a person takes if they know they're about to pass. "Thank you, I love you" to the people who've contributed to their lives. Finding that state inside a person brings them closure and freedom. Everybody wants to be loved and appreciated for who they are and I find that's one of the greatest healers. I'm interested in taking a person all the way there. I'm not interested in forgiveness – I'm not interested in apologies and those kinds of incomplete levels of awareness. They are still assuming there's something disassociated from them that caused their so-called problem. They are still labelling their event as evil without good and this incomplete awareness keeps them in bondage. I now know there is a way of getting beyond such illusions and I've found a way that works.

After watching you work with people, I certainly understand what you are saying. I can also understand someone reading this and not understanding how a person can experience a traumatic event and shortly thereafter say they wouldn't change anything.

I've worked with so many people from around the world that I am certain that I can obtain such results. I once processed eleven incest cases in a single weekend in Calgary, Canada. It became an incest weekend of sorts. And I had a strong debate on that Sunday with a twelfth woman attending who put sexual perpetrators in prison and refused to finish the method. She had been incested as a child and was still bitter, angry, and full of hate fifty years later – you could see she was still in a self-imposed prison. I said, "Why don't we take advantage of this weekend and clear everybody, including you. Does anybody have a problem with that?" The eleven women and I went one after another and there were cheers all over the room as they broke free. However, this one woman was absolutely angry and repulsed because she saw women who could once again love. She was just angry and refused to work the method. She was holding onto her desire for revenge for her earlier event punishing men and doing it under the disguise of legality and social responsibility. It was very obvious and the whole room was trying to tell her maybe it would be wise to have her complete the method and dissolve her anger. However if she completed the method her whole career could be undermined in her mind. She couldn't let go of her career because she's a well-known leader in that field. She couldn't possibly complete the method and come to appreciate and love the man once involved that she imagined she hated. Sometimes there are secondary gains that people cling onto while they play their victim roles and those secondary gains have to be addressed if they are really going to be ready to make the necessary effort to break through.

Could you imagine if she had embraced the Demartini Method, switched and gone in the other direction and assisted people – through your unique approach.

That's exactly what I was trying to have her see. She could be a leader in this new movement, method, or approach. You could see it in her mind-questioning it, but she just couldn't do it. There were too many benefits of her previous way of viewing these sexual events. I told her, "I'll sit with you privately, assist and help you on that objective, if you would like it." I could see that she was thinking about it approximately ten per cent, "I would love to do that, I wish I could get out of my prison" and ninety per cent, "No I've got to defend my prison, I have been hurt and want to protect others and get revenge." It was really interesting and educational to watch. The whole room could see it too and nobody was fooled by her game. It was very obvious. Nine out of the other eleven women stood up and gave a testimonial outlining exactly why they were saying thank you to their previous so-called perpetrator for their *Breakthrough Experience.* The lady was just shocked. She is famous in her field because of what she went through and was doing in the courts, so I said, "Did you ever thank him for your success"? "Oh, don't go there," she slammed. I did get her to look inward and contemplate a new alternative way of viewing an ancient set of social and sexual interactions.

If I had not seen what you do in person I wouldn't believe it or understand it. It's hard to comprehend the healings, the stories, and the traumas that last so long. What can someone do with their story to move on, rather than living their story over and over again?

Most of the defensive attendees believe they have been wounded. They hold onto their wounds and try to live their lives through their wounds, and even try to punish other people through their wounds – a lot of them, including this litigious psychologist. I once had a therapist in San Francisco who literally started screaming in the *Breakthrough Experience* saying, "This is outrageous and how could you say there is one benefit out of such an evil act?" As she screamed another woman stood up and addressed the group of attendees, saying, "Look, I've been sitting here for the last four hours and I've been finding an unbelievable amount of insights about my life, people I've met, and the drive I've had, as well as the accomplishments that I've had because of the sexual event. The things that came out of my sexual event I have now realized there are a pair of opposites at each moment. This has been the most freeing experience I've had. So, because you choose not to do it and you want to be the victim and you want to be angry about this, just know that's fine. But right now don't judge us for actually letting go of our previous incomplete perceptions and being grateful for this because I'm actually getting to the point where I'm going to go and say 'Thank you' to this person." The therapist was going absolutely insane and stormed out. She could not handle being around those that would not support her victim mentality. It has been stated for centuries that pity wants a party.

Well it's like you say, do the process and see the event through new eyes and create new perceptions – why remain in hell if you can release it?
Well they have to be getting benefits out of staying within their victim story or they would not speak out against new alternatives; there are always unconscious motives underlying these types of reactions. People continue to do things when they receive more advantages than disadvantages, more rewards than risks.

The traditional method of dealing with sexual abuse or assault is to identify it, try to catch and maybe punish the perpetrators, and expect the victims to bury their memory or to relive their story, over and over again. Most people don't even press charges because they know they will be re-victimized. There's no relief for them. What do you think about traditional therapy or what I've just said?
I think it's part archaic, myself. If I had just one anecdotal case I'd remain quiet, but after assisting in hundreds of cases and some of the most extreme cases of sexual trauma that you could imagine I'm absolutely certain it is a matter of hours for many traumas to become cleared, once you know the right questions. It does not take years to get the story dissolved. It's a matter of knowing the right questions. People aren't asking the right questions. They instead believe the idea and construct that something terrible occurred. They buy into the idea that people are hurt and need

compassion and sympathy and have little resilience. But perceptions of the mind are always paired and therefore whenever there's a torture, there's an accompanying ecstasy and the accompanying ecstasy is a dissociated ecstasy that is actually there to compensate and to survive the so-called perceived torturous events.

What happens is, unless you put those two poles of the mental magnet together, you won't get to the true story. You don't get to what's actually going on in the mind and the event. I'm a firm believer in asking the right questions to help people see things from a perspective where they can be poised again. No therapy is ever complete until cause equals the effect in space time. Until we own our own initial dynamic in the equation, we're going to be in a vicious cycle and we are not going to get anywhere. We have to understand the whole situation. In the *Demartini Method* people see how they attract and experience opposites to make sure they break their addictions to one-sided desires. That variable is not added in normal psychological therapies and until it's put into the equation, psychologists are going to be searching for one-sided answers in a dead end system.

When I have a rape case and I identify all the components of the rapist that the raped are judging, you'll see that the raped are simultaneously addicted to their opposite. When they actually realize that and see who's playing the opposite role at the moment, it is liberating to them, it's a release. They're actually thankful because they realize they are liberated from some incomplete perception that doesn't truly exist, a delusion in their mind. It's hard to comprehend until you see it live. It's just truly mind blowing.

I understand. However, I see critics asking or shouting in your face: "If it's so easy to get over something so traumatic, isn't it like condoning what the rapist or the child molester does?" Does it mean they should get less of a punishment because they're contributing to the evolvement or development of the person violated?

Well, I get that response pretty well every week when I am doing a case of rape or incest. But, I think there are many variables here. One thing I have certainly observed is the greater the degree of suppression and repression of certain behaviours in our society, the higher the concentration of its opposite behaviour in a select group of people to compensate.

I've said for a few decades that what the collective society represses, the selective society expresses. And the more society collectively represses and labels something bad, the more it gets concentrated and expressed in a handful of people that become labelled the villains. The villains are actually outlets, steam pressure releasers, for collective society's repressions. In that context they serve a purpose in society – in a way that we don't normally think about. So, to condemn them completely is not to understand how collective society helps create the very things that they are condemning.

At the same time, in a collectively repressed society with established values, ethics, rules, and laws, governing authorities are responsible for enforcing these laws and the selective minority are going to therefore pay the price and become constrained in their expression and in some cases incarcerated. I'm not negating the idea of having the condemned expressers put in prison, but in the prison I think it is wiser to have them go through the same method that will help them understand their portion of the complete dynamic and also the sources of their dynamics so as to educate and clearly neutralize the need for their concentrated expression. The prison environment is generally not conducive for those incarcerated to have such an education or transformation. What often happens is the incarcerated receives a Pygmalion label and they end up further manifesting the behaviours and repeatedly slip through the cracks again as an outlet for the collective. But if you actually go into the prison and know what you are doing, you can transform some of these people's lives, and if the collective society is further educated, you reduce the polarity of the sexuality in society. The probability of them being able to function again in society is real. The traditional approaches are under a division model, the perpetrator-victim, predator-prey model. In my opinion, that's not going to effectively solve such a paradox. It's going to keep perpetuating the paradox and the underlying repression-expression dynamic. The whole construct that's driving this is the moral or value split. If people actually understand and have the two people that are intertwined each go through the process, amazing things can happen. This paradox is not limited to sexuality, it applies to other social dynamics as well – the collective poor and the selective rich, the collective ignorant and the selective knowledgeable, the collective disempowered and the selective empowered. These dynamics are governed by, "the law of the many and one" or the dynamic equilibrium of complementary opposites.

I've seen people who've been in prisons transform their lives. Sometimes they have had a series of events in their life they felt were hopeless and unfair. Yet when those same events were all perceptually transformed and emotionally cleared, some of their own anger and desire for extreme antisocial expression was also cleared. There are two poles within the criminal justice system. One that says that criminals are victims of their society and that we need to be kind to them and try to help them through their emotionally trying experiences. The other pole says that they are hardened evil criminals and they need to be stopped, punished, and sometimes even killed. The people in society whose values are really or possibly directly challenged are generally going to be hard on these criminals. The people whose individual values have not been affected by them are going to be easier on them. There are many variables in society that determine the results.

If an individual experiences a sexual event that they initially perceived to be traumatic, when they actually balance or dissolve their emotional charges concerning it, they and the resultant outcome can actually be transformed into an event that can be appreciated and even loved. An amazing *healing* can be the result. If an individual focuses on how the sexual event can serve what is truly and inwardly inspiring to them (and there's now a way of achieving that), then there is a way of transforming their life. I work with individuals and groups and bring about transformations weekly. I've watched true and lasting transformations in people's lives. I've spent almost forty years of my life working on this and I think there is now an alternative method that can be observed and studied as is the case now at the Imperial College in London. With the *Demartini Method* there is an alternative. This does not mean we are not to temporarily put the selective "expressers" into prisons and keep them separated from the collectively repressed society. I'm not negating that as a temporary action. But to just stop there, and just leave them in prison and label them bad isn't enough, and to perpetuate the innocent victim model is not going to awaken the world to the ever present balance.

Individuals who have experienced sexual events such as incest and rape that I've taken through the *Demartini Method,* become transformed in their perception: grateful and freed. I once worked with a woman that had been both raped and impregnated twice, and had avoided a third attempt. We sat in the *Demartini Method Training Program* that was conducted in South Africa and actually processed both events, including the abortions, in front of the whole group. It was just amazing to see the final transformation and yes it also ended with gratitude and love. The mother of the woman was watching and participating in the entire transformation. Tears of gratitude resulted.

I've now known her for five years and she's a completely different person. Prior to the method she was frightened and wanting to commit suicide. None of those feelings or desires are present now. This is doable and reproducible. I'm just amazed how the old perpetrator and innocent victim model is still persisting. It's just astonishing. The results of the *Demartini Method* will become socially recognized and its efficiency and effectiveness will be another new model for transformation and growth.

In our society we view and hear about so much violence and sex in the media. One side believes this programming contributes to the abuse and the violence and protests loudly; the other camp disagrees or doesn't want to talk about it. Which do you feel it is?

Both. As long as you have a violent story enter into your mind that is socially labelled *terrible,* you will have little alternative but to either be neutral about it and ignore it, be negatively charged about it and stress over it, or see it as an outlet of expression and be entertained. Once it is taken in and then neutralized and seen from a balanced and whole perspective, a different story emerges and you can actually become grateful for the entire story. At that point there's no need to affirm or deny it, or express or repress it. It just becomes an event that initiates a "thank you" for it will always be accompanied by its complementary opposite. There was a lady attending the *Breakthrough Experience* this weekend. You were there. Her husband had died last November. Now, you saw her before the *Demartini Method* was applied, she was an expresser of

grief: it wasn't major grief, but it was still grief. I think you can remember and acknowledge that.
Yes.

At the end, what did she have?
She was thankful her husband had passed after his long illness. She didn't have any remaining grief. I was actually doing the method on myself as I was listening to you work with them.

Why were you doing it?
To help myself. I was grieving the loss of a friend – so, I did it on her.

If you know how to ask the right questions, amazing results can be shown. Years ago I was interviewed by a noted psychologist in South Africa on her own two-hour national radio show. The topic was dealing with death and grief. There was another female guest on the show who was considered the *compassionate friend*. She was the founder of the Compassionate Friends organization. She believed individuals should be remorseful and grieving over the death of their loved ones for the rest of their lives. I thought to myself, "Gosh, this seems a bit extreme."

A grieving man who had just lost his wife called into the radio station and I had the opportunity to take him through the *Demartini Method* live right on this psychologist's radio show. The woman of Compassionate Friends thought I was terrible for putting him through such revealing questions like: "Now that your wife has just passed, what specific traits are you presently missing?", "Who in your life is now demonstrating those same traits, one or many, to the same degree?", "What were some of the downsides of your wife's original traits that are now missed?" and "What are the benefits of the newly emerged traits now found in others?" I worked with him live on the radio for about twenty minutes. I couldn't get him all the way through the method in the time allotted, but it was clear that it was helping him dissolve his grief. He was regaining his composure and feeling present; that was different than when he started. The woman from Compassionate Friends attacked me and my method and said it was dangerous and cruel. "You can't put people through this. They are deeply suffering and grieving." She was projecting her own grieving onto the man. She was still grieving a child she had lost twenty-two years earlier and even still had a room with all his clothes and toys where she went in and cried every day. When the psychologist asked the man if my questioning served him, he claimed it had and wanted my contact details, so he could follow up further with the method. Not one individual I have interviewed desires to have those remaining after their death to be grieving and in sorrow. They want their loved ones to get on and fulfill their lives to the fullest.

When people go through the *Breakthrough Experience*, their initial stories and perceptions become changed. Asked if their stories are the same afterwards they say no every time. So, the story is different. Why would I let them run a story that's not even true? It's fictional. Why would you want to give them the power to run stories that are fictitious, that are then keeping them in bondage, when they could ask the right questions to get to the real facts and help them get to a point where it's not painful and then run that story when it is ended in a state of gratitude? The truth does not require sorrow or forgiveness, only thank you.

Does it matter if the trauma happened many years ago?
It doesn't matter. Time is irrelevant, although time can sometimes add additional distortions which have to be dissolved.

I first heard about you as the *grateful* guy in the movie, The Secret. Last weekend you said something about how great awareness occurs when we are grateful – can you expand on that statement please.

I think that any challenging event can be transformed once we ask the right questions and expand our awareness. Every event can result in a state of gratitude. Gratitude opens up the gateway of our heart and allows us to see things through an even broader perspective. Seeing things from a full and more broadened perspective will eventually lead to gratitude.

When somebody attends the *Breakthrough Experience* and they feel hurt or have resentment over some event, they have an incomplete view, a biased perspective. If it's not balanced, they're going to stay stuck in their story and they're not going to have gratitude. Once we broaden their awareness through questioning and have them see their reflection in the event – what role they're playing, the dynamics involved, and the opposite benefits that occur synchronously – they end up saying, "Wow, thank you. I'm grateful for this now." The illusion promoting the concept of forgiveness deserves to be transformed into "thank you for giving me this experience." That's the only place forgiveness has a place in my teachings. Thank you for giving me the opportunity to experience this.

What effect do values have on healing?
Well, values are the most significant cornerstone of healing that I know. Your values determine how you evaluate and respond to events. Stress is one of the biggest factors in wellness and illness. Stress is the inability to adapt to a changing environment. The two sides we face in our environment are biological and originate from the earliest prey-predator environment. Anything that supports our values, we call prey, which helps us build. Anything that challenges our values, we call predator and it can lead us to be destroyed. We are basically faced with attractive things we're infatuated with, things that build us up, and repulsive things that we resent because we think they will destroy us. If we can balance our equation and find the benefits in the things we think are going to destroy us, and the drawbacks of things that we think are going to serve us, and neutralize them, then the source of stress is dissolved. The fear of loss of that which we are infatuated with (prey-food) and the fear of gain of that which we are resentful to (predator) are the sources of our stress.

The critics are going to say you simplify difficult things.
They don't always study applied physiology.

They may see you as being uncompassionate or non-emotional. Do you not have any feelings for the trauma these people are going through? You are not coddling.
Why would I do that? It's not the truth. That traumatic event is not the whole truth. It's only half the truth. Why support their one-sided delusion? I don't find that productive. Think of it in this way, people come into you with a disorder and if you buy into their disorder, you're both disordered. You come in with order, and if

you can help them see the order, they're now transforming their perspective into order. It's that simple. You don't let disorder run order, you let order govern disorder. Compassion is often one wounded person rescuing or enabling another. I prefer to dissolve the illusion and get them back in touch with their reason. I am filled with gratitude and love. I am just not weighed down with emotional illusions. Therefore, I go into a session knowing there's already a hidden order and balance. There isn't a case I'm aware of that I haven't helped someone bring back the balance and see the order. I don't buy into, "Oh, you poor thing." I don't find that in any way productive. I have feelings for them, I have love for them, and I have gratitude for the opportunity to work with them. I am absolutely certain if I stay with them, they're going to have gratitude and love in turn when they too are balanced. So, why would I buy into something that's a myth – fictitious and an incomplete awareness with a biased perception – when I can help them see the whole picture and actually have a point where they're poised and grateful? So no, I don't buy into the story because I know the story is about to be dissolved. If people say I'm brainwashing them, no I'm not. I'm asking them questions to make them look at facts – perceptions they initially overlooked. Did I impose anything this weekend?
No.

I just had them ask questions and had them look again to see things they weren't originally seeing. As they see things they didn't see, their perspective changes quickly and becomes balanced, then they feel their heart pump and say, "Wow, thank you." I don't have to impose anything. I never say you have to do this and that's the whole truth, I just ask what the other side of their event is. It's there, I'm certain about that. They always come back and say thank you for pushing them past their illusions.

It was Ralph Waldo Emerson who emphasized that crying for sympathy for somebody, instead of hitting with rough electric shocks, keeps them in their bondage. So, I'm not going to support their illusive bondage. I'm not going to sympathize and play that role. If they want that they can find some wounded therapist to listen endlessly to their woes. As I stated previously, compassion is one wounded person supporting another wounded person. I think it would be wiser to say that I'm not a cold, clinical person, I'm simply one who truly cares and loves what I do transforming people's lives. I'm not sitting there cold-hearted. I'm thinking, "What's the other side? Let's go back there and look again." The result is an open heart with tears of gratitude and love.

Thanks for clarifying that for the reader because if someone just looks at what you're saying, people could say you're harsh. It is completely different and difficult to explain to someone who has not experienced the method.
I get all kinds of responses from people. I am considered both a hero and a villain. I openly embrace them both. Until we do, we can't love ourselves.

A fifteen-year-old girl that's been beaten or raped can sit here with me for an hour or two, or possibly three hours at the maximum, and leave with a completely different perspective and become open-hearted and less likely to commit suicide or self-harm. I do similar cases nearly weekly.

How do you feel this interview will be received?
I think it will be received like most discussions about new and original ideas; in two ways: it will be supported and challenged. Some will say, "I don't believe that. That's insane." Others will say, "Maybe there's something to this. Let me investigate it further." If people do investigate, hopefully they have enough skepticism and cynicism to be cautious and enough openness to be explorative – society needs a healthy balance of both. For every gullible and vulnerable individual, there's a skeptic and cynic to counterbalance. Both assist in the world and both make sure that knowledge refines itself through time. I think we need the combination of both when it comes to my method. Both reactions will serve me in refining the method through time and polish its effectiveness. You need to have the supporters and challengers in a balanced manner in order to have growth. That's what keeps me refining what I do to make sure I am delivering quality products and services. I'm sure that will happen from this interview experience and there will be some whom will benefit from it. There will probably be somebody who might be perturbed by it too. But if there are growing numbers of people who are being served through the use of it, then that's my chief aim.

By doing the ABCs in life and not the XYZs, we master our lives and in turn dissolve challenges in the world, in pursuit of greater ones. Helping people to feel that they have meaning and purpose in their lives and that they can be inspired, and showing them a new science of how to do that, is an amazing contribution to have the opportunity to fulfill. I've seen so many lives that have been in apparent vicious cycles and I've also seen when they have learned how to dissolve their cycles and clear them all. I've seen people do extraordinary transformations. So, I presently just spend my life focusing on my mission of service. I'm just an inspired man on a mission doing whatever I can to be of service to the world.

Anything that any individual could be confronted by in their future we now have a way of processing it and breaking through it. The *Demartini Method* is a tool that individuals can use for the rest of their lives and when they do, they will be able to put order back into their awareness, be grateful and just sit in awe. Why not? It was Albert Einstein who basically emphasized that it was enough for him on a daily basis to contemplate and sit in awe about the intelligence that permeated the universe. Well that is true enough for me. Each day that I am able to explore just a small portion of the universe and see the magnificent, elegant, mathematical order that's there, that's hidden from most individuals' first appearance, and discover such an intricate elegance – that allows me to remain inspired in my work. I believe that elegance is sitting inside every experience. There is a beautiful hidden order in all of life.

Well, I'm grateful to meet you and to be able to attend the Breakthrough Experience this weekend. Can you leave us with an affirmation on being grateful?

Certainly. No matter what you've done or not done, you're worthy of love, and there's nothing but love, all else is illusion. If you take the time to ask the right questions and reveal to your awareness what your intuition and inspiration are constantly calling you to be aware of, you will discover this, and you will be grateful for your life and you'll do extraordinary things.

Advocacy

Please

Sheldon Kennedy is a former national hockey league player who came forward as a victim of sexual abuse in 1996. In 1998, he rollerbladed across Canada to raise awareness and funds, raising over $1 million that was ultimately donated to the Canadian Red Cross Abuse Prevention Services. With a movie and book to his credit (*Why I Didn't Say Anything - The Sheldon Kennedy Story*), he now serves as a spokesperson for violence and abuse prevention programs with the Canadian Red Cross and his own company, Respect Group Inc. Sheldon was instrumental in the recent opening of the Calgary Child Advocacy Centre in Calgary, Alberta.

Respectgroupinc.com
Sheldon Kennedy

Hi, Sheldon, thanks for talking to me as you wait for your flight.
Hi, Deb, how are you?

I am doing very well, thank you. I really appreciate your agreeing to be interviewed at the last minute. I'd like to focus on the legal aspects and solutions part of your expertise in the area of sexual abuse, if that is okay.
Sure, I think we're past the horror stories. It's about looking for solutions now.

There are more and more people working toward that now and that's a large part of what this book is about. Working collectively we can accomplish so much more.
Well, absolutely.

Our time is very limited so let's get right to the questions. You demonstrated a lot of strength coming forward and pressing charges against your perpetrator, Graham James. What was it that ultimately moved you to take legal action?
There were a few things. I was at a point where my life was falling apart. My wife at the time was pregnant with my daughter and I knew I was never going to be the father, or the person, that I wanted to be. I kept seeing Graham outside the locker room when I was playing for the Calgary Flames. He was coaching the Calgary Hitmen and there were always younger players hanging around. Nobody was doing anything to warn the guys, so the bottom line was, I needed to take steps to protect them. If I was going to keep

living I needed to charge him because I was on the verge of feeling like I didn't want to be around anymore.

Those are big motivators. The fear of re-victimization is a big contributor to the fact that so many people remain silent and don't come forward to press charges. Do you have any regrets, in terms of taking the legal action that you did?

Not at all. When I look at the changes that have been made around the world since the Graham James case sixteen years ago, they've been absolutely huge. We talk much more openly about sexual abuse issues in this country. I think the Graham James case was the catalyst for creating conversation and change. It's about holding people accountable. Kids know when something is wrong. When they come forward they need a safe place to talk about what happened to them. I don't think kids are thinking, "Oh, I hope he gets life in prison." A lot of times they need to get some clarity in their mind – the abuse is not their fault and that needs to be made clear to them. That's the most important piece for the kid.

There are two parts: one is the legal side, and the other is gathering resources to help kids and their families turn their lives around immediately after coming forward. Give them a chance to live their life again. Often when we wait until we're adults to report the abuse, we're dealing with not only the trauma of the abuse, but the way we have lived our lives because of the abuse. The wreckage we leave in our path is a huge problem.

Exactly. You mentioned providing resources immediately after. Give me an example of a few resources you would like to see.

We are accomplishing a lot here in Calgary. Three days ago we opened the Calgary Child Advocacy Centre: it's the first one of its kind in Canada. We have signed working memorandums of understanding between Alberta Health, the Calgary Police, the Crown Prosecutor's Office, and Child and Family Services, and they're all working together under one roof. We have twenty-five thousand square feet and the goal is to do everything through a one-stop shop. We want to do one interview with a child – not four or five, which is currently what happens. If the interview is done well the result will be more convictions and longer sentences.

We have the legal side as well as the services for the kids to begin to start building their life back and give them a chance to deal with the abuse. If we focus on dealing with the abuse, we've helped the kids and will save a lot of money in the future. When we don't deal with abuse early on the kids may end up in a government-subsidized program, whether it is our criminal justice system or mental health system, or they end up dead. At the Centre our goal is to be the best we can be when they walk in the door to begin the investigation and the best we can be following the investigation.

I'd like to mention the conversation we've been having with governments. One of their pillars is the Victim's Bill of Rights – they're finally looking at prevention and early intervention. Finally, we have that ball at the top of the hill and people understand the issues better. What we're dealing with is an invisible trauma. It was hard for people to wrap their heads around the type of damage and trauma sexual abuse causes because they couldn't physically see it-unlike when somebody with two broken legs comes through the door and we can visibly see the damage. Too often abuse has been overlooked, but we're at a point now where we understand that our prison systems are filled with kids who have had terrible experiences.

You're absolutely correct. You're touching many valid points.

Deb, it's important for people to have conversations like this one to share information. Many new policies have been passed into legislation since I came forward. Bill C-10 was passed (otherwise known as the Omnibus Crime Bill). This includes mandatory minimum prison sentences for drug offenders and harsher penalties for violent crimes and sexual assault. That bill gets tougher on crime. We're actually hearing government talking about prevention and early intervention and working with the victims, the Victim's Bill of Rights – we haven't heard that language before. It was all about rehabilitating the criminal – what about rehabilitating the victims? Most of the victims of this type of crime are turning into criminals when we don't deal with the trauma. The Victim's Bill of Rights is on the agenda for this term and it is very important. The ability to start shaping these bills, and keeping them simple, is critical, because the issues are confusing enough already.

Are you familiar with Erin's Law in the States? There's a short piece about her in this book.

I was on a call with her and I'm going down to Washington DC and speaking at a conference with her in March. She is doing good work in the educational system. Why wouldn't every adult, custodian, bus driver, parent volunteer, and teacher in our school system be mandated to understand sexual abuse, bullying, and harassment?

We talk about empowering the bystander, yet there is no mandate that a teacher has to have an educated understanding. If we walk up and down the hallways of schools and ask teachers if they can give a definition of abuse, bullying, and harassment and their legal and moral responsibilities around it, the odds of getting the right answer aren't very good. Yet we're all expected to do the right thing.

People have put blinders on and created paranoia around these issues. We have to create a confidence through consistent education and a standard definition or model of abuse. There's too much of a grey area now: "You're abusing my kid because they didn't get a C on a test" or "You're abusing my kid because they didn't make the Triple A Hockey Team" – that's not abuse. But there's no clarity on the definition and no standard within organizations; therefore it's hard to hold people accountable and it's hard to have a conversation.

You could have remained anonymous and chosen not to battle your case publicly. I knew who you were because I'm a hockey person; I knew you were the troubled guy and wondered why you couldn't get your act together. Did you come forward intentionally?

I don't know that I made a conscious decision. People I knew leaked something to the local paper. I had always felt I was alone and I had no idea there were others going through what I was going through. Then all of a sudden I had an outpouring of support. Many people came forward. It was unbelievable. I didn't expect that then, almost seventeen years ago.

There was a lot of support, which at the time seemed like a surprise. I mean NHL hockey guys.

It was unbelievable. I thought, "Here's an opportunity to make some change." From day one I've never had a publicist; I've never had anybody. It has been me and Wayne, and if people want to do an interview they can track me down. (Wayne McNeil is a former volunteer President of the Sheldon Kennedy Foundation, Sheldon's business partner, and co-founder of Respect Group Inc.) My purpose from day one has been to keep pushing for change – it's all about action. I don't want to hear lip service. What are we doing? What are we actually going to do to make this better? Put it this way; I didn't carry my lunch kit to the end of the lane thinking this is what I was going to do for a living. There have been lots of times I didn't want to do this, but people kept bringing me back and I've never really been allowed to get out of it.

That's my story in a sense. Sometimes trying to avoid a recurring theme in your life is futile. I think you are meant to do what you are doing – you sound so passionate as you're talking.

You know what? I'm having fun now. Look at the issues, for example, bullying; it's the flavour of the week now. We were engaged in that back in the day when it wasn't the flavour of the week. It was a tough grind to draw attention to it; now it's not. It's fun for me now because people are listening. I really enjoy what I'm doing, being able to shape change and being able to get people on the same page and have them understand.

We're in a lot of different places today with these issues, but I look at them all the same: sexual abuse, physical abuse, verbal abuse and bullying. They all affect kids the same way. We need to break down the silos and stop just focusing on bullying or sexual abuse. They derive from an imbalance of power and it all affects kids the same way. We need to start talking about them the same way.

What advice would you give someone who's thinking about charging their perpetrator and what were some of the biggest obstacles or challenges that you faced?

Things have changed a lot since I came forward, like the general understanding of these issues. There was also a lack of understanding from the police force and other institutions that dealt with this type of crime – today we are a lot more aware. People who provide services are more aware, and a lot more understanding when a child or an adult comes forward, now. There has been a major shift. More people are going to believe and support you today. The police organizations I've worked with across the country take sexual abuse very seriously. People should feel safe to come forward and deal with abuse. Doing this is important because it's how we get our power back.

One thing that really bothers me is when someone comes forward and people say they are a victor or the difficult part is done. To me, that's when the person becomes the most vulnerable, because they have it in their minds that after coming forward everything's going to be okay. The reality is, when you come forward things get worse because now the secret is out of the bag. All your feelings and everything else turns upside-down and sideways and life becomes a gong show. All you want to do is shove your stuff back in that treasure box, but you can't.

That's probably the most vulnerable time in an individual's life. I believe a victor is somebody who has his or her power back. That might be two or three years down the road. When someone is hanging off a bridge by a rope they are not a victor.

What should the individual be doing during that vulnerable time?
After they come forward they need a really good support system, and that's what I'm pushing to create. It's really important that they keep talking through their issues. Who knows where they are in their life: drugs, alcohol or who knows what? It's important to know if they need to be in therapy. At this time they are very exposed and vulnerable.

People often try to deal with sexual abuse by themselves because they feel ashamed, but it's important to seek community.
There are several groups working with people who have experienced abuse. If you can get into therapy, go. It's important to do that as soon as you disclose. When you talk to the police and press charges against your abuser, it's not over. I can't emphasize that enough – the reporting is absolutely just the beginning of your vulnerability. It will take a few years to change your feelings, because your mind has been trained otherwise. Research shows that your brain rewires when you've been exposed to trauma as a kid. You have to retrain your thoughts.

Is it worth going through all that?
Absolutely, you have to. Change of any sort is hard and it takes a

long time. For us to live a certain way for twenty years and think we're going to get better in three days is a joke. It takes a commitment to change and get better. We live a certain way – with fears and detachment disorder and there are going to be things we have to work on. Until we commit to getting our power back, the perpetrator has it.

In 1997 James pled guilty to 350 sexual assaults against two players; you were one of them. He was sentenced to three and a half years in jail and that means he served a few days for each assault. That's not justice. How do you explain the depth of the effect of sexual abuse to someone who doesn't understand the impact?

I think social media has exposed how much abuse has actually occurred in our society. We understand the damage when we see kids committing suicide and when we look at the research about the criminals in our prison systems – a large proportion of them were abused as kids. Researchers are starting to connect brain trauma and the way kids react. It takes a long time to collect data in order to make those important conclusions.

In Canada, I don't think we're ever going have the same sentences as in the US, where an offender can receive several hundred years. Bill C-10 is a positive step, but the most important piece and our best defence is to educate and empower the masses within our communities and organizations. For every Graham James, there are five hundred other predators and we'll never catch all of them. Perpetrators and pedophiles rely on the public's ignorance and indifference.

Sheldon, do you think forgiveness is necessary or even attainable in most cases of sexual abuse, in order to heal?

I don't know. I get asked that question quite a bit, Deb, and to me forgiveness is about getting your power back and doing the work. I like the quote, "Faith without work is dead." In other words, you can pray to win the lotto all you want but if you don't get off your butt and buy a lotto ticket, you don't have a chance. Doing the work means the perpetrator doesn't have power in your life anymore; it means you are not consumed by what happened and that's about moving on. Do you forgive them? I don't know. I don't really understand that whole thing, forgiveness. I don't like that. I don't think it's okay to say, "It's okay you did that, let's move on." I think forgiveness is about doing the work.

What's the greatest lesson you've learned because of the sexual trauma you experienced?
It's keeping life simple – commit every day to being better. I'm under no illusion that I'm perfect, but I know I'm a lot better than I was fifteen years ago. It's about being the best person I can be and trying to push for as much change as possible. It is staying open-minded and believing the key to these issues is keeping it simple. I think sometimes we want to complicate things too much.

How can someone like a spouse or a family member best support someone who is struggling and acting out because of sexual trauma?
Often we want to give direction. When I was rollerblading across Canada to raise money and awareness I thought I had to save or help everybody that disclosed to me. I found the best thing I could do was listen. When they need a hand, guide them, be there for them. Sometimes they need you to be there to talk about something completely different. Just listen and if they need you, show up. It's not rocket science; keep showing up and don't try to fix them. When it's court time, show up at the court. We can't take their pain away, but we can show up and we can be there – that's the key.

If you were talking to a group of kids in a high school, what would you say are the initial signs of the grooming phase kids should be aware of?
No matter what anybody tells you or who they are, it's inappropriate for an adult to be touching you sexually, hurting you physically or degrading you emotionally. Most perpetrators gain a kid's trust and are known – they are not the boogie man jumping out from the corner. They are your aunt, uncle, dad, mom, teacher or your hockey coach. I tell kids there are people who will listen to them and that they should talk about it if someone tries something on them.

Tell the readers about the centre and what happens if a child calls for help.
The Calgary Child Advocacy Centre was mine and Wayne's idea when we visited a similar centre in Denver, Colorado, three years ago. We brought the concept forward and were suddenly joined by seasoned experts in the field and leaders in our community, both government and corporate. Our incredible Board raised the funds we needed to build the Centre. When a child or the child's support

person phones in, the call is handled by the Child and Family Services on-site authorities, the police are there, and everything is in process. Everybody is working together. As soon as a child or their support person calls. We don't have to call elsewhere or say, "Sorry, we can't talk to you." We start talking to them immediately and decide whether there will be a criminal investigation.

Can a child call just for advice?
If a child phones and discloses something, we have a legal responsibility to report child abuse. If he or she is disclosing that they've been sexually abused at home, we're going to send someone there and probably arrest the offender and begin to build a case – why wouldn't we do that? We can't sit back and let a kid phone us and tell us they've being sexually abused at home and leave it. When the Centre gets the call, they send out experienced officers to handle the situation in a professional way, with the child's well-being in mind. We need to be able to step in because often the kids don't have the courage to do more than call us. They're obviously reaching out and telling us for a reason.

Exactly. Do you have anything else you'd like to share?
Our motto at Respect Group is "Empower the Bystander." We have trained over two hundred thousand people. It's mandatory education for coaches, parents, and adults working in schools across this country. We believe the most important prevention is to educate and create standards within organizations.

People traditionally have not wanted to get involved in other people's business, even when they suspect something might be happening. Who wants to be connected with the stigma and taboo of sexual abuse?
People don't want to get involved in a lot of stuff because they are frightened. Once they learn about it and understand it and can recognize it, they will become a lot less fearful. That's why we want to educate people working with our youth – ninety-eight per cent of whom are good people. Let's not focus so much on catching the bad guy, because if we can empower and educate people to support the individuals that are coming forward, I think we're in a lot better place.

What is your main focus now?

Creating programs. Our programs educate thousands and thousands of people every year. Go online and find "Respect Group Inc." We have "Respect in the Workplace," "Respect in School," "Respect in Sport" and "Respect in Sport for Parents." I also helped create the "Speak Out Program" with Hockey Canada.

You've made an amazing, incredible contribution. You have turned a difficult situation into something that benefits many.
Yes, I guess I've done some good things.

Absolutely. We went a little bit over our time so I'll just say it's been great talking with you. I appreciate your time, congratulations on the Child Advocacy Centre, and I hope to see you at an event in Toronto someday.
That would be great. Thanks, Deb.

Making a Difference – Erin Merryn

www.erinmerryn.net

Deb Maybury

One person can make a difference. Erin Merryn's decision to take action will change how children deal with sexual abuse in the future. She has demonstrated that you are never too young to help others and to create change. Erin is orchestrating a movement that is long overdue. Her commitment to educate children about sexual abuse on a national scale is remarkable, daunting, and inspiring. She is speaking for so many who do not have the courage or maturity to break their silence. Erin often says, "We teach kids tornado drills, fire drills, bus drills. We teach them nothing about sexual abuse."

Erin was sexually assaulted by two different men over a six-year period and remained silent. She stated, "I didn't have the words," until her younger sister described their cousin as being gross: "I knew exactly what that meant and I couldn't believe that I was staying silent in this horror." Together they told their parents, but that was not enough for Erin. She has made it her mission to speak out on behalf of all children and remove the stigma and shame from survivors and give them a reason to speak. She wants children to know that abuse is not their fault.

At age twenty-five, she helped create a bill requiring schools to educate children about sexual abuse. The name of the bill is Erin's Law. The State of Illinois was the first to pass it and as this book is being finished, Erin's Law has been passed in six states. The bill requires age-appropriate sexual abuse and assault awareness and prevention for students starting in pre-kindergarten. She has the support of Governor Quinn, of the state of Illinois as well as many other politicians, celebrities and survivors, and over ten thousand Facebook fans.

Erin is the author of two books, *Stolen Innocence* and *Living for Today*. Her list of appearances includes *Oprah, The Today Show,*

CNN, *Montel*, and *Good Morning America*, as well as at high schools, colleges and community events. She has also been featured in publications such as *Glamour* magazine, *Time Magazine*, *CosmoGirl Magazine*, and the *Chicago Tribune*.

As more people learn about Erin's efforts travelling back and forth across the United States, it is my hope that this bill will gain more momentum and eventually Erin's Law will spread to other countries.

Erin says, "I will not stop until this is passed in every single state. If it takes me to my last breath on this earth I will do it. I have finally found a positive way to heal my life."

Thanks Erin.

FACSA Foundation
(Family and Friends Fighting Against Child Sexual Assault)
Connie Lee

Growing up in an abusive home where we were hungry, neglected, beaten and raped, I finally grew up to understand how we cultivate a multigenerational epidemic of child sexual assault. For I too married a great guy who turned out to be abusive to the children we conceived together. I knew I could not rear my children in an abusive environment, so I left when they were five, four, and one. I had no job, no money, and no place to go, but God provided a way. I was able to put us all through college and bring up my children with good Christian values.

Right after our divorce, my daughter came home from her father's house with gonorrhea. She was four years old. While in court the local pediatrician said, "If she had used the same towel that he had used, she could have caught the gonorrhea from the towel." He received no sentencing, no probation and no counseling, and we received no justice. The judge ordered her to see her father every other Thursday in a public place with his parents present, and the boys could visit their father every other weekend. Fast forward twenty-five years, my granddaughters were showing signs of abuse. My children believed I lied about their father, for if he had done something they believed he would have gone to jail. I reported to the local Child Protective Services (CPS) and law enforcement but nothing was done. The local CPS representative said I was not even a mandated reporter so I had to fax my credentials to her. This is the broken nightmare of a system our children have to endure.

I founded the FACSA Foundation to fight for families and provide resources we never had, providing pro bono attorneys and counsellors for children of sexual assault and their families. We also conduct prevention and education of child sexual assault and human trafficking presentations to local communities. When I began, I had never run a non-profit, but knew it was divinely inspired and God would provide if I let Him guide. After the painful knowledge from witnessing the signs and symptoms of child sexual assault and seeing my grandchildren not being protected, I decided I had to do something. I mortgaged my home to get a decent vehicle and began my own healing journey while on the Shattering the Silence Tour and Documentary Project. I began a thirty-six-city winter tour across the US to teach community leaders, parents and grandparents how to be the frontline defense for their children, with local advocates in each area. Currently, we are on the spring/summer one-hundred-fifteen-city tour, and I am so excited to see the change we will all make together. We are changing the social stigma of child sexual assault and changing public policies. We are conducting current research of community needs and assessment; educating communities on prevention and education of child sexual assault by hosting free conferences with local advocates. We are filming a documentary with survivors' stories across the nation. It's about how to heal from any trauma. We aim to help people to thrive rather than just survive. It is time we learn to live rather than merely exist.

We will host a "Million Survivor March" in Washington D.C., September 28 and 29, 2013, at the Jefferson Memorial. We hope you will join us on this incredible adventure! You can email me, Connie Lee, at facsasavethechildren@hotmail.com or go to our website FACSAFoundation.org. You can also follow us on Twitter and Facebook at facsafoundation.

I left home with only $300, a wing and a prayer, but God provided donations along the way. Never let funds, or anything, keep you from taking action on your dreams today. Just take a step and God will lead and direct your paths: to follow humbly, and walk boldly and courageously where He leads. "Never Let Your Fears Override Your Dreams!"

Final Thoughts

I suppressed tears when my older brother told me my niece had been raped. That was the last thing I anticipated when I wrote this book. I had prepared myself for everything – except hearing that. I told him I was sexually violated as a young child so he wouldn't be surprised; I didn't anticipate my surprise.

That's the thing about sexual abuse, it's an epidemic but it still shocks us when we find it in our own backyard. It bites us fast and hard. The memories can cripple us just when we think we are in control of our lives – they shake our foundation, challenge who we are and reprogram how we think. Innocence is no more, trust is broken, anger builds and silence rules.

I am not a therapist though I did spend four years studying psychology only to discover I didn't have any desire to listen to people's problems. Funny how things change – I needed twenty-five years to come to the realization that I not only wanted to listen, I needed to.

It would be easy to write a hundred pages and still fail to convey all that I have observed and learned during the process of creating *Unlock The Door*. As I struggle to write these final pages I keep asking myself what I intended this booked to accomplish: people to have a forum to reveal their stories publically, an informative resource, an introduction to unique healing modalities I stand behind and for the book to be a means of connecting those who have experienced sexual trauma. Overall, I wanted those violated to feel better after reading the book than before – I wanted people who are suffering to realize they are not alone.

Everyone will take away their own insights from these stories. My most heartfelt discovery is that people who have experienced sexual trauma often experience debilitating emotions because they believe they did something wrong or should have done something different. The *what if I had done this or that* combined with an infinite number of *why did he or she do this to me*, result in a quandary of inner conflict and self-sabotage. Those who habitually question their reaction to the abuse are stuck in the unmerciful memories endlessly identifying *as* their story. Because this observation was such a surprise, I would like to point out four reactions to being sexually violated: freeze, flight and fight and pleasure. I will address the latter first.

I added pleasure to the well known freeze, flight and flee theory because some people, who were young when they were first exposed to sexual abuse, found the touching physically pleasing. Not all sexual abuse is aggressive, violent and painful. Some perpetrators, as unhealthy as they are, seduce their victims gently. For those who had a pleasurable response, the adverse emotional shift came when they were older and discovered the experience was a violation. "It was pleasurable and *that* is why I'm upset at myself," one individual said. In Tim's chapter he states, "I wanted it and couldn't wait to go back and play our games." Later he says, "When I was ten or so years sober I forgave my babysitter for molesting me. Not for what she did, but I couldn't hold onto that resentment anymore. I gained some freedom from the grip of her. I was able to forgive myself for what I thought I was responsible for."

The human body reacts when stimulated and body betrayal (physical arousal during sexual abuse) often results in shame and guilt. However, like Tim said, "I was a child. I wasn't in any way responsible, no matter how my body responded." It is imperative to understand, the individual violated is not responsible for the actions of the perpetrator – ever! You did what you were led to do at the time and you need not feel badly about your response. Furthermore, we are often silenced not by the sexual trauma, but prior to it, as Gabor Maté stated in the foreword, "That voice had already been silenced – that is why they don't know what to do with the trauma: in fact, that *is* the trauma." That is why educating children with proper language skills to discuss sexuality is so important. Children often don't possess the cognitive maturity and confidence to reveal sexual abuse or have someone they trust and feel safe enough with to report the violation to.

Often people say their reaction to childhood sexual trauma was to freeze – stare into space, pretend to be asleep or dissociate. I vividly recall freezing as well as being confused and not knowing what to do, let alone say. Deep in my core, I desperately wanted to escape and screamed, "Stop. Why are you doing this?" and "You are gross," all the while my body was limp and my voice non-existent. This is an unfortunate example of not knowing what to do, so doing nothing.

Freezing leaves many feeling ashamed because they didn't actively try to get away. Yet, what most don't appreciate is, freezing is a survival tactic when there appears to be no escape. A bird caught in a net may freeze and appear calm or dead as you approach it, though it is extremely frightened. Some people who were violated question their behaviour and blame themselves for freezing without realizing their reaction was not only instinctual but also a viable attempt to protect themselves. That self-blame turns into guilt and anger when the reality is, fighting back and fleeing weren't possible.

Children, in particular, are easily overpowered both physically and psychologically. They are suffocated by the shock of the molestation from a perpetrator they likely know and trust. If the violation is in the home, running away can be a very frightening proposition and not an option until the child is mature enough to consider it practical. Physically fighting could actually cause more injury to a child. A woman stated that after the first time her father overpowered her and raped her she no longer felt anything. The enormity of the violation robbed her spirit and vitality and attempting to fight back was futile. Typically fighting isn't realistic because of the insurmountable strength difference and hierarchy of psychological power.

Regardless, many victims experience perpetual shame because they didn't fight or flee. For that reason, I want to emphasis that fighting and fleeing wear many disguises. Because you didn't engage in a physical fight or pack your bag and leave doesn't mean you didn't consciously or unconsciously fight, flee or ask for help. In fact, you probably did and nobody was aware enough to notice or wanted to take the initiative to investigate their suspicions. Several contributors to *Unlock The Door* attempted to flee in various ways. For example Stewart, Charmaine, Stephanie and Dorothy, to name a few, all told someone they were *touched* and were disregarded. Sexual abuse remains a stigmatization and people often still do not want to deal with the consequences or get involved in the outcome.

There are many symptoms a child or adolescent may display when experiencing sexual abuse. (Refer to the list of potential sexual abuse symptoms following the final thoughts). Children want an adult to rescue them but do not reveal the abuse because of fear, not wanting to get their perpetrator in trouble or not knowing who to tell. Therefore, it is the responsibility of every adult to be aware and watch for signs of abuse – not to over-react, but as Art Lockhart advised, watch and ask questions. Sadly, too often when children do in a sense fight back by telling on their perpetrators, they are not believed or the sexual abuse is minimized or hidden. This not only causes immeasurable pain, it's an absolute breach of trust.

Sexual trauma interrupts a time when children trust wholly, are vibrant, curious and full of life. They do their best to persevere, regardless of their initial reactions and unknown future. Their innocence is forever shattered and replaced with coping mechanisms stretching from isolation and alienation to insurmountable hostility. Trust erodes as one's voice disappears and the tragedy is, without those two, healing from and overcoming the inner mayhem caused by sexual abuse is impossible – to recover and heal one must have the courage to trust and speak.

Healing encompasses taking responsibility for your healing, accepting what happened without condoning or necessitating forgiveness, integrating a past with sexual abuse into your full life's experience without dragging around the ball and chain and ultimately harnessing the energy to serve others. All this is not realized single-handedly. Telling your story is never painless, though it does get easier with time.

I am honoured that the contributors in this book trusted me with their most private thoughts and feelings. Some asked if I had experienced sexual abuse, some asked if I was sharing my story too – most just wanted to get the weight of years of silence off their chest. I am grateful to have spent countless hours listening to thirty-nine contributors (as well as those who shared around the book's periphery). The result is the privilege to share over a thousand years of insights, wisdom and knowledge.

Throughout the writing of *Unlock The Door* I have immersed myself in the area of sexual abuse in an attempt to comprehend all aspects of this issue – there is so much to learn and share as we collectively move toward solutions. I've listened to horrendous stories and unforgiveable actions. Yet, despite witnessing individual pain and suffering, sadness and despair, fear and helplessness, I have been impressed by the magnificence and determination of the people. Their contributions, selflessness, community spirit, transcendence, desire to help others and need to make a difference has been an inspiration and a constant reminder of the resiliency of the human spirit.

I Am Who I Am
Stephanie

I want peace. I have survived sexual and emotional abuse. I have experienced unconditional love. I am weak. I have so much strength. I am a mouse. I am a warrior. I have hurt. I have love. I'm lost. I want guidance. I've made mistakes. I can learn from them. I have flashbacks. I get frustrated and angry. I cry. I breathe. I listen. I have a voice. I just want to be heard. I cry. I laugh. I care for others. I do yoga for me. I am vulnerable. I am valuable. I see dark. I am creative. I have deep pain. I meditate. I journal. I read. I struggle with the dark. I love the sun. I run up the stairs. I look over my shoulder. I breathe. I dream. I'm living my dream. I believe. I smile. I hurt. I hope. I'm proud to be a wife. I'm thankful for my husband. I am a mother. I cherish my children. I am blessed with my family. I protect them. I run. I don't want to look back. I'm happy. I don't want pain. I want freedom. I value time. I'm settled. I'm a mess. I'm calm. I breathe. I love the beach. I want change. I have created change. I've created me. I am peace.

We shall draw from the heart of suffering itself the means of inspiration and survival.
Winston Churchill

Deb Maybury and *Unlock the Door*

Deb Maybury vividly remembers lying awake one evening in November 2011 asking herself how best to combine years of learning and teaching into one meaningful area that would allow her to serve and educate others. She remembers thinking, "What's the purpose of all this?"

Deb had spent the nine months up to September 2010 training for and raising money for the Sears National Kids Cancer Ride, in which a group of cyclists pedal from Canada's West to East Coast. To be accepted onto the team, Deb transformed herself from a non-cyclist to an accomplished one. Completing the ride was an incredibly exhilarating experience, followed by the deep low that inevitably follows such a physically and emotionally intense event.

Despite having met two important personal challenges in 2011, the nagging issue remained: What's the purpose of all this? As Deb pondered her question, memories of her childhood sexual abuse surfaced. In a troubled state she felt compelled to get out of bed and write *her story,* for the first time. She seldom thought about those experiences, so why now? Suddenly, the idea of a book of personal memoirs about sexual abuse began to take shape. She saw that book in the hands of thousands of people who have been sexually abused and think they are alone. Then she understood.

Deb believes that all her experiences led her specifically along the path toward writing and becoming involved in the process of Reveal, Connect and Heal – eliminating the taboo and stigma that is sexual abuse. Those years of overcoming challenges, working on personal growth and sharing those lessons with others made creating *Unlock the Door* possible. In Deb's words, "This project has been the biggest challenge I have ever encountered and the greatest reward and gift I have ever received."

.

Potential Symptoms of Sexual Abuse

- gradual or sudden change in behaviour: isolation, becoming introverted, withdrawal, fearfulness, agitation, excessive crying, depression, low self-worth
- aggressive/disruptive behavior
- cruelty to others/cruelty to pets
- recurring nightmares; disturbed sleep patterns, fear of the dark
- regression to more of an infantile behavior (bed wetting, thumb sucking, excessive crying)
- unusual interest in and/or knowledge of sexual matters
- expressing affection in ways that are inappropriate for a child of that age, sexual acting out/inappropriate sexual play (with self, other children, adults, pets, toys)
- fear of a certain person or an intense dislike of being left somewhere or with someone, trying to avoid a familiar adult
- unhealthy/odd attachment to a specific person
- loss of or lack of interest in friends, school, sports, other activities,
- difficulty learning in school/inability to concentrate/short attention span/may appear to have a learning disorder/appears to be hyperactive (may even be diagnosed as ADD / ADHD), sudden change in school performance
- extreme and/or unexplained anger, delinquent behavior
- self-destructive behaviour/self-harm/self-mutilation (cutting, burning)
- seductive behaviour/promiscuous behaviour
- eating disorders, addictions (drugs, alcohol, sex, pornography)
- anxiety
- lack of trust in self & others
- difficulty forming relationships/poor peer relationships/avoidance of relationships
- signs of PTSD (Post Traumatic Stress Disorder)
- suicidal thoughts/attempts and/or suicide

Sexual trauma leaves tracks that lead to different places as we sort through how to cope with disturbing memories.
Deb Maybury

Resources
Updated resources at:
unlockthedoorbeyondsexualabuse.weebly.com

Canada
The Gate House
http://www.thegatehouse.org

Silence to Hope
http://www.silencetohope.com

B.C. Male Survivors
http://bc-malesurvivors.com

Fredericton Sexual Assault Crisis Centre
www.fsacc.ca

Canadian Centre for Male Survivors of Child Sexual Abuse
www.cc4ms.ca

Loretta P. Merritt, LL.B., LL.M.
Lawyer
Civil sexual, physical and emotional abuse and assault cases
www.torkinmanes.com

USA
Rape Abuse & Incest National Network
http://www.rainn.org

National Child Abuse Hotline
http://www.childhelp.org

Envision Counselling & Support Centre
www.envisioncounsellingcentre.com

Kids Help Phone
http://www.kidshelpphone.ca
1-800-668-6868 Canada

National Teen Dating Abuse Hotline
1-866-331-9474 USA

National Child abuse Hotline
1-800-422-4453 USA
Survivors of Abuse Recovering
http://survivorsofabuserecovering.ca

Childhelp's National Child Abuse Hotline
1-800-422-4453

Male Survivor
www.malesurvivor.org

National Domestic Violence Hotline
1-800-799-SAFE (800-799-7233)
TDD 1-800-787-3224

Pandora's Project
www.pandorasproject.org

FACSA Foundation (Family and Friends Fighting Against Child Sexual Assault)
(318) 539-2571
facsasavethechildren@hotmail.com

United Kingdom
The National Association for People Abused in Childhood
http://napac.org.uk

Hotline: 0808 2000 247

Help for Adult Victims of Child Abuse
www.havoca.org

Ethnic Survivors Forum
www.ethnicsurvivorsforum.org (Scotland)

Kingdom Abuse Survivors Project
www.kasp.org.uk (Scotland)

The Survivors Trust
www.thesurvivorstrust.org (Warwickshire)

Little girl, young boy

Hey, what you doin' to that child when you're alone?
You don't know I know, but I've been watching all along.
I wonder how you look that stranger in the mirror.
And how you dismiss that child's pure sweet tear?

What you're sowing is choking the seed.
If only the divine would intercede.
Send a message clear and stern.
But my doubt is my certainty you'll never learn.

I once was that little girl and I knew that young boy.
I once was that little girl, knew that young boy.

Maybe that babe will grow strong, determined and wise.
But health, love and trust are all compromised and
I don't see remorse in your cold, cold empty eyes.
Should I be surprised?

Cause, you never hurt that little girl,
You didn't harm that young boy.
You didn't hurt that little girl or harm that young boy.
In your mind.

Don't know why I get involved in all this stuff.
It's not like I can do much.
But my heart it aches and my mind runs wild and I
wonder if once upon a time you were that child.

Were you once that little girl? Did you know that young boy?
Were you once that little girl, know that young boy?

I once was that little girl and I knew that young boy.
I once was that little girl, knew that young boy.
You didn't hurt that little girl, you didn't harm that young boy.
You didn't hurt that little girl or harm that young boy.
In your mind.

Don't know why I get involved in all this stuff.
It's not like I can do much.

Deb Maybury

http://unlockthedoorbeyondsexualabuse.weebly.com/

www.debmaybury.com

Made in the USA
Charleston, SC
05 June 2013